Growing Readers

Units of Study in the Primary Classroom

Kathy Collins

Foreword by Lucy Calkins

Stenhouse Publishers

Portland, Maine

Stenhouse Publishers
Portland, Maine

Stenhouse Publishers
www.stenhouse.com

Library of Congress Cataloging-in-Publication Data
Collins, Kathy, 1964–
    Growing readers : units of study in the primary classroom / Kathy Collins; foreword by Lucy Calkins.
        p. cm.
    Includes bibliographical references and index.
    ISBN 1-57110-373-2 (alk. paper)
    1. Reading (Primary) I. Title.
    LB1525.C68 2004
    372.4--dc22   2004049180

Cover and interior photographs by Angela Jimenez
Back cover photo by Amy Ludwig VanDerwater
Cover and interior design by Martha Drury

Manufactured in the United States of America on acid-free paper
10 09 08 07   9 8 7 6 5

To Carol and George Collins,
Who encouraged me to start

To Ian and Owen Fleischer,
Who ran with me to the finish

Contents

Foreword

I have waited a long time for this book. Katherine Paterson describes the writing process like this: "Writing is something like a seed that grows in the dark . . . or a grain of sand that keeps rubbing at your vitals until you find you are building a coating around it. The growth of a book takes time . . . I talk, I look, I listen, I hate, I fear, I love, I weep, and somehow all of my life gets wrapped around the grain."

For ten years I've watched Kathy as she grew toward this book, and now an exquisite, rich book is finally here, layered with all that she has learned through the past decade of working with little readers and their teachers. Kathy writes that when "we closely observe our students, we learn about them, of course, but we can also learn about our teaching."

Kathy's dreams and struggles with teaching are evident throughout the pages. She tells us of her alter ego, Ms. UltraOrganizo, the teacher she dreams of being, the one who writes neatly all the time, keeps her files up to date, and has socks and earrings that match every holiday, including Earth Day. She shares the "aha!" moments, those times when the stars align, the instruction is effective, and the children respond in ways that make a teacher want to run and tell everyone what just happened. But Kathy also admits her struggles and candidly shares what she learned from the things that did not work in her classroom. She is not afraid to talk about what's hard, and we learn that it's often how we reflect on the challenges we face that show us the way on our journey to become the teachers we dream of being.

Kathy has been my traveling companion since 1993. She now leads the Teachers College Reading and Writing Project's work with primary reading, coaching all our staff developers and overseeing the work we do in primary reading in hundreds of New York City schools. Each month, Kathy sends 400 coaches from New York City schools a new installment of curricular support.

To those coaches and the Teachers College Reading and Writing Project, Kathy is something of a rock star. People love her mix of self-deprecating, uproarious humor and her nitty-gritty knowledge of teaching. When Kathy leads a conference day or teaches an advanced section in our institutes, the cavernous auditorium will inevitably be full: people know that her teaching will always be practical, fresh, and fun.

I met Kathy fifteen years ago when she was studying in the Teaching English as a Second Language Program at Teachers College and needed a job that would help with tuition. She started working part-time answering telephones at the Project, and within a few months, I'd recruited her to join our tiny team of preliminary researchers who set the stage for the Teachers College Writing Project to become the Teachers College *Reading* and Writing Project.

Kathy is the most brilliant researcher I've ever known. She watches kids with such empathy and attention that she can later reenact what each child said and did so faithfully that the child in all his or her idiosyncrasies comes to life. This means that when Kathy visits a classroom, she carries episodes from the classroom to the conference table, putting this little bit of life on the table for all of us to study, rewinding and replaying the episode as we explore it for all the insights it yields.

Our years of collaborative research led us to develop the ideas on teaching reading that I've written about in *The Art of Teaching Reading* and that now inform instruction in the thousands of schools with which the Teachers College Reading and Writing Project has worked. The ideas came alive not only when doing our research, but also when Kathy decided to take the ideas and put them into practice herself by teaching first grade at P.S. 321. Her classroom was our laboratory; we followed in tow, and it was not unusual for six of us to be in Kathy's classroom, learning from her teaching. One year, we brought Gay Su Pinnell to work with our team, growing new ideas together on guided reading, conferring, and interactive writing, and a good deal of that work was done in Kathy's classroom.

When it was time to write *The Art of Teaching Reading*, I knew I could not write it alone. Kathy was my collaborator in that book. She is the heroine of all my chapters on primary reading, and her words and wisdom fill the book with strength. Since then, Kathy has been my collaborator in our newest endeavor as she leads the primary reading component of our efforts to support New York City's new demands for professional development. A year ago, the chancellor of the New York City schools held a press conference at P.S. 172, a Teachers College Reading and Writing Project school in Brooklyn. "The approach to teaching reading and writing in this school needs to be for all of New York City's children," he said, suggesting that every school in New York City needed to turn away from basals and give children the opportunity to learn to read from literature and their own writing.

And now *Growing Readers* can become the seed to wrap your teaching around, nurturing your own experiences in the light of an author whose fresh and original teaching reflects her deep, deep understanding of young children and reading.

Lucy Calkins

Preface

Every July I teach at the Summer Institute on the Teaching of Reading at Teachers College, Columbia University. Hundreds of teachers, principals, and staff developers from all over the world take time from their summer vacations and make the journey to New York City to participate. Many of these educators return year after year to take advanced sections, while the rest are new to the teaching of reading within a balanced literacy framework.

When we instructors lead sections for the educators who are attending for the first time, there is a place where many of us begin: "Would you take a few minutes to think back on your reading lives, and jot some notes about the reading events you remember—the good ones, the bad ones, and don't forget the ugly ones." Sometimes the teachers need an example of a reading event because, for most of us, reading events aren't nearly as memorable as, say, getting a driver's license or sharing a first kiss.

I often share two of my stories to help the teachers remember their own. Until eleventh grade, I considered myself a good reader for a couple of reasons: I liked to read, and I read a lot. It was that simple. In eleventh-grade English, however, things changed for me. My class was reading *The Return of the Native* by Thomas Hardy. My teacher talked about this book in ways that made me believe I was missing a lot of pages from my copy. I struggled to find the deeper meaning of the story, which he made seem so obvious. My teacher talked about symbolism in the book as if the publisher had kindly included a little Symbolism Alert! icon in the margins of the text itself. I felt I was reading this book through opaque curtains. The metaphors, symbolism, and deeper meanings my teacher talked about were just not clear to me.

Adding to my dismay was my belief that everyone else in the class could see what I could not. Until that year of eleventh-grade English, I had never thought much about who I was as a reader. Sure, I knew I *loved* to read, but because of this experience I began to wonder if I *could* read. I worried that I didn't understand much of anything, especially the kind of literature that was supposed to be preparing me for college.

That time in my reading life is etched into my mind. Those dark days of eleventh-grade English signified a shift in my feelings toward books and reading, and toward my own intelligence. Besides adding to the angst of high school, this experience had a profound effect on me. In college, I ended up avoiding literature classes as much as possible because I wasn't confident that I could handle them.

As I share this story on the first day of the institute many teachers nod sympathetically. The looks on their faces tell me that this story sounds familiar. "It wasn't all bad," I assure them as I begin to share another, happier story from my reading life. I tell them how my mom used to take my two younger brothers and me to the town library every month or so. Once we got there, she'd let us split up, something that never happened anywhere else. Somehow, the library felt safe and trustworthy, unlike a shopping mall crowded with shoppers or a large supermarket full of candy, aisle displays, and glass jars. The library provided an early taste of independence, which I savored.

I ventured off on my own to gather books that would sustain me for the month. I had a system. I simply began at A in the children's fiction section and walked toward Z with my head at an angle so I could read the titles on the spines of the books. I'd pull a book from the shelf and quickly assess whether it made the cut. My sophisticated method of assessment was to judge the book by the cover and to occasionally read the blurb on the back. After a while, my mom would call to my brothers and me, and it would be time to go. Before I approached the checkout desk, I'd dutifully open up my books and stack them like Pringles™ potato chips so the librarian could easily insert the date cards. She'd smile at the step I saved her, and I'd smile back, knowing that I was set for the next month. This story, like the first one, is not about one momentous event in my life but about a series of experiences that as a whole contributed to my relationship to reading.

Sharing these stories helps teachers recall some of their own stories. As they jot down their reading memories, they inevitably uncover long-forgotten events and feelings about reading. Then we share the reading memories with each other. We listen to stories about lying cuddled up beside a parent and being read to until sleep arrived. We hear about the thrill of sneaking grown-up books off parents' bookshelves and whipping through the pages quickly to get to the juicy parts before getting caught. Often, through someone else's story, we're reminded of the pleasure of finding the first book that we just couldn't put down, the joy of finding an author to love, the pain of being forced to write a report after every book in fourth grade, the horror of being asked a question in English class, and so on. I began to realize that whenever teachers share their stories, it always seems that most of the happy reading events happened outside of school.

As you may expect, many of our difficult or painful reading experiences took place in school. People talk about the terror of having to stand in front of the class as they read aloud paragraphs full of hard words from social studies textbooks. They tell of the struggle to read required books that couldn't hold their interest or understanding, about the anxiety of taking pop quizzes to prove whether they had done the previous night's reading homework.

The point I want to make is that many of us grow to love reading in spite of what happened in school, not because of it.

First grade, in particular, holds a lot of stories. For many of us, it was the time and place we remember learning to read, but not loving to read. When I think back to that time in my own life, I realize that my home reading life and my school reading life never crossed paths. In school I sat in a semicircle with five other "purple" readers. My teacher chose the book we would read, and she'd slide a copy across the table to each of us as if she were dealing cards. And it was like playing cards. Some of us would bluff. I would try to predict the part I'd be asked to read aloud instead of concentrating on the story. I don't remember one book that I read in elementary school. I just remember trying to get reading right.

At home, in the meantime, I was lying belly down on the floor with my grandpa's old geography encyclopedias. I spent hours reading, in my six-year-old way, the one on Asia. Oh, how I studied the picture of the Japanese lady standing on an arched bridge in a brilliant kimono with a parasol in one hand and a baby tied to her back. It made me want to live in Japan (which I eventually did). I can still find that book in my parents' house, and even today I get the feeling of wanderlust when I turn to the page with the dazzling lady on the bridge.

Back in school, however, the reality is that we primary-grade teachers bear the pressure of making sure children learn to read. If a child isn't reading with fluency and accuracy and at a particular level by the middle of first grade, all kinds of alarms go off—at school, at home, and most sadly, in the child's head. On the other hand, for many of our strong first-grade readers, school reading can be an exercise in quantity over quality due to a growing emphasis on reading levels, number of books read, and standardized test scores, even for our youngest readers.

I'm reminded of an end-of-the-year celebration I attended a few years ago. The principal was presenting awards to the top readers in first grade. Abby, my friend's daughter, received a gold-sealed certificate for reading 427 books. She was one of three first graders who read over 400 books that school year. After the celebration, as we were leaving the school, I asked Abby which book was her favorite. "I don't remember," she said as she licked orange Cheez Doodle powder off her fingertips. Of course, Abby was a strong reader, and as the years pass, she always remains at the top of her class. But I wonder today if she has any favorite books or authors, or if she's still reading as if she were in a race.

I believe that we primary-grade teachers have an important dual challenge. We need to teach children how to read, but we also need to teach them how to fall in love with reading. We need to teach children the skills and strategies that strong readers use, but we also need to teach them the reading habits that they will keep long after they leave our classrooms. Many of us have found that the independent reading workshop is a component in our teaching of reading that allows us to meet this dual challenge. The independent reading workshop makes it possible to teach children the reading skills and strategies to get through texts while also guiding them toward independence, intention, and joy as readers.

Many people understandably wonder what kind of independent reading life is possible for a six-year-old. "They're just learning! How can we expect them to learn to decode well and also to build an exciting reading life?" teachers will say. "That's a lot of responsibility for us to take on with everything else." I agree. It is a huge responsibility, but what could be more important?

At the Summer Institute, Lucy Calkins, the founding director of the Teachers College Reading and Writing Project, asks teachers what hopes they have for their young readers and writers. Most teachers say they hope their students will read and write throughout their lives. Nobody ever says that they hope their students will continue to make dioramas of their favorite scenes from books they've read or that they will remember always to write a book report when they finish a text. Nobody says they want their children to continue to make story webs or to write alternative endings for books. Instead, our deepest hopes are for our students to grow into the kinds of people who are deeply affected by books, who carry books on vacations and subways, who turn to books for information and solace, who list reading as one of their favorite things. Well, then, if these are our hopes, doesn't it make sense to foster them in the place where reading often begins? Yes, right here in our primary classrooms!

In this book, I share ideas for launching and maintaining an independent reading workshop in your classroom in a way that not only teaches children how to read but also shows them why to read. Although other literacy components occur throughout the day in a balanced literacy classroom, such as writing workshop, shared reading, interactive read-aloud, and so on, in this book I focus mostly on the work we can do in units of study during independent reading workshop that will help students grow as readers. My hope is to create a vivid image of the teaching and learning that can happen throughout the year within the independent reading workshop.

In the first chapter, I share some beliefs about teaching and learning that are necessary to support the independent reading workshop. Next, in Chapter 2, I describe the independent reading workshop and the other components of a comprehensive and balanced literacy program that work in conjunction so that our students can grow into strong, well-rounded readers. In Chapter 3, I describe the possible units of study in a year-long curriculum and how the independent reading workshop changes and grows from September to June.

In Chapters 4–8, each unit of study described in Chapter 3 is laid out clearly with a possible curriculum and samples of mini-lessons and reading conferences. In these chapters, my hope is to describe the units of study in a way that enables you to envision them in your own classroom.

Before each chapter on a unit of study (Chapters 4–7), I provide a Getting Ready section to suggest some of the behind-the-scenes work you can do to prepare for the upcoming unit of study and to plan for the teaching.

Writing this book took a very long time (my family and my editor are nodding and quite possibly rolling their eyes right now). As I worked on it, my husband and I moved from Brooklyn to Buffalo to Manhattan. I had a baby, and I'm expecting again. I cut my hair very short and then let it grow back again. The Yankees stopped winning the World Series.

Although these changes affected me on a personal level and have provided convenient excuses for not getting my book done sooner, there was another major change that profoundly affected my work on this book: I left my classroom at P.S. 321 in Brooklyn to become a staff developer/reading consultant at the Teachers College Reading and Writing Project at Columbia University. As a result, you will notice that my voice in the book switches between that of Ms. Collins, first-grade teacher, and Kathy, staff developer.

In the midst of writing this book, when I made the change from teaching in my own classroom to working with teachers in their classrooms, my stories also changed from those I experienced to those I observed. It is my hope that my work as a teacher and as a staff developer will combine to make the ideas in this book clear, accessible, and helpful to you as you make plans for the independent reading workshop in your classroom.

As you read through this book, I hope you feel the presence of the children and educators with whom I've had the privilege of working. Their humor, sincerity, and hard work have inspired me, both in and out of the classroom; without them, there would be no book.

Acknowledgments

If you look at the pages in this book at a particular angle under a special light, you'll see the faces and hear the voices of the people who have informed my thinking and inspired my words. They belong to the communities of thought, practice, children, and family to whom I owe so much.

For more than a dozen years, my community of thought has been the Teachers College Reading and Writing Project, and I begin my acknowledgments by thanking Lucy Calkins, the founding director. In every interaction with Lucy—a study group, a phone call, a quick chat—I learn something new or rethink something familiar. Back when I was deciding whether to write this book, Lucy encouraged me to take on the challenge and made me believe I actually had something to say. Throughout the writing process, she offered advice when asked, guidance when needed, and feedback when I was ready for it. Over the years, Lucy's professional and personal generosity has enriched my life immensely, and I am deeply grateful for her time, support, and friendship.

I want to thank Laurie Pessah and Kathleen Tolan, the deputy directors at the Teachers College Reading and Writing Project. I admire the way Laurie manages to strike a healthy balance between work life and family life and how she fits about thirty-six hours into a twenty-four-hour day. Kathleen has taught me how to turn ideas about teaching, learning, and staff development into practice. Both Laurie and Kathleen give so much of their time to help others do their jobs well, and I thank them both for all of their support and encouragement.

Every Thursday the Project staff meets in study groups to fuel our work with teachers and children. Everyone contributes to the ideas and direction of our work in schools, and I am particularly grateful to the K–2 staff developers. A huge thanks to Kim Ethun, Jessica Fairbanks, Ian Fleischer, Amanda

Hartman, Christine Holley, Mara Kaunitz, Alison Kilts, Marjorie Martinelli, Enid Martinez, Marika Paez, Stephanie Parsons, Hannah Schneewind, Shanna Schwartz, and Jory Zand for kindly sharing their good work. And to Joe Yukish, a senior advisor for primary reading at the Project, for being especially helpful in deepening our knowledge of the reading process and working with individuals.

Thanks also to Beth Neville, the assistant director, and Amber Boyd, Maurie Brooks, Denise Capasso, Karen Curry, Tasha Kalista, Wairimu Kiambuthi, Mary Ann Mustac, Bibinaz Pirayesh, and Kristine Widmer for their abundance of patience and lack of attitude, even in the midst of our most hectic, million-things-going-on-at-one-time seasons.

Donna Santman and I shared a year at the Project before I left to teach in my own classroom. Although Donna has always taught older students, her ideas about teaching and learning have greatly influenced my work with children, teachers, and the primary-grades curriculum. Randy Bomer, a former co-director at the Project, made me think hard, watch closely, and ask questions, helpful survival skills for any kind of situation.

I also thank Carl Anderson, Lydia Bellino, Teresa Caccavale, Linda Chen, Mary Ann Colbert, Lynne Holcomb, Gaby Layden, Ginny Lockwood-Zisa, Leah Mermelstein, and Cheryl Tyler, Project study-group and think-tank members, for thinking aloud and teaching me to look at the big picture and the small details of instructing young children.

I am grateful to the teachers I've worked with in leadership groups for graciously sharing their teaching challenges and victories. Many of the ideas in this book have grown in their company. I especially want to thank Rebecca Applebaum, Christine Comeau, Allyson Daley, Bernadette Fitzgerald, Amanda Hartman, Elyse Kerber, Karen Salzberg, Amanda Sarno, Stephanie Parsons, Evelyn Summer, and Sophie Trecker for all that we accomplished together in our groups on reading centers and whole-class studies.

Because of my work with the Project, I've had opportunities to learn from a variety of literacy educators. The time spent in the presence of Nancy Anderson, Kylene Beers, Katherine Bomer, Randy Bomer, Brian Cambourne, Marie Clay, Ralph Fletcher, David and Yvonne Freeman, Ellin Keene, Brenda Parkes, Gay Su Pinnell, Kathy Short, Frank Smith, Diane Snowball, Sandra Wilde, and many, many others has been both instructive and inspiring.

As I grew closer to finishing this book, I was fortunate to meet almost every week with a study group of wonderful New York City literacy coaches. I want to thank Bonni Cohen, Mary Croft, Florence Delgado, Stephanie Durham, Lois Grabash, Maria Guzman, Linda Kasarjian, Mary Lauritano, Kathleen Maher, Jacqueline Morison, Silvana Ng, Barbara Pinto, Myrna Rosado, Beverly Sanders, Marge Smith, and Karma Suttles for all I learned about units of study and methods of staff development through their work with teachers.

The next community I want to thank is P.S. 321 in Brooklyn, my community of practice. After working at the Project for several years, I decided to go back to the classroom. I wanted to teach at P.S. 321 because I longed to work alongside dedicated educators who believe in the abilities of all children. I also wanted to work closely with Liz Phillips, who was the early childhood coordinator at the time and has since become the principal. I had gotten to know Liz through a couple of Project study groups. I admire her integrity, wide-angled thinking, and her ability to say what's on her mind in helpful, constructive ways. She trusts teachers and provides us with the materials and instructional support needed to do the job that our students deserve. Liz has been one of the most important people in my teaching life, and I'm so grateful to her for many reasons, including her friendship.

I'd like to thank the past and present assistant principals, Caroline Forlano, Richard Goldstein, and Beth Handman, for their constant instructional support and kindness. Whether we needed more bright-green construction paper from the supply closet, help with planning a social studies unit, or back-up in dealing with a challenging situation, Caroline, Richard, and Beth were always close at hand. Lastly, I thank Peter Heaney, the former principal, who hired me at P.S. 321 in the first place. What a gift that was!

My colleagues at P.S. 321 have made an enormous impact on my teaching life, and simply walking into their classrooms is a learning experience. I'm grateful to all the first-grade teachers through the years for everything they taught me, but I'd like to specifically acknowledge the core group with whom I taught the longest: Kristen Jordan, Eve Litwack, Connie Norgren, Stephanie Parsons, Lisa Ripperger, Hannah Schneewind, Tracy Tashima, and Jessica Borg Weinberger. Thanks especially to Jessica for the incredible year that we worked side by side in an inclusion classroom. She taught me so much about classroom management, organization, and working with children with special needs.

Of course it wasn't just the first-grade teachers at P.S. 321 who were important to me. I learned so much about early childhood teaching when Phyllis Allen, Renée Dinnerstein, and Bill Fulbrecht moved up from kindergarten to teach first grade. I drew inspiration from the humor and clarity of Alice Ressner, the wisdom and experience of Phyllis Bilus and Karen Sachs, and the creativity and dedication of Tom Lee and Mike Rogers. Thanks also to the rest of the teachers, aides, and staff at P.S. 321, for showing me how to create an environment conducive to learning well and teaching responsively.

The communities of children I've worked with are at the heart of this book. I'm so grateful to the students at P.S. 321 for reminding me how lucky I am to be a teacher, and for showing me daily that I still have so much to learn. I thank their families and caregivers for all of their support and participation in the life of our classroom.

When I left the classroom to become a primary reading staff developer, the teachers and administrators at P.S. 29 in Queens, P.S. 29 in Brooklyn, and Westminster Community School in Buffalo opened their classroom doors to me and allowed me to get my "kid fix." So much of what I learned working alongside the teachers in these schools has become part of this book.

Thanks to the folks at Stenhouse Publishing for providing the opportunity to write. Philippa Stratton saw the book before I did, and she knew how to keep me moving along in spite of my pregnancies, relocations, and job changes. When Martha Drury got her hands on the manuscript, it finally felt like a book to me. I appreciate her expertise, creativity, and care in its design. Brenda Power and Cathy Mere were two of the early readers, and their suggestions and encouragement kept me moving through the tricky parts. The work of Alice Cheyer, the copy editor, was helpful, and I appreciate her attention and fine-tooth comb. I thank Tom Seavey and Doug Kolmar for getting this book out into the world and into teachers' hands. Angela Martinez joined me at P.S. 321 to take the photographs, and I was thrilled by her unique perspective and fresh eye. I want to thank one of my former students, Talia Groom, for joining us to take photographs as well. I am grateful to Jenna Laslocky, Eve Litwack, and their first-grade students for allowing us to take pictures in their classrooms.

Thank you to my family. I want to express my deepest gratitude to my parents, George and Carol Collins, and my brothers, George and Tom, for all of their love and support from the very beginning. They always knew I'd become a teacher. I am incredibly thankful for their sacrifices, their ability to find humor in the most unlikely places, and for the lessons they've taught me about working with and caring for others.

Last, and most important, I am so thankful to have had a writing partner alongside me the whole way. Ian Fleischer cheered quietly, listened supportively, waited patiently, and cooked regularly. He made it possible for me to carve out writing time, helped me keep my focus, and gave me so much to look forward to when I finally finished.

And now I'm done, my love, so let's play!

Creating Classrooms for Learners, Thinkers, and Talkers

Chapter 1

RECENTLY I WAS ON THE SELECTION COMMITTEE for assistant principal at my school, P.S. 321 in Brooklyn. Part of the committee's responsibility was to comb through the resumés and personal statements of the educators who wanted to be considered for the position. I read the files with curiosity, putting myself in the place of these applicants who were trying to create an image of themselves on paper.

Looking at the beautifully designed resumés, I was fascinated by the variety of ways these educators had found to describe their methods of teaching reading and writing: "balanced literacy," "comprehensive literacy," "workshop approach to literacy," "process," "phonics-based," "literature-based," and so on. But the names used for literacy approaches rarely left me with a picture of what the applicants really meant and believed about the teaching of reading and writing.

Fortunately, another part of the application required the candidates to describe their beliefs about teaching and learning. This was where they could really define themselves. Some people wrote lush paragraphs full of classroom anecdotes, while others wrote succinct statements that went straight to the point. After reading about a dozen of these personal statements, I started thinking about how I would answer the question, What are your beliefs about teaching and learning? I realized it is not as simple to answer as it seems. Even though I have strong ideas about teaching and learning, and strive to put my beliefs into practice every day, it can still be difficult to articulate them.

To answer this question for myself, I considered the times in my own life when I've learned best and the conditions that were present in those situations. Then I had to expand my thinking, because there are so many different kinds of learning styles that we have to imagine the conditions that make learning possible for all learners, not just for learners like ourselves.

This book is meant to help teachers launch and maintain an independent reading workshop in their classrooms. However, the independent reading workshop does not happen in isolation from the rest of the day. It's crucial for us to consider the whole day of our teaching, the classroom tone and expectations we set from arrival to dismissal, and our belief system about teaching and learning.

So before I get into the nuts and bolts of the independent reading workshop, I share here some of my beliefs about teaching and learning that seem most important to make the independent reading workshop, and indeed all components of the school day, effective for all learners. These beliefs include

- The ongoing pursuit of knowledge
- The importance of safety and consistency
- The importance of providing opportunities for independence
- The power of a print-rich, talk-rich, inviting classroom
- The value of clear and high expectations

I invite you, too, to think about your beliefs about teaching and learning, and to consider the ways your beliefs are evident throughout the day in your classroom practice. It's important for us to check in with our own belief systems on occasion to make sure that what's happening in our classrooms reflects our beliefs about best practices.

The Ongoing Pursuit of Knowledge

We teachers have a huge responsibility to know our subject matter, our students, and our teaching. These three things are always evolving, and it's our job to keep up with the changes.

As teachers of reading, we need to know what's going on in the field of reading beyond our district's prevailing model. This means we have to continue to educate ourselves about the reading process and learning issues. We need to be sure our knowledge base about reading is ever-growing and that it leads us to more inquiries in our teaching. The best teachers I know never feel like they've mastered it, and so they keep trying to figure things out. It's as if there's a carrot forever dangling in front of them.

It's helpful to talk to colleagues about our teaching. Although it may feel more comfortable and affirming to talk to like-minded colleagues, it's also important to talk to teachers who might do things differently. Listening to those who have different ideas keeps us open-minded, and it can help us clarify, strengthen, and amend our own beliefs and practice.

I can't emphasize enough the power of being part of a supportive network of teachers. I've been fortunate to be involved with the Teachers College Reading and Writing Project throughout my teaching life. Lucy Calkins, the founding director, provides many different venues for teachers to come together to share ideas, study with experts, confront difficulties, and perhaps most important, to know we're not alone.

This idea of continuing to learn about our subject matter and learning from our colleagues, of course, extends to learning about our students. I listen closely to everything my students say, especially when they don't know I'm listening. I watch my students' interactions with classmates and other adults throughout the day in order to add more details to the picture I have of each child.

When we closely observe our students, we learn about them, of course, but we can also learn about our teaching. One of my former students was also one of my most important teachers. I noticed that Shakeem seemed reluctant to participate during lessons and class discussions. I didn't consider him to be shy, and he was a strong student, so it seemed sort of strange that I rarely heard his voice. I talked to Shakeem's parents about how quiet he was and how I was trying to get him to participate more. They were surprised to hear this. "He's usually very outgoing and doesn't seem intimidated by groups," his parents told me, as they recounted different situations in which he had partic- ipated with enthusiasm. We were puzzled, so I began to watch closely for times when Shakeem did express his ideas in class.

I noticed that he often participated during math lessons. During literacy work, however, Shakeem was silent. He rarely contributed to a book talk or offered insight during a writing lesson. My theory was that Shakeem didn't feel as comfortable stating his opinions on more amorphous topics as he did answering questions that had a definite right or wrong answer. My theory was that he liked the security in knowing that he was right. I felt as if I had uncovered a little project to work on in my classroom.

The project required that I not only think about Shakeem and his participation but also reflect on my teaching. If I were to encourage Shakeem and other learners like him to participate more, I would need to fine-tune certain aspects of my teaching.

I realized that instead of having whole-class discussions during book talks in which the same handful of children tended to participate, I needed to provide more opportunities for my students to "turn and talk" to a partner. For children like Shakeem, it's not as threatening to share an opinion with a friend as it is to do so in front of the whole class, and talking to a partner also provides a venue (as well as an expectation) for children to share their thinking about books. When I have my students turn and talk, I can scoot around and listen to what they are saying, so I hear more ideas than I generally would in a whole-group discussion.

In addition to watching students as a way of reflecting on our teaching, it can be very informative to watch our teaching on videotape. As miserable as it is to see and hear myself on videotape, I try to take the high road and focus more on my teaching than my bad haircut or fashion faux pas. I look for places in my teaching where I could be more explicit or concise. I've also found that it can be just as informative to focus the video camera on the students in order to watch their reactions, responses, and levels of engagement as we teach.

I often ask those with more expertise to observe my teaching so that I grow as a teacher. I remember struggling with transitions with one particular class. It felt and looked like Grand Central Station when my students were going from one thing to another. There were materials everywhere, a noise level that rivaled rush hour, and more tattling than I care to remember. I decided to slow down the transitions into their smallest pieces to calm things down.

After a few days, I knew it wasn't working. I needed another pair of eyes, so I asked Liz Phillips, my principal, to help me out. (I realize how lucky I was to have the kind of principal whom I could trust to watch me in action during what I considered one of my weakest classroom moments.) Liz helped me see that in my effort to create calmer transitions by slowing them down, I was actually increasing the tension. "Pick up the pace a bit and don't wait for stragglers. Just get the next thing started, and they'll begin to move faster when they know you won't be waiting for them," she suggested. What a difference in my class in just a couple of days!

The beauty of a job like teaching is that there are so many opportunities to learn and change. Our job reinvents itself when we get a new class each fall, change grades, or develop a new curriculum. We model all day long as we teach, but perhaps the most important thing we can model is how to learn. I believe that we teachers have to be the most insatiable learners out there.

The Importance of Safety and Consistency

The best places to learn in are safe, consistent environments. It goes without saying that the classroom must be physically safe. After all, who could concentrate on learning long division if a clanging fire alarm and the smell of smoke offered ominous distractions? Besides physical safety, teachers must also provide a safe emotional environment. Our students need to believe that we like them and believe in them no matter what—no matter whether they act up on the playground, struggle with their handwriting and math facts, or vomit all over the magnetic letters. Children in the primary grades are still so new at school, and we need to provide the kind of safe environment where they'll be willing to face challenges and take on risks. They will be more likely to do so if they know their attempts and approximations will be supported and respected.

In safe learning environments, learners are invited (and encouraged) to take risks without fear of ridicule or retribution. We need to make it comfortable for our students to try out and strengthen their new skills, both independently and in the company of others. As I write this, I'm having scary flashbacks of a time when I took a risk in an unsafe learning environment. I'm remembering my seventh-grade experience with the clarinet. The middle school band had just begun practicing together, and I decided to join. I had been playing the instrument for a couple of years or so and believed I was doing okay.

One day at band practice, we were in the middle of some piece of music. All of a sudden, my teacher marched over to me, wildly tapped his wand on my music stand, which knocked off my Bonne Bell Lipsmacker®, and yelled at me for making a mistake. "Don't you ever practice?" he snarled at me in front of the whole band. As you might imagine, I felt as small as a piccolo as I sat there wishing both the teacher and the clarinet out of my sight.

My wish came true because soon after that experience I quit the band and stopped playing the clarinet altogether. Okay, maybe I was a little sensitive back then, and perhaps I overreacted, but it was seventh grade, after all. When I told my teacher that I was quitting the clarinet, he didn't acknowledge what had happened in band practice, nor did I. It seemed that he didn't even remember. But to me, it was a huge event in my musical life. It may have even prevented me from being a soloist with some highly regarded philharmonic orchestra!

Although this story offers an extreme example of an unsafe environment for risk taking and is not characteristic of most early elementary school classrooms, I've been able to distill something from the experience that instructs my own teaching. I know it's important to keep my impatience in check because what might seem to me to be a weak or careless attempt at something by a student might really be a huge step for him. And when I feel the words, "Haven't I taught that 750 times?" about to issue from my mouth, I remember to swallow them. I remind myself that sometimes it may take 751 times for a student to understand something, or perhaps I need to come up with another way to teach that particular thing. In any situation, students need encouragement and instruction, not annoyance or criticism, from their teacher.

It's also crucial that the way everyone relates to each other be safe as well. The expectations for interactions should be clear, and known and consistent consequences should follow actions or words that violate community standards.

In a recent column by a parenting expert, a mother wrote in about her concern that her eight-year-old daughter was acting fresh and disrespectful to adults: "Kids today are so different. When I was little, I never would have rolled my eyes at my parents or walked off in a huff when they asked me to do something." The parenting expert responded that it's not that children today are so different, it's just that when the letter writer was a child, she couldn't get away with acting disrespectful, her parents didn't allow it. Nor should we.

In our classrooms, it's likely that children will tattle or tease, roll their eyes, or get in a snit over something, but just because it's likely doesn't mean it has to persist. We need to make sure our students understand that disrespectful behavior directed at anyone, whether it's subtle like eye-rolling or overt like talking back, is not acceptable. The respect in our classrooms must run between the teacher and students as well as among the students themselves. We need to not only teach our students but also show them exactly what we mean by respect so that everyone can enjoy their learning life in the safety of the classroom we share all year long.

I've grown to believe in the power of consistency within and across school days as another way of creating a safe environment. One year, I had the privilege of teaching an inclusion class with Jessica Borg Weinberger. Although Jessica and I shared many ideas about teaching, our approach was often very different. Jessica is highly organized, and she thinks through classroom studies and lessons in a step-by-step fashion. She imagines possible obstacles and problems ahead of time, and figures out ways of dealing with them in advance. I, on the other hand, tend to jump right into something and work through the difficulties along the way. I always have my goals in sight but don't necessarily map out the way to get to them.

One of the most valuable lessons I learned from teaching side by side with Jessica is the importance of consistency. Her years of experience in teaching students with special needs proved to her that consistency creates comfort, which leads to better opportunities for learning.

Jessica and I would plan out each day together right down to the smallest details, and after a couple of weeks of school I remember worrying about how routine our morning routines had become. Our morning meeting always had the same features, and the work that followed was always in the same order. I was secretly concerned that the children would get bored by the regularity and that this would turn into a classroom management headache.

But when I took a close look at our class during morning meetings, I saw that the students were engaged throughout the meeting and during all of the regular routines that followed. There was always a lot of participation and energy, and the children never said, "This again?" I came to realize that although the structures and organization of the morning meeting and the routines remained consistent, what happened within them each day had variety, joy, and humor. The work within these structures grew and changed over the course of the school year, although the structures themselves remained constant.

Because the routines stayed more or less the same, our class was free to improvise and create challenges within them. Jessica and I were not constantly distracted by teaching a different way of doing things in addition to teaching new content, and the children were not bogged down trying to figure out what we expected of them. Because of the consistency of our mornings, there was a lot of constructive variety and joyful learning.

Workshop teaching offers consistency. From the earliest days of the year, our students know that we begin independent reading workshop with a mini-lesson (Calkins 1983) and that their job during the lesson is to listen and think about how it will affect their independent work. After the lesson, our children expect and look forward to time to read on their own, and they know that we will circulate among them to offer instruction, support, and guidance in reading conferences. When work time is over, our children put their materials away and return to the meeting area for a teaching share time. When we follow these routines day after day, our students can use their energy to grow as readers and learners rather than to figure out what we expect them to do. And we, in turn, can focus our energy on teaching, not managing, our independent readers.

The Importance of Providing Opportunities for Independence

In workshop classrooms, children get a lot of time for independent work. Whether it's writing, reading, math, or art, we begin with a mini-lesson to teach about a skill or strategy that will help students with their independent work, and then we send them off to try it. In reading, this means that after a mini-lesson my students go off to read self-chosen books that are at an appropriate level of difficulty for them to grow stronger as readers.

During independent reading time, the children are not left to sink or swim, nor is the classroom a free-for-all without direction. Quite the contrary. There are clear expectations for what they need to do during their independent work time and consequences for when they don't use their work time well. And for teachers independent reading workshop is certainly not a time when we sit back with a cup of coffee to do paperwork.

We do very important teaching while the children read independently (or with partners). From ongoing assessments we have a good idea of what we need to teach each of our students so that they develop into strong, careful readers. We use this knowledge to plan whole-class mini-lessons that will set children up for a successful independent reading time. During independent work time, we confer with individuals and partners to offer individualized direct instruction. We may also pull together small groups of children to help them through challenges or to challenge them to take on more as readers. Because the range of learners in any classroom is so vast, the children's work may vary greatly. On a given day, any number of children meet success or struggle, and it's our responsibility to offer all of them the support they need to grow as readers and learners.

During the time when learners are working at a task independently they can learn to solve problems, develop resiliency, and become resourceful at helping themselves. This is not just learning to read: it's learning for a lifetime.

The Power of a Print-Rich, Talk-Rich, Inviting Classroom

Think about the classrooms in your school. Now picture the one that is the kind of space that you'd want to teach in—the model classroom. We all know teachers who create classroom spaces that could be featured in an interior design magazine, and teachers who have a knack for plucking the perfect short bookshelf for the classroom library from someone's curbside trash. Then there are those who sew beautiful curtains for the windows and who paint over the institutional beige walls to create a warm and welcoming space. And I can't forget to mention the teachers whose classrooms are so clean I'd eat a birthday cupcake off their floors.

At P.S. 321 several classrooms fell into each of these categories. Teachers would leave their classroom doors open after school in an unspoken invitation to look around at each other's classes. There were a few classrooms that I loved to visit in the peace and quiet of late afternoons. I'd stand in the middle of the room, soaking in the wonderful learning spaces, hoping to borrow their great ideas for my own classroom. On bad days, I tried hard not to get overwhelmed and racked by teacher envy when I looked at the differences among the classrooms. I had to remember that creating inviting classrooms through design and decoration is certainly an important part of arranging the classroom environment, but it is just one of the parts. Beyond rocking chairs, ambient lighting, and pretty carpets, what elements in the classroom environment lend themselves to strong literacy work and a feeling that reading and writing really matter in that room?

❖ *Children's seating is arranged in groups.* In most all of the workshop classrooms I've seen, there are tables for four to six children spread throughout the room. At these tables, children of mixed abilities can talk about and make sense of their work together. Of course, many times children need to work quietly at their own seats, and during these times, the classroom is quiet so that all learners can concentrate and do their best work.

❖ *There is a meeting area where the whole class can gather.* The meeting area in many workshop classrooms is designated by a carpet remnant that is large enough for every child to sit comfortably. The class gathers at this meeting space for mini-lessons, teaching share time, read-alouds, and book talks. When our youngest learners gather in close around the teacher for lessons, it's easier for them to focus on what the teacher is saying and demonstrating. The teacher can more easily "read" the room when children are gathered in front of her, and this helps her figure out where to slow down, where to clarify, and where to speed up within a lesson. She can be more responsive to the whole class when they are close as she teaches.

By contrast, if children sit at their own seats during a lesson while the teacher teaches from the front of the room, many of our youngest students have difficulty maintaining attention and focus during the lesson. For these children, the distance from their seat to where the teacher is standing as she teaches may leave the child feeling as if the teacher is across the world.

❧ *Children have access to materials they need.* In classrooms that are designed for rich work in literacy, there is a prominent and welcoming classroom library for the children to find books that will help them grow stronger as readers, encourage them to develop a reading habit, and inspire them as writers. There needs to be a range of books available that includes leveled texts so that children can choose from a variety books at their independent reading levels. The baskets of books in the classroom library also need to include books that hold children's interests, pique their curiosity, and simply make them want to learn to read. The best classroom libraries have a variety of genres, picture books, nonfiction texts, and authors represented on the shelves. In subsequent chapters, I provide more details about building and maintaining classroom libraries.

Children have access to the materials they need to do their work in workshop classrooms. This means, for example, that there is a writing area with pencils, felt-tipped markers, a variety of paper choices, staplers, paper clips, scissors, and the other tools that writers need to write, revise, edit, and publish. For art, the supplies are within reach in an art area so that the children don't have to follow the teacher around asking for another pipe cleaner or more magenta paper.

If we hope our students will work independently, the most basic place to start is to teach them how to gather the materials they need to do their work. We have to teach them how to use the classroom supplies in a way that is considerate of the community. We need to teach them to be economical. ("No, we don't need thirty-five staples to make a booklet because then we'll run out of staples too fast. It really only takes three staples. Let me show you how to do it.") We need to teach them how to neatly take out and put back supplies so that other people can find and use them.

❧ *A print-rich classroom has print all around.* A classroom with strong reading and writing work going on is inevitably print-rich. There are charts around the room written by the teacher and students that detail the work of the class. There are books, lots and lots of books, in the classroom library and in other places around the room. There are books about turtles near the turtle tank, books about math near the math materials, and books about artists in the art area. Near the block area, there are books about buildings and structures. Almost everything in the classroom is labeled with words and pictures, and writing supplies are accessible all over. Children's work is easy to find around the room; it's hanging on clotheslines that criss-cross the room, tacked to bulletin boards, and taped to closet doors. Just one minute in a print-rich classroom would tell a visitor that this is a space for readers and writers.

In our sincere effort to create a print-rich environment, there is a possibility that we may overdo it. It's important to look around our classrooms from the children's perspective because sometimes our rooms can be overstimulating. I suggest that teachers sit in the meeting area or pull up a chair at the children's tables and look around the classroom from the point of view of a child in the class. I try to do this every month or so to clean house. I remove old charts, clean up bulletin board displays, and make sure there is some white space in the room so that my students aren't overly distracted by the decor.

I suggest that premade charts and signs found in teacher stores and classroom supply catalogs do not convey the same feeling as those created by the teacher and students. I know this is mostly a matter of personal taste. But it's worth emphasizing that we don't have to be graphic designers or calligraphers to create attractive charts and signs for our classrooms. All we need is a steady hand, a box of markers, and some photographs of the children that we can affix onto the charts to illustrate the points on the charts. For example, when we teach our children about the community standards and expectations for behavior, it makes more sense to me to co-create a chart with my own class rather than to rely on some generic ready-made chart designed for any classroom anywhere. When we make our own charts, we can use the shared language of our classrooms and illustrate the charts with photos and children's writing and drawing.

❖ *A talk-rich classroom offers time for discussions and chats.* When I was a student, I was a teacher pleaser. I rarely got in trouble, but if I did, it was for talking. One particularly horrifying moment took place in the cafeteria when I was in third grade. The lunch lady was standing on the stage using the microphone. All of a sudden she singled me out in the sea of other kids who were crinkling wrappers, trading sandwich halves, and snapping their *Happy Days* lunch boxes open and shut. The lunch lady yelled at me to stand up, and she made me take the walk of shame. I had to walk all the way across the cafeteria while everyone watched, go to a wall, face it, and wait for my teacher to come and pick up the class. I never really understood what I'd done wrong. (I was talking during lunchtime, go figure!)

In class, I knew better than to talk. I didn't talk at all during work time. We would sit at our desks, diligently work away on our worksheets, and raise our hands to answer the teacher's questions. When my teacher read aloud *Bedknobs and Broomsticks*, we sat at our desks and listened closely so that we could answer her comprehension questions at the end. I rarely knew much about the other girls and boys in my class because our opportunities for conversation were so limited.

So, now that I'm the teacher, I've made my classroom very different. Reading time is not a silent time. The reading workshop is punctuated with talk about books, in hushed voices, we hope. Students read quietly and privately, and then have opportunities to share their thinking about books with their reading partners, in small groups, and in whole-class discussions. Of course, we teachers have to set standards for conversations and model the kinds of book talk that deepen comprehension.

We also need to make sure there's time for children to talk to each other without some curricular agenda. I know a teacher who prides herself on the number of songs her children know and sing on the school bus during field trips. "It keeps them busy on the bus, so they don't go nuts," she says. Believe me, I can understand the allure of keeping children busy as a management tool, but I wonder if kids should just be let alone sometimes to talk to each other, for the sake of building social skills and community. They need daily time to talk with each other without us acting as directors or facilitators of their conversations.

The Value of Clear and High Expectations

Because we want our students to be readers for life and not just readers in school, our expectations must be high. They must also be clear and rigorous. After all, we're aiming to affect lives and thinking habits, not just test scores and state rankings.

Donna Santman, a teacher at I.S. 89 in Manhattan, has been talking about rigor in classrooms for years. For instance, she says, children often tune out during read-aloud time no matter how compellingly and beautifully we read aloud. This is discouraging because many of us work so hard to make read-aloud time engaging and to improve the children's talk about the books we read aloud. We work on teaching children to retell well, to follow lines of thinking during read-aloud time, and to carry on focused conversations. We transcribe or videotape the book talks, and congratulate ourselves when we review the wonderful comments some children have made.

But, as Donna points out, if we look beyond the profound comments of a few children, we see a greater number of children who are not present in these conversations. Some tune out intentionally, and some just because they don't know how to listen. In one of her demonstration lessons, Donna raised this issue with the students. Many admitted that their minds often wandered as their teacher read aloud. Some said it was really hard to follow the story. And there are other children who are challenged during read-aloud time because of English language issues or auditory processing difficulties.

Donna's observations help us realize that we need to teach children how we want them to work during read-aloud or any other time. Just sitting nicely on the carpet and looking at us as we read aloud is not enough. We have to teach them how to actively listen, and then work on getting everyone involved in the conversations. In order to help the children meet our high expectations, we need to model, demonstrate, and tell them exactly what we expect them to do.

Often the things we expect our children to do seem so obvious and simple to us teachers. We say things like, "Listen as I read," or "Point under the words as you read," or "Open to page 13 in your handwriting workbook," or "Take only one tissue at a time," or "Use your quiet voices." These kinds of directives embody performance expectations, yet the children may not understand exactly what we mean. "Listen as I read" could mean a thousand different things on any given day. A child could be listening to his stomach growling, to the car alarm outside the classroom window, to the child next to him who keeps clearing his throat. A directive seemingly as obvious as "Open to page 13" can be challenging for children who don't yet know two-digit numeration or understand number order. For other kids, the distance between page 1 and page 13 is vast, and they may make quite a few pit stops at pages of interest as they flip through the book. For these reasons, especially with our youngest learners, we need to make our expectations for their work crystal clear by modeling, demonstrating, and explicitly teaching them exactly what we want them to do.

Turning Our Beliefs into Practice

Get a few teachers in a room, and it's easy to talk the talk with regard to beliefs and philosophy. But the real test of our beliefs is when we walk the walk in our classrooms. It's one thing to say what we believe, but it's quite another to do what we believe, especially when mandates from far away ask us to compromise or change the way we do our jobs. Regardless of the curriculum, whether it's a new math program or a mandated approach to reading, there are fundamental ways of being in our classrooms that enable us to follow our beliefs as professionals and to follow our hearts as teachers of children.

I learned this lesson recently when I worked with a teacher who was struggling with independent reading in her classroom. "My kids love to read, but it feels like party time during reading workshop. They talk, walk, and daydream. All I seem to be doing is trying to get them settled in to work. How can I get them to work more independently?" she asked me one day after school.

We sat down and looked at her typical day and talked about the way she teaches other subjects. We discovered that reading time is the only time all day that her students need to be self-initiated enough to work independently. During writing time, they have writing prompts and assignments to direct their work, and during math, they have workbook pages. During art, they all make the same kind of project, like the tissue paper Halloween ghosts staring down at us from the light fixtures.

This teacher struggled with independent reading workshop not because she is a bad teacher or the independent reading workshop is a bad idea. It became clear that the problem was that the work habits and motivation the children needed to be successful during independent reading workshop were anomalies in this class. The children didn't know how to handle independent work time during reading because they were not expected to work independently at any other time during the school day. Because this teacher truly believed in the value of the independent reading workshop, we thought about ways she could allow children to be more self-motivated and independent at other times in the day. What a huge job she was taking on! She was trying to change her practice to more closely match her beliefs about teaching and learning.

The point of sharing this teacher's story is that it shows how our teaching in one subject is affected and dependent on the way we teach other subjects. This means that we must teach into our independent reading workshop throughout the day, even during math or science, recess or story time. The habits of mind we want our children to use at reading time need to be valued all day long. In other words, we can't just turn on a particular belief system for a particular subject. It's vital to check in with ourselves to make sure our beliefs (and knowledge) about teaching and learning are evident in our classroom practice all day long.

My hope, as you've read this chapter, is twofold. I hope that you've had a chance to reflect on your own beliefs about teaching and learning. I think it's so important and helpful for teachers to reaffirm, clarify, and revisit this essential issue. I also hope that you'll find what I've said here about my beliefs to be reflected in the classroom stories and teaching ideas throughout this book.

Even now, as I move on to write the next chapter, I know that this chapter can never really be finished. As I add years to my teaching life, I'm sure I will also add to and revise my beliefs about teaching and learning. Our work in classrooms is ever-changing, and our beliefs about our work also evolve and grow through our experience, through our struggles, and through our victories. How lucky we are to be teachers, to work at something with such inherent variety and such profound importance.

Experiences in Literacy Throughout the Day

Chapter 2

WHEN I WAS A CHILD, MY YOUNGER BROTHER played soccer in our town league. time, there were no girls' teams in the area. I would watch his games sidelines wishing that I could run right out on the field and race for the ball. There must have been a lot of us sisters watching our brothers play because the following year a girls' soccer team was started in our town.

I played soccer every summer and each school year as I grew up. I had many teammates, a variety of coaches, and winning and losing seasons. When I think about a particularly successful team on which I played, I realize that the coaches of that team knew a lot about soccer and about working with children: our practices were well planned and organized, and the coaches spent time teaching us the skills we needed to play soccer well, such as dribbling, passing, trapping, and heading the ball. But that wasn't all. We warmed up, scrimmaged against each other, and played exhibition games. They also fostered a sense of community among the players and the families, and all of us, grown-ups included, looked forward to game nights and tournament weekends. During games the coaches were kind, supportive, and helpful from the sidelines. They took a well-rounded, balanced approach to coaching soccer as they taught us to become not just better soccer players but better athletes and sportswomen as well.

I think successful reading instruction has similarities to successful soccer coaching. They both require a well-rounded approach. A child won't learn all there is to know about reading simply by learning the print-sound code (Clay 1991). In the same way, a child won't learn how to play soccer by learning only how to dribble and pass the ball. On the other hand, children don't learn to read by putting a book in front of them and hoping for the best, just as a soccer player doesn't learn how to play by stepping onto a field and kicking the ball around when the whistle blows.

In teaching reading, we need to provide many types of functional practice and experiences that will support children's growth (Goodman 1996). In classrooms everywhere, teachers find that a balanced approach to literacy instruction offers a variety of ways for children to become well-rounded and strong independent readers and writers. Although the focus of this book is the independent reading workshop, it is worth noting that in balanced literacy classrooms teachers make time in the day for other components of literacy instruction as well. These components include shared reading, interactive read-aloud with accountable talk, story time, phonics and word study, small-group work (guided reading or strategy lessons), interactive writing, and writing workshop.

My purpose in this chapter is to provide an overview of, and a vision for, the independent reading workshop and to suggest other literacy components that will complement, enhance, and strengthen the work that your students can do during their independent reading time, in school and anywhere else they find themselves lost in a book.

What Is an Independent Reading Workshop?

In many classrooms around the country, teachers have given careful consideration to ways and methods of providing their students with time to read independently, and of course, their conceptions differ. Imagine that right now, you and I are going on a professional journey together (paid for in full by our districts, of course). Our quest is to step inside classrooms and observe what's happening in the name of independent reading so that our vision of the independent reading workshop becomes clear. Okay, grab your notebooks and let's go.

Our first stop is at my school, P.S. 321 in Brooklyn, where I'll show you the independent reading workshop in my classroom. My students are gathered in the meeting area, looking at and listening to me as I teach a mini-lesson on a comprehension strategy that proficient readers use. Each day I begin independent reading time with a mini-lesson like this one in which I offer whole-class, direct, explicit reading instruction. I wrap up the mini-lesson (which typically takes less than 10 minutes) by sending the students back to their reading spots for private reading time. It takes a minute or so for the room to settle. The children have their own plastic file holders with several books inside. They are reading a range of texts, from easy books with one line of text on a page to chapter books, because each child is reading a book at his or her independent reading level. I assess the children often so that I can guide them toward the books that match them as readers. As the children read independently, I offer individualized direct instruction during one-on-one conferences with readers. I take notes about each child during these reading conferences.

After 20 minutes I tell the children it's partner reading time. I briefly remind them of one of the ways we've learned to talk well about books. The children quickly move around to meet with their reading partners. The noise level in the classroom has risen slightly as the children begin reading together and talking about their books with their partners. During partner reading time, I confer with some partners and then I gather four children for small-group direct instruction. Today, I'm supporting a small group of readers in a guided reading session because, based on my assessments, they are ready to move to the next level of text.

After about 10 minutes of partner reading time, I stand up and again get the children's attention. "First graders, I hate to say it, but reading time is over." There is an audible group sigh, and a couple of children plead, "Just another minute, we have to finish talking about this page!" I smile and tell them to use a sticky note to save their spot so they can continue their conversation tomorrow. Then I say, "Please put the book you're going to read at home tonight in your take-home bag, and bring your bag and your body to the meeting area for share time." For the next few minutes the children gather again in the meeting area, and I share some of the great work I observed during reading time today.

During this visit to my classroom, you witnessed instruction throughout the independent reading workshop. The instruction began when I modeled and demonstrated a reading strategy in the whole-class mini-lesson. Then, as children worked independently and with partners, I coached and instructed them during reading conferences. I pulled a small group of children together to offer more assessment-based instruction. Finally, during the teaching share, you saw that I reinforced the day's lesson by sharing some of the ways children were successful with the strategy I taught.

The next stop on our journey is my old elementary school, where independent reading is known as silent sustained reading or SSR. As we go into a classroom, we listen as the teacher instructs the children to take their SSR books out of their desks. "Remember that this is a quiet time," she reminds them. As we look around, we notice that the children are reading a huge variety of books, and the room is very quiet.

I used to look forward to SSR time when I was a student. We only had it twice a week: on Wednesdays after library time, and on Friday afternoons, and it was exciting because our teacher would let us read any book that we brought in or borrowed from the library.

Let me be honest here: what excited me most about SSR wasn't necessarily having time to read my own book. What I really looked forward to was the possibility of "getting the call." My teacher randomly picked children who would get to be her helpers during SSR time. Oh, how I hoped my name would be chosen! I loved to be a helper and do things like use the staple remover to take down the construction paper jack-o'-lanterns with accordion legs in order to make way for cornucopias and five-finger turkeys. I longed to be the one to collate and staple homework packets for the following week. Unfortunately, during those many SSR times when my name wasn't picked, I had trouble concentrating on reading my book. I was distracted as I watched my lucky classmates hand masking-tape loops up to our teacher as she stood precariously on bookshelves putting up the maps of the continents we had colored during social studies. During SSR time, the teacher may or may not be teaching reading. My teacher spent SSR time catching up on the other work she needed to do with the help of some eager children. It seems that often SSR time is less an instructional opportunity and more of a management structure that enables teachers to get some other things done while children are quietly looking at books.

Our next stop is a first-grade classroom during literacy center time. The teacher is meeting with a small group of children for guided reading at a cashew-shaped table. The rest of the children are working in small groups around the room. Some are plugged into the tape recorder at the listening center, and others have Big Books and shared reading texts spread out on the floor. A group of children are practicing spelling and making words with magnetic letters. Almost everyone seems busy and engaged. As we continue looking around, we see a group of children sitting at a table with a basket of books in the middle, all reading books from the basket and debating about who has the scariest Halloween costume. This conversation about costumes began when two of the children were looking together at the book *Rattlebone Rock*.

I ask the children what they are doing at this center. One child looks up and says, "It's the independent reading center. We're reading *Rattlebone Rock*. This is the browsing basket." Again, like SSR time in the previous classroom, the independent reading time in this classroom is a management structure that enables the teacher to do something else, in this case, to meet with guided reading groups. The teacher is not teaching directly into the children's independent reading because she is working with one guided reading group after another. When she finishes the second of the three guided reading groups, she transitions the students into another center.

The next school we visit is in a district where independent reading is called DEAR time, or "Drop Everything And Read." During DEAR time everybody in the school, including the principal, the custodian, and the guidance counselor, stops what they are doing to read something, anything. As we walk around the school, we see adults reading catalogs, professional literature, district memos, magazines, novels, and newspapers. We see children sitting in their seats reading a variety of texts as well. The building is relatively quiet as everyone focuses for a while on his or her own reading.

The obvious power of DEAR time is that a school becomes a community of readers. It's exciting for children to see grown-ups around them reading, in much the same way as it can be thrilling for children when a teacher joins a game of tag at recess or the principal sits beside them in the cafeteria and eats her lunch. During DEAR time, however, if everyone is dropping everything to read, no explicit reading instruction is going on. Of course, the power of modeling reading is important, but we have to ask, "Is that enough?"

Now, as our journey nears its end, let's talk about what we observed. In each of the classrooms I've described, the children were, in fact, reading self-chosen books independently. One of the main differences, however, between the independent reading workshop in my classroom and independent reading time in the next three examples (SSR, independent reading during literacy centers, and DEAR time) is the absence or presence of direct, explicit instruction. In some classrooms the only instruction children receive during independent reading time is on management and procedures, because the teacher is engaged with other tasks (e.g., her own reading, her to-do list, or guided reading groups). By contrast, during the independent reading workshop, the teacher provides whole-class, individual, and small-group direct, explicit reading instruction to her students. In addition, when children read independently during independent reading workshop, they read just-right books, which are books that match their independent reading levels. Children can read their just-right books with fluency, comprehension, and at least 90–95 percent accuracy (Calkins 2001).

I hope our imaginary visit to my classroom gave you a vision for what an independent reading workshop looks and sounds like. In the chapters that follow, I provide specific information about the teaching and learning that goes on during this time.

Guiding Principles of the Independent Reading Workshop

During independent reading workshop, the teacher actively works with his students to teach them the skills and strategies they need to grow stronger as readers. Lucy Calkins often refers to the independent reading workshop as the heart of our reading work because it's the time in the day when children have the opportunity to orchestrate all they know about reading in order to read their own just-right books (Calkins 2001).

For now, to provide an overview, here are what many teachers consider to be the seven guiding principles of the independent reading workshop within a balanced literacy framework.

- Readers have time to read just-right books independently every day.
- Readers select their own appropriate books.
- Readers take care of books.
- Readers respect each other's reading time and reading lives.
- Readers have daily opportunities to talk about their books in genuine ways.
- Readers don't just read the words but also understand the story.
- Readers' work in the independent reading workshop is replicable outside the classroom.

Readers have time to read just-right books independently every day. Common sense (and life experience) tells us that getting better at anything requires practice. I don't think anyone would disagree that in order for children to become strong independent readers, we need to allot them the time to practice reading on their own, with our guidance and instruction, of course. In primary classrooms, this might mean that in September, after a mini-lesson, children read independently for 5 to 15 minutes daily. By the end of the school year, their stamina for reading independently will increase to allow 30 or 50 minutes, including private reading time and partner reading time. Throughout the year, while children are reading independently, we teachers have reading conferences with individuals, partners, and small groups to offer individualized direct instruction.

Readers select their own appropriate books. Every day during independent reading workshop, my first graders read just-right books, which they've selected from our classroom library. These are books at the children's independent reading levels, which means they can read them independently with 90–95 percent accuracy, fluency, and comprehension. When children choose their own just-right books, they will have more interest and investment in their reading (Short and Harste 1995; Holdaway 1979; Smith 1987). And when they choose books that are at their independent reading levels, they will grow as readers.

To support children's choosing just-right books, at least 30–40 percent of the classroom library is leveled according to a gradient of text difficulty. In many classroom libraries, teachers use a color dot system to indicate the level of the texts in the leveled portion of the library; for example, the easiest books that share the same text characteristics may have yellow dots on the cover and be located in a basket with a yellow dot on its label. We need to teach our students where they'll find their just-right books in the leveled library, and this is based on our reading assessments.

There are many leveling systems that teachers and schools use to uniformly level texts from one class to another. In my teaching, I rely upon the Teachers College Reading and Writing Project leveling guides (Calkins 2002).

In addition to the leveled portion of the library, classrooms with independent reading workshops always have libraries filled with a range of books, in terms of level, topic, and genre. It's important for our students to know that there is a world of texts beyond the leveled library in which they can pursue their interests and develop new ones.

In addition to just-right books, we also encourage children to choose interest books, which may or may not be at their independent reading levels. So, for example, a child might choose to read a couple of nonfiction books on insects if that is a particular interest. Another child might borrow a Mem Fox book because her teacher has read it aloud. During independent reading workshop, the children's reading time is spent with their just-right books, but we also provide opportunities, either added on to independent reading workshop or at another time of the day, for children to explore a wider variety of texts.

In the chapters that follow, I offer more details about the classroom library, systems for students' book choices, and managing the whole system.

❖ *Readers take care of books.* When I was a child, I was mesmerized by three of our Christmas tree ornaments. They appeared so fragile and beautiful that I wanted to look closely at them. Each year, my mother would tell my brothers and me the story of these glass orbs, how they were ornaments from when she and my uncles were children, and she'd remind us that they were very special to her. She'd let us hold them before she gently hung them on the highest branches of the tree. I remember feeling that I needed to be so careful with those ornaments, not only because I'd get into trouble if they broke but also because my mom would be so sad if anything happened to them.

I spend some time early in the school year encouraging children to feel about books the way I felt about those three ornaments. I want my students to learn and to believe that books are special, worth taking care of, and meant to be shared with other people for many years. On a practical note, this is important because classroom books cost hundreds of dollars and need to last from one year to the next.

I teach my students how to take care of books and why it's important to do so. I also teach them how to keep the classroom library organized for all readers by putting books back carefully into the correct basket. Taking care of books and the organization of the library is a community matter in workshop classrooms.

❖ *Readers respect each other's reading time and reading lives.* One of the greatest challenges for teachers who launch independent reading workshop is the management of the time, so it's of great importance for children to understand the expectations for how they need to work. Children learn how to use quiet voices during reading time as well as how to stay focused on their books and what to do when they finish a book. We spend time teaching these expectations during our September unit of study, Readers Build Good Habits (see Chapter 4).

Also, we teach children to respect the differences among readers in the classroom. In independent reading workshop, all the children are reading books that are just right for them, so there is often quite a range of texts being read in any one class. In our inclusion class, Jessica, my co-teacher, and I had children reading books with one line of patterned text per page alongside children who were reading chapter books, so it was extremely important for us to talk to students about how we all have different reading needs and tastes, just as we all have different heights, hair colors, or numbers of loose and missing teeth.

❖ *Readers have daily opportunities to talk about their books in genuine ways.* During independent reading workshop, after private time when children have read by themselves, we provide time for them to meet with their reading partners to read together and talk about their books. In order to have a conversation about a book, one needs to have had some thoughts as one reads, and this is what we want children to do whenever they read—have thoughts and talk about them with other readers. This time to talk and think about books with other readers helps children make meaning and supports deeper comprehension.

In our classrooms we do a lot of work outside of the independent reading workshop to support children as they learn to talk well about books. During shared reading and interactive read-aloud as well as during reading workshop mini-lessons, we teach our students the kinds of things readers can think and talk about, we show them how to use text evidence to support their thinking, and we model how to have good conversations that stick with one idea at a time and that include each partner's ideas.

The authentic conversations we make time for during partner reading time grow out of children's own thoughts and ideas as they read. From early in the school year, our students learn that thinking about and understanding what they have just read is a big job for readers and that it's fun to talk about one's ideas with others. In other words, the conversations between reading partners are not prompted by the teacher.

Instead of expecting very young children to regularly write reports or synopses or to answer comprehension questions about their books, we teach them how readers make sure they understand texts by thinking as they read and talking about the stories with others.

❖ *Readers don't just read the words but also understand the story.* Typically, once children crack the code and read the words in their books with relative ease, they begin to race through books and just keep moving from one to the next. For many children, reading seems to become nothing more than word digestion; there's little time for savoring the text, for thinking about the story, and for connecting it to what they know about their lives, the world, and other texts (Keene and Zimmermann 1997). We make it clear that reading is much more than decoding the words in books, that the big job for any reader is to understand and to follow the story.

We spend a good portion of the independent reading workshop teaching children how readers hold themselves accountable for understanding their stories, and we teach them ways they can help themselves if they don't understand.

❁ *Readers' work in independent reading is replicable outside the classroom.* The independent reading workshop is meant to closely resemble the reading work children can do when they are not in our sphere of influence. We want to provide time for them in school to practice the things they can do whenever or wherever they are reading. For this reason, independent reading workshop is packed with reading, thinking, and talking, which are the authentic, functional, and purposeful things that proficient readers do throughout their lives.

We don't make time during independent reading workshop, especially in the primary grades, for children to do lots of writing about their reading. For one thing, our youngest readers are also our youngest writers, and expecting them to write often about their reading can be too demanding. In lieu of regular writing assignments, we provide time for children to talk about their reading. It's easier for them at this stage to convey their thinking orally than in written form, and talking about books is much more common in real life than writing about them.

That said, I do acknowledge that there are district mandates about having children write about their books, so I understand that teachers may need to provide time to do that. I would just keep it separate from independent reading workshop.

Structure of an Independent Reading Workshop

The independent reading workshop has a predictable structure:

Structure of an Independent Reading Workshop
- Mini-lesson (10 minutes or less)
- Independent work time with instruction
    Children are engaged in private reading time.
  Teacher provides instruction during reading conferences and small-group work.
- Mid-workshop teaching
    Children are engaged in partner reading time.
  Teacher provides instruction during reading conferences and small-group work.
- Teaching share time (about 5 minutes)

The children in my classroom know that independent reading workshop starts when the class gathers in the meeting area for a mini-lesson. After the mini-lesson the children go to their reading spots for independent work time. This work time begins with children's reading their own just-right books, first by themselves during private reading time and then with their reading partners during partner reading time. Reading partners read books together and talk about their books. Sometimes, between private reading and partner reading, the teacher may do some very brief mid-workshop teaching to remind or teach children about something that will help them in their work with partners. After partner reading, the children know that they will gather again in the meeting area for a teaching share time.

Mini-lesson

Imagine now that it's late September. In my classroom it's time for independent reading workshop. I gather the children in the meeting area, which is a 9' × 12' rug bordered on two sides by the classroom library bookshelves and on one side by the chalkboard. I sit in a chair with the chalkboard behind me, an easel to my left, and a basket of books to my right. The children sit in front of me, next to their reading partners. My class knows what to do and what to expect during this mini-lesson because the expectations are the same for any mini-lesson, whether it's for writing, math, art, science, or social studies. They know that a mini-lesson is a time for them to learn something new that will help them with their work. They know that a mini-lesson is not a time for big discussions, getting a drink of water, or checking the Velcro on their sneakers. Of course, in early September I had to teach them about the expectations I have for behavior and participation during mini-lessons.

The mini-lesson by that name was first conceived in the context of the writing workshop (Calkins 1983). During this time a teacher directly instructs the whole class on a skill, strategy, or habit that they need to learn and use during independent work. Mini-lessons are brief, explicit teaching opportunities that follow a certain "architecture" (Calkins 2001):

Architecture of a Mini-lesson
- Connection
  - Connect today's lesson with yesterday's lesson
  - Connect today's lesson with ongoing unit of study
  - Connect today's lesson with students' work
  - Connect today's lesson with an experience outside of school
- Teaching point
  - Present verbally
  - Demonstrate or model
- Active engagement
  - Children try out a skill or strategy with a text
  - Children act like researchers as they watch a demonstration
  - Children plan work out loud
  - Children imagine trying a skill or strategy
- Link to ongoing work

The idea of a mini-lesson's having an "architecture" arose when Lucy Calkins and her colleagues were studying the characteristics of the most successful mini-lessons. They realized that there seemed to be a kind of rhythm or predictability that characterized the best ones.

Connection

A mini-lesson often begins with the teacher's making a connection that grounds the work of today's mini-lesson in the ongoing work the children have been doing.

He might connect today's lesson with yesterday's lesson or with an ongoing unit of study, saying, for example, "Yesterday we learned that one of the things readers can do to figure out the words in their books is to check the picture and think about what's going on in the story; today I want to show you another way that readers can figure out words in their books," or "For the last week or so, we've been learning about lots of things readers can do when they get to tricky parts in their books; today I want to teach you another thing you can do when you get to a tricky part."

Or the teacher might connect today's lesson with his observations of student work or with an experience he has had outside of school, for example, "Yesterday, during partner reading, I noticed that Ryan and Ben were helping each other with tricky words in their books, not just jumping in and telling each other the words but figuring them out together; today I want to teach you what they did to be such great reading teachers for each other," or "Last night I was reading a book about when George Washington was president, and something happened to me that I know happens to you—I came to a really tricky word that I didn't know at all and had to do some work to figure it out; today I want to teach you what I did because I think it will help you, too."

Teaching Point

The next part of a mini-lesson is making the teaching point, in clear language and by demonstrating or modeling exactly what is meant. Telling children what we want them to do is not enough. Research suggests that demonstrating and making our teaching explicit provides children with powerful examples and a vision for what their own work should look like during independent reading workshop.

The teaching demonstration is often cued by the teacher's saying, "Today I want to teach you how to. . . ." Then, after stating the teaching point very clearly in language that children can understand, the teacher moves into the demonstration: "Let me show you what I mean." Often the teacher will alert children that they need to pay close attention to the demonstration by saying, "Notice how I . . ." or "I want you to watch what I do."

Active Engagement

After the demonstration the teacher provides an opportunity for guided practice (Pearson and Gallagher 1983), a chance for students to try out the skill or strategy right then and there. I use the term "active engagement" for the guided practice portion of the lesson. While the children are trying out the skill or strategy, the teacher assesses whether they have made sense of the teaching point. There are several ways to conduct the active engagement portion of the mini-lesson.

Providing a text for each child (or pair of children), the teacher might say, "I want you to try this strategy using these books." It helps if the books are easy or familiar to the children so they are not distracted by the novelty or challenge of an unfamiliar text. Or, the teacher might ask each child to bring a just-right book to the meeting area and try out the strategy using that.

Another method to accomplish active engagement is to ask children to be researchers while they watch a demonstration by the teacher: "Right now, I want you to watch me closely while I try. . . . Notice how I. . . ." Then, after the demonstration, the students talk to their partners about what they noticed the teacher doing. Or, giving a negative example of what should *not* be done, the teacher might say, "Watch me as I try to figure out one of the words on this page. If you notice a way to help me, put your thumbs up."

Children may also restate the teaching point to their partners, plan with their partners how they will use a skill or strategy in their own reading, or imagine themselves using the strategy that has been taught. Guiding their concentration, the teacher might say, "I want you to imagine that you take out your just-right book, look closely at the cover, and think about the title."

The active engagement portion of the mini-lesson needs to be quick so that the mini-lesson doesn't turn into a long, drawn-out session, and it needs to provide an opportunity for children to try out, right then and there, the skill or strategy emphasized in your teaching demonstration that day. In the chapters that follow, I've included examples of mini-lessons reflecting a variety of methods for active engagement.

Link to Ongoing Work

Finally, in the last part of the mini-lesson, the teacher makes a link to the students' ongoing work. She restates the teaching point and reminds students to use the strategy themselves during independent reading or any time they are reading, whether at home or in school: "Whenever you're reading, whether it's here in school or at home or on the subway, I want you to remember to use the pictures in the story to help you figure out the words, just as we did today."

Sample Mini-lesson

The following is a sample mini-lesson that I've done late in September, with comments interspersed to highlight the parts of the mini-lesson mentioned in the previous section.

Readers, I can tell you guys are so ready to get really strong at reading the words in your books. So many of you told me that you just can't wait! Yesterday, Joci even said, "Can we get to the words now? I'm ready for it."

I bet lots of you feel like Joci. Give me a thumbs-up if you feel ready for the words, like Joci. [I look around to see everyone giving me a thumbs-up.]

Good, because for the next few weeks, we're going to work really hard at becoming strong readers who figure out words and understand the stories in the books we read. Today, I'm going to teach you something that careful readers do first to get their minds ready to read the words in their books. I'm going to teach you that careful readers look closely at the covers of the books to get their minds ready.

I *connected* today's lesson to things I've heard the children say and to the unit of study I'm launching—Readers Use Strategies to Figure Out Words. I invited guided participation by having children give me a thumbs-up rather than asking, Who feels like Joci?

Today I want to teach you how readers get their minds ready to read the words in their books by using information from the cover. Careful readers look closely at the information on the cover, the title and the picture especially, and think to themselves, "What might this book be about?" [I show a book.] This helps them get their minds ready to read.

Hmm, before I just jump right in to read this book, I'm going to get my mind ready. The title says, "How to Make a Sandwich." Oh, look at the picture on the cover. What is that? It looks like peanut butter. I'll bet this book is about how to make a peanut butter and jelly sandwich. Now I feel more ready to read the words in the book because my mind is ready.

Okay, readers, did you notice how I read the title out loud and thought, What might this book be about? Did you hear how I looked at the picture on the cover for clues? And all along I kept thinking, What might this book be about?

My *teaching point* is that readers get their minds ready to read a book by looking at the cover and using the information on it to think about what the book might be about. I *demonstrated* how to do this by thinking out loud as I used the cover to get ready to read. I purposely chose a book similar to what many children in the class would be reading during independent reading time. Before beginning my demonstration, I *told them clearly* what to watch for. I used consistent language throughout. After the demonstration I refocused the children's attention on the strategy by saying, Did you notice . . . ?

Okay, now I want you guys to try it. I'm going to show you a book, and I want you to think about the title and look at the picture while thinking to yourselves, What might this book be about? [I put an unfamiliar Big Book on the easel and read the title to the class.] Look at the cover, think about the title, and look at the picture. Remember to think to yourselves, What might this book be about? [I give them half a minute to do so.]

During *active engagement* I gave the children a chance to try out the work I want them to do on their own. I used a new Big Book for this demonstration because I wanted to replicate what they would need to do with unfamiliar books.

Turn and talk to the person sitting next to you about your thinking. What might this book be about? [I listen in to a few partner talks.]

I gave them time to talk with their partners about what they were thinking rather than asking the whole class for volunteers to participate.

Readers, I listened in and learned that you really thought about the cover of the book. You said the title out loud, and you noticed the picture. The title and the picture on the cover helped you imagine what the book might be about, so I'll bet you would be all ready to read the words in it.

When they talked to their neighbors, I listened in to report back what I heard them say. This is more efficient than asking, What did you think? If I had asked this, only a few children would have had the chance to share their thoughts. When I asked them to turn and talk, everyone had the opportunity to share their thinking.

Readers, whenever you're about to read a book, remember that you need to think about the title and the cover picture to get your mind ready to read the book. Think to yourselves, What might this book be about? Today, I'm going to be looking for careful readers who do that, careful readers who think, What might this book be about? I'm sure everyone is going to try it because it's such an important thing for readers to do.

During the *link to ongoing work* I restated the reading work I had taught them to do in this lesson. I told them I expected them to do this whenever they read.

Other Considerations for Effective Mini-lessons

It's important to follow a consistent architecture in our mini-lessons, whether it's similar to the one I described or another method used regularly in the classroom. When we have a consistent approach to mini-lessons, planning becomes easier, teaching becomes more efficient, and the students come to know what to expect so that they can better focus on the skill or strategy that we're teaching.

Of course, the language and tone of my mini-lessons will inevitably differ from other teachers'. After all, we each have our own way with students, and we have to teach in ways that feel comfortable and natural. Throughout this book, I provide sample mini-lessons, and my intention is for readers to use these as templates rather than as scripts for their own work with children.

Although we need to account for differences in teaching style, the following suggestions can help every teacher conduct effective and inspiring mini-lessons:

- *Limit student talk.* Sometimes, in our effort to hear children's voices, we may invite too much student participation during mini-lessons. I used to do this; then my mini-lessons would stretch too long, and the children would become fidgety and unfocused. Joanne Hindley, author of *In the Company of Children*, says that the mini-lesson is the time for the teacher to talk and to teach. She provides other times in the school day for children to talk about their work, but during mini-lessons she does most of the talking. We can allow a certain level of participation during mini-lessons, but it should be guided and controlled.

- *Keep connections brief.* The stories we use to make a connection should not be too elaborate or grand lest they distract from the teaching point. I once shared a story that involved baby aspirin, my younger brother, and ipecac. Needless to say, my students were so morbidly interested in the story that they entirely missed the teaching point I was trying to make. So, keep the connection part of the mini-lesson brief, not much more than half a minute long.

  As well, don't turn the connection part of a mini-lesson into a Q&A session by asking things like, "Readers, who can tell us what we've learned about figuring out hard words in our books?" Teachers often do this in an attempt to assess children's knowledge. Unfortunately, these Q&A sessions don't really provide an accurate assessment, and they almost always turn the mini-lesson into a drawn-out, meandering event. If a teacher feels she must remind students about the things they've learned already in the unit of study, she might instead say something like, "We've been learning about how to figure out hard words in our books. One thing we've learned is. . . ." When the teacher does the work of reminding the class, the connection goes much faster and the lesson stays on track.

- *State the teaching point simply, and reiterate it.* Sometimes, in our efforts to be crystal clear, we may overexplain the teaching point. It always works better to state the teaching point concisely and repeat it throughout the lesson. It also helps to regularly cue the teaching point by saying something like, "Listen closely . . . today I'm going to teach you how to . . ." or "Today you'll learn how to. . . ." When we cue the teaching point this way, children become conditioned to focus on what they're going to learn in this mini-lesson.

  I like to imagine that when my children get up from a mini-lesson and go to their independent work, the teaching point is playing over and over in their heads like a song. For this to happen, I use consistent language to describe the teaching point, both during the lesson and in reading conferences.

- *Demonstrate the teaching point.* After expressing the teaching point clearly, it helps to demonstrate it, especially from the perspective of a six- or seven-year-old child. To cue the demonstration, the teacher can say, "Let me show you what it looks like," or "Watch me as I show you how to do it."

- *Use a familiar text.* To demonstrate the teaching point, it's helpful to use a familiar text rather than a new one. An unfamiliar text might distract students because they tend to focus more on the novelty of the new text rather than on the strategy or skill they are learning.

- *Match the active engagement to the teaching point*. It's important for the active engagement to match the teaching point so that children have the chance to practice the same skill or strategy that was demonstrated.

To wind up the active engagement, a teacher could ask children to report back on what they just did, but this might draw the mini-lesson on too long. More helpful is the teacher's stating what she noticed children doing during active engagement: "Okay, readers, eyes up here. I noticed some good work. Some of you were. . . ."

Independent Work Time with Instruction

After the mini-lesson, I send the children out of the meeting area back to their reading spots for *private reading time*. In my classroom the children's regular seats are their reading spots. I know many teachers who let children sit around the room in cozy nooks and comfortable chairs for reading time. I love that idea, but typically it's been hard for me to start out the year with children reading around the room. I find it easier to manage the room, especially at the beginning of the year, when children sit at their tables. Then, later in the year, when children know exactly what's expected of them during reading time, I let them choose places other than their own seats for reading.

On the other hand, some teachers have found that having all their students at their tables or desks can create its own set of management problems because the room might get too noisy or the children might distract each other. These teachers find it more effective to let children read in spots that are spread throughout the room. Where children read during reading time is an individual decision teachers make based on the class temperament and their own comfort.

During private reading time, the children in my class read just-right books that they've chosen from the classroom library. Once a week, they shop for the books that they will read throughout the week, and I guide each of them toward the books that are at their independent reading level. In the chapters that follow, I explain in more detail how children choose their books.

The room is quiet during private reading time, but it's not completely silent. First, most young readers are still reading aloud to themselves, so there is a quiet buzz in the room during private reading time. Also, I let students talk quietly with the person sitting next to them if they need quick help with something. Other teachers I work with do expect private reading time to be silent, and they discourage children from talking to their neighbors during this time. This again is a decision teachers can make based on their tolerance for noise and the temperament of the class.

During private reading time I have reading conferences with individual readers. After private reading time, which increases from 5–10 minutes in September to 35–45 minutes in June, I stop the class for mid-workshop teaching. I might say something like, "Readers, I have to stop you. It's time to meet with your reading partners. Right now, take your books and your book bin, and go to your partner reading spot for partner reading time. Remember, today you will want to show your partner the cover of your book and tell him or her how you got your mind ready to read."

Mid-workshop Teaching

During mid-workshop teaching I remind the children how to use the particular strategy I taught, or teach them something specific to support their work in partnerships. This mid-workshop teaching is based on the needs of the class at the time.

After the brief interruption the children get up and move around the room to meet with their partners for *partner reading time*. Some teachers might begin private reading time by having partners sit near each other on chairs back-to-back, so that when it's time to transition to partner reading, they just need to turn their chairs around. In my classroom children go to their own seats for private reading time, and I tend to assign partner spots, so that each day partners know where they will meet. Again, this is an individual decision based on what works best for the teacher and the children.

During partner reading time the noise level in the room does go up a bit as children read together and talk about their books. Even so, it's important for a teacher to be consistent and clear about how much noise is acceptable. Especially early in the year, I briefly stop my class when the noise rises above a tolerable level. I want them to internalize their own volume monitors so that, as the weeks go by, it becomes less necessary for me to interrupt their work (and my reading conferences) to remind them to lower their voices.

Often during partner reading time, I pull together a small group of children for either guided reading instruction or a strategy lesson. When I don't teach a small group during partner reading time, I continue to walk around the room and conduct reading conferences, this time with partners rather than individuals. The chapters that follow explain setting up and managing reading partnerships in more detail.

Reading Conferences

During the children's independent reading workshop, teachers have very challenging work to do, too. While the children read privately or with partners, the teacher moves around the room providing direct instruction. In order to do this, we need to know our students as readers, a variety of ways to support their reading development, and how to teach the strategies they need to grow as readers.

I rely on two resources to guide me with reading conferences. Carl Anderson's book *How's It Going?* is full of valuable information about conferences in general and writing conferences in particular. Lucy Calkins's *The Art of Teaching Reading* details the kinds of conferences we might have during independent reading workshop. I also refer to other professional literature to help me imagine a repertoire of things I could teach in conferences (see appendix).

When I work with teachers new to independent reading workshop, it's always the case that reading conferences are the most challenging part of the workshop. Teachers often wonder what to say or what to emphasize when they sit alongside readers in their classrooms. As we watch children read, it can be overwhelming: there are a million things to teach them within a single conference.

I begin by providing an idea of how a typical reading conference might go. First, it's important to say that I move to the children rather than having them come to me. In other words, I meet them at their tables and their reading spots instead of asking them to join me at a conference table. When I move around the room for reading conferences, I am able to subtly manage the class because my presence in different places is effective. When I'm walking over to Atelah to confer with her, I can tap Jacob on the back as I pass him if I notice that he seems distracted or unfocused. Also, when I meet Atelah at her reading spot, the conference she and I have can inform the other readers at her table.

It's my goal to have conferences that last less than 3–5 minutes. In order to meet this goal, my conferences, like my mini-lessons, tend to follow a sort of architecture. As I sit alongside a child, I review my notes from our last conference and then observe the child as she reads. I jot some notes about what I see (and don't see). I then begin the interaction by offering some kind of compliment to the reader. This is an important yet often overlooked part of a conference. When we learn to begin a conference with a compliment, it trains us to watch our children and see their strengths. Often, as teachers of reading to new readers, we tend to focus on the skills or strategies that are missing. It's easy to sit alongside a child and feel overwhelmed by all the things the child needs to learn, but when we see only what's missing, we can't truly meet our students where they are as readers. Also, a compliment is just plainly a kindly and encouraging way to begin the interaction required in a reading conference.

So, after doing a little research and complimenting the reader, I move quickly to teach the student a skill or strategy that he needs to help his reading improve. Just as in a mini-lesson, it's most effective to decide on one teaching point for a reading conference. I make this decision by prioritizing the child's needs and picking the strategy or skill that will help most at this time in his reading life.

Having decided on the teaching point, I demonstrate just what I want the child to do, and I watch her as she tries it within the conference. At the end of the conference, I restate the teaching point and remind the reader to use the particular skill or strategy from this point forward. This summary is similar to the "link to ongoing work" portion of the mini-lesson.

As I confer, I take notes on my interaction with the reader. At first, when I was new at conferring, it was hard to observe, teach, and jot notes at the same time. But I've gotten better at it, and it helps me to remember that the purpose of my note taking is to inform my teaching.

In my conference notes, I make sure to jot down the compliment I offered the reader so that I can keep track of what's going well. I note the teaching point of this conference and the other needs of this reader so that I can address them in the next conference or within a small-group strategy lesson with other readers who share that particular need.

Sample Reading Conference

The following is a sample reading conference, with comments interspersed to highlight the parts of the conference just described.

As I sat alongside Julian, I quickly *reviewed my notes* from our last conference to remind me of what we had worked on and what Julian might still need to learn. I *listened and observed* as he read a few pages of his text.

My goal is to leave the child better off at the end of the reading conference than when we started. So, I need to consider the possibilities for what I might teach. Based on my notes from previous conferences and on listening to Julian read, I knew we could work on several things. But today, I decided, my *teaching point* would be that when Julian was figuring out tricky words, he should go back and reread the text smoothly. I knew from previous conferences that Julian tended to rush while reading and to stop to think about what he had read only when asked to do so. I decided to teach him to slow down and reread the tricky parts smoothly because this would support his comprehension and fluency. I also decided on what *compliment* to offer. I jotted all this down in my conference notes.

Julian, I noticed that when you were reading, you used lots of strategies to figure out the tricky words in your book. Like, when you came to the word cleaning, *I saw you check the picture, make the sound of the first letters, and take a guess. You said, "clening," but then you fixed it because that didn't make sense. I liked how you didn't just give up as you were reading.*

I made a specific *compliment* based on what I observed Julian doing as he read. The compliment is analogous to the connection in the mini-lesson, and it starts off the reading conference in an affirming way.

Julian, I noticed that when you were doing that hard work with some of the words in your book, you kept right on reading. It gets a little messy when readers stop to work on words, and when reading gets messy, it can be hard to understand what's going on in our books. So, today I want to show you something that careful readers do to make sure their reading is clean and understandable. Readers go back and reread the parts where they had to do lots of work. Let me show you what I mean.

I'm going to go back to one of the pages where you did some work on words, and show you how careful readers go back and reread so that their reading doesn't sound so messy. Watch me do this.

I returned to the page where Julian had worked hard on a word, and I *demonstrated* how to reread it smoothly.

Julian, did you see how when I stopped to work on a word, my reading got messy? Did you notice how I went back and reread? It helped me get back into the story again.

I *explained* briefly what I had done, noting the benefit of using the strategy.

Now, I want you to go back and reread a part where you worked hard to get the word. I want you to reread it so it sounds clean, not messy, because this will help you better understand what you're reading. Right now, I want you to go back to this page and reread it to clean it up.

I offered the student a chance to *practice the strategy*. I made sure to use *consistent language* throughout the conference, and I remembered to explain why the strategy is important.

Wow, Julian, that sounded really clean. I'll bet it was easier to understand, too. Well, rereading the parts that you work hard on is a really important thing to remember when you read. When your reading is clean, not messy, it's so much easier to understand what you're reading. I want you to do this from now on, okay?

I complimented Julian on his success and *restated the teaching point*. I also made clear my expectation that he would use *this strategy from now on* as he reads. If he had not been successful, I might have demonstrated for him again and asked him to try it once more.

Throughout the chapters that follow, I provide examples of reading conferences that correspond with particular units of study.

Teaching Share Time

After private and partner reading time, my students gather together again for the teaching share time. After partner reading time I say to the class, "Readers, guess what? It's time to meet again for share time. But first, pick out the book you're going to read at home tonight, and put it in your take-home bag. Do that now." The children select a just-right book from their own book bins. "Okay, put your book bin away and bring your bag to the basket in the meeting area, and we'll get together for share time."

The children gather in the meeting area, put their take-home book bags in the proper basket, so that they can be passed out at the end of the day with the homework folders, and take a seat for teaching share time. Many teachers have moved away from the round-robin way of conducting share time, in which each child shares something that they did during reading time. We've found that this kind of share takes a very long time, and the children tend to tune out after the third or fourth description. Instead, many teachers have come to view the share time as another teaching opportunity. I often think about it as a mini-lesson, jr., although it doesn't follow the mini-lesson architecture as described in a previous section. Here are a few different ways that teachers might conduct the teaching share time.

Share Time as a Mini-lesson Reinforcement

Sometimes during independent reading workshop, share time may be used to reinforce the teaching done during the mini-lesson. For instance, I might say, "Today we learned how readers use the cover of a book to help them get their minds ready to read. I want to show you the great work that Selena and Michael did to get their minds ready to read their books." I would show the class what the students had done by acting it out. Then I might say, "Okay, everyone else, turn and tell your neighbor how the cover helped you get your mind ready to read your book today."

Share Time as a Mini-lesson Add-on

When we confer with readers, we may notice that they do something that can supplement the teaching we did in our mini-lesson. In such a case, I might say, "Today I taught you how readers get their minds ready to read by looking closely at the cover picture, saying the title out loud, and thinking what the book might be about. Well, today when Alex was reading, he noticed the author's name on the cover. He had a book by Joy Cowley, and I heard him say, 'Hey, Joy Cowley. I bet this book is going to be silly.' That was so smart of Alex to notice the author's name so that he could get even more ready to read his book. So I guess we can do a few things: Say the title out loud. Look at the cover picture. Notice the author. Think, What might this book be about? Hey, we should start a chart called Things to Do to Get Our Minds Ready to Read a Book, shouldn't we?"

Share Time as a Mini-lesson Preview

Often, during reading conferences, I find that I taught a child a skill or strategy that I had planned to teach the whole class in the next mini-lesson. Then I might use share time to preview the mini-lesson: "Today we learned how readers take a close look at the cover of their books to get their minds ready to read. We learned that it helps to say the title out loud and to look at the picture on the cover. But, you know what? Today Eliza discovered something else that helped her get her mind ready to read. She took a sneak peek inside the book, right, Eliza? Well, tomorrow, I'm going to teach you all how you can do just what Eliza did, how you can take a sneak peek into the book to help get your minds ready to read."

Share Time as a Problem-Solving Opportunity

Some days, the independent reading workshop doesn't turn out as planned. Usually, when this happens, it's a workshop management issue, and the children need to be reminded of what's expected of them. The share time is a good time to have this kind of talk, for example: "Readers, today we were supposed to be working on getting our minds ready to read by looking closely at the covers of our books. But a few kids told me it was hard to concentrate because it was pretty noisy. I even had to interrupt conference time to remind you to use your library voices. I thought we all knew how to use our library voices during reading time. Right now, turn to your neighbor and talk about what it means to use your library voice during reading time and why using library voices is so important." The teacher listens in as children talk briefly. "Okay, I heard you guys say that library voices are quiet voices and that we use library voices so we don't distract other readers. We have to remember that if we're going to have a reading workshop where all readers can concentrate on their work. Right now, I'm going to add another 5 minutes to reading workshop, and we're going to practice using our library voices. Then tomorrow I expect that reading workshop will be much quieter because I'm sure that you'll remember to use your library voices."

In this chapter, I've given a broad overview of the independent reading workshop. The chapters that follow look more closely at the work units of study composing independent reading workshop throughout the year.

Other Components of a Balanced Literacy Framework

Before moving toward a more detailed examination of the independent reading workshop, it's important to acknowledge that there are other components throughout the day within a balanced literacy framework in which we teach children to read, to write, and to be active thinkers and eager learners.

A balanced literacy framework is likely to have the following components as part of the daily approach to teaching reading and writing:

Components of a Balanced Literacy Framework
- Independent reading workshop
- Writing workshop
- Shared reading
- Interactive read-aloud with accountable talk
- Story time
- Small-group work (guided reading, strategy lessons)
- Word study (phonics, spelling)
- Interactive writing

If we think of the independent reading workshop as the heart, then we might think of the other components in a balanced literacy framework as the circulatory system that delivers the "goods" to the heart.

The other components of balanced literacy listed above work in service of independent reading time; they are not ends in and of themselves. After all, the goal of shared reading is not to help students be good at shared reading. We use shared reading as a supporting component to teach students the skills, strategies, and habits they need to be strong independent readers. In the same way, the main purpose of interactive read-aloud is not to teach children how to be good at interactive read-aloud. Rather, we use the interactive read-aloud as a component to model and teach the reading habits and comprehension strategies children need in their own independent reading. In other words, the reading children do in these other balanced literacy components is meant to transfer to the reading children do independently during reading workshop. And the work children do during independent reading workshop is meant to transfer to the reading children do outside the confines of the classroom.

Because the emphasis of this book is on the independent reading workshop, I only outline here the essential aspects of the other components. Many professional books detail the rich and important teaching that can be done within these components (see appendix).

Writing Workshop

The writing workshop follows the same structure as the independent reading workshop—it happens daily and begins with a mini-lesson followed by independent work time and a teaching share time. During independent writing time the children write or revise texts about self-selected topics while the teacher offers individual and small-group direct instruction during writing conferences and strategy lessons. During independent writing time children have access to the materials they need to write, revise, edit, and publish the pieces they've written.

The writing workshop provides valuable support as our youngest students become stronger readers by providing opportunities to develop letter-sound knowledge, word-level (lexical) knowledge, syntactic knowledge, and semantic knowledge (Clay 1998). Many of the skills and strategies our students need to control in order to be successful readers are also taught during the writing workshop. As children compose writing, they have another way of learning about letter-sound relationships, the structure of texts, reading with fluency and comprehension, and the joy of literacy.

Shared Reading

Shared reading, developed by Don Holdaway (1979), is a time in the school day that replicates the experience of a parent's reading a bedtime story to his child. During shared reading teachers gather their students around an enlarged text, such as a Big Book or a poem. All the children can easily see the text and illustrations, and the teacher and students together read and think about the story or poem, just as a parent and child might do as they interact with a book. The reading work during shared reading is shared between the students and the teacher, with the teacher offering significant support as the children lead the way. During a shared reading session the teacher may spend some time working with the students on a focused teaching point, although she needs to be flexible and follow the students' interests and inquiries within the text.

In many classrooms the shared reading session begins with the class reading a familiar text together to warm up and then reading the text they are working on together for a set of days. Finally, many teachers expose the children to a new text at the end of a shared reading session. This new text will become the work text in future shared reading sessions.

Interactive Read-Aloud with Accountable Talk

No matter what side of the reading debate one is on, both sides agree that children need many opportunities to listen to texts read aloud by adults. The interactive read-aloud with accountable talk provides time for the students to listen to and talk about wonderful books that are most likely beyond their independent reading levels. Often early childhood teachers decide to begin the year reading picture books out loud, and then they move on to chapter books. During interactive read-aloud with accountable talk, the teacher models the work that careful readers do to comprehend texts and to foster ideas and theories about stories and characters.

Because the teacher is doing the reading, children can concentrate on using strategies for comprehension and having accountable conversations about the text. The conversations that children have about the read-aloud texts serve as models and scaffold the kinds of conversations we want them to have with their partners during the independent reading workshop. The interactive read-aloud is a time when we can model for the children what they will be able to do themselves as readers in the not-so-distant future.

Story Time

In addition to read-aloud with accountable talk, I try to have at least two other times in the day when I read aloud to my class. These story times provide opportunities to expose children to wonderful literature, beautiful story language, a range of vocabulary, and beloved authors. Story time is also an opportunity to read aloud texts that I could later use to make some kind of teaching point. For example, I make sure to read aloud books, such as *Shortcut*, that I can later use to mentor my students during writing time. I want to ensure that they have had a chance to listen to and enjoy the story as literature before I use it to serve a teaching purpose for writing workshop or other content areas.

Even though my story times may not have the same teaching rigor as the interactive read-aloud with accountable talk, I still model my thinking and provide opportunities for children to talk about the text.

Small-Group Work (Guided Reading, Strategy Lessons)

There are many versions of small-group work, so this component is particularly hard to describe in a brief manner. In many of the classrooms I've worked in, teachers tend to do small-group work in the form of strategy lessons (Goodman, Watson, and Burke 1987) or guided reading sessions (Fountas and Pinnell 1996). In *The Art of Teaching Reading* (2001), Calkins charts some of the differences between strategy lessons and guided reading. I've found it helpful to think of strategy lessons as being efficient opportunities to gather children who need extra support with a particular skill or strategy. I tend to bring children together for guided reading sessions when they are on the verge of moving to or have just begun reading a more difficult level of text.

Word Study (Phonics, Spelling)

It's important to spend time each day systematically teaching our students about letter-sound relationships, spelling, and strategies for encoding and decoding words. There are many methods, approaches, and programs for teaching these things (see appendix).

When we plan word study and phonics instruction we must ensure that we teach children how to transfer what they learn during this time into their own writing and reading work. After all, what good would it do if our children knew digraphs but didn't have opportunities to use them in their own writing? And just because a child can make the /ch/ sound in a whole-class phonics lesson does not mean that she will know what to read if the word *choose, change,* or *exchange* is in the text. We must always contextualize the work we do in word study with the work that readers and writers do in their own texts.

Interactive Writing

During an interactive writing session, the teacher and students co-create a text and "share the pen" to write it on chart paper or sentence strips. In my class, for example, during our neighborhood study, we visited the local veterinary hospital, and when we got back to class, we decided to write a thank-you note to the veterinarian who had given us the tour. Together, we decided what we'd write, and we co-wrote the text on a large piece of chart paper. I called children up to the easel to do some of the writing while the other children sat in the meeting area trying to do the same thing on the dry-erase boards.

This interactive writing session provided an opportunity for me to teach the children about the genre of thank-you notes and to focus on how writers stretch out words to make sure they get the letters in the middle. In most interactive writing sessions the teacher chooses a focus for teaching children something they need to know for their own writing or reading.

Scheduling the Literacy Day

How to schedule the literacy day is one of the most frequently asked questions at workshops and presentations, and it's one of the hardest questions to answer. Every school has particular issues, such as overcrowding, so that in some buildings first graders have to go to lunch at 10:15 a.m. in order for the school to cycle all the students through the cafeteria. In other places, teachers are forced to have a 90-minute literacy block with every single minute mandated by the administration. Still other schools have one half-day per week off for children so that teachers can have professional development. This doesn't include field trips or school assemblies. There must be hundreds of permutations of burdens that teachers endure with regard to scheduling, so I acknowledge that it can be almost impossible to propose a schedule good for everyone. Having said that, I share herewith a possible classroom schedule:

Sample Schedule for a Literacy Day

8:30 a.m.	*Arrival,* morning jobs, library time
8:45	Morning meeting
9:00	Shared reading
9:15	Independent reading workshop
10:05	Word study
10:15	Writing workshop
11:10	Interactive read-aloud with accountable talk
11:30	*Lunch and outdoor play*
12:15 p.m.	Quiet time, free reading
12:20	Math workshop
1:15	Social studies, science, art, choice time
1:45	Preparation
2:35	Story time
2:50	Homework, pack up
3:00	*Dismissal*

Arrival, Morning Jobs, Library Time

Children arrive and do morning jobs. As they do their morning jobs, I greet them, gather notes, try to check homework, and do all the usual first-thing-in-the-morning tasks that teachers have to do. After children finish their morning jobs, they may go to the classroom library and read anything with anybody until it's time for the morning meeting to begin.

Morning Meeting

During the morning meeting in the class meeting area, we go over the schedule for the day and do the quick math work that our math program requires. Three days a week, we do interactive writing via a kind of morning message.

Shared Reading

In the class meeting area, we start with a familiar shared text to warm up and then work on the current work text, which we use for several days. A few times a week, I end the session by introducing a new text that we'll use as a work text in the future. The texts I most often use for shared reading are Big Books, short poems, or interactive writing pieces that we've created.

Independent Reading Workshop

After shared reading and before beginning the independent reading workshop, I ask children to leave the meeting area to get their independent book bins and take them to their seats. This gets them up and moving before they come back to the meeting area for a mini-lesson.

Word Study

No matter what method you use to teach word study, phonics, and spelling, it is crucial to facilitate the transfer of these skills to children's own reading and writing. They need to understand that the things they learn during word study will help them as they write and read. I incorporate handwriting and letter formation practice into the word study session.

Writing Workshop

After word study and before beginning writing workshop, I ask the children to leave the meeting area to get their writing folders and writing tools ready for writing time. Again, my purpose is to get the children moving, if only briefly, so that they'll be ready to focus on the writing mini-lesson. Writing workshop follows the same structure as reading workshop: mini-lesson, work time, and then share time.

Interactive Read-Aloud with Accountable Talk

In the class meeting area, students sit next to their read-aloud partners to listen to and talk about the book I'm reading aloud. This is an opportunity to work on comprehension and conversation strategies. I read a variety of types of texts, including picture books, chapter books, short stories, poetry, and nonfiction throughout the year.

Quiet Time, Free Reading

When the children return from lunch, I give them 5 minutes or so to calm down and read anything from their book bins. They may talk quietly to the children sitting next to them about their books.

Math Workshop

Our math program begins with a mini-lesson and then work time, just like the reading and writing workshops. At the end of math time, I try to have a brief share time, but I admit I don't do it consistently.

Social Studies, Science, Art, Choice Time

In my school, we alternate between social studies units and science units throughout the year. So, if we are immersed in a four-week science unit, I tend not to do social studies at the same time. I believe strongly that children need regular opportunities to create art and to learn about the different art-making media, so I try to ensure that we have at least a period or two of art each week. Also, it's important that we broaden our view of art to include not only the visual arts but also music, drama, and dance.

Fortunately, my school is committed to providing young children with choice time at least a couple of times a week. During choice time, children might do things like build with Legos and blocks, work on their own writing or reading projects, explore math materials, cook, create art, act in plays. In an ideal world, children would have time each day for art, choice, and recess, but in reality, if I can fit these things into the schedule two or three times a week, I'm (sort of) happy.

Homework, Pack Up

I quickly go over the homework assignment and pass out homework folders and take-home book bags.

When we plan out our schedules, fitting everything in on a daily basis can feel like we're trying to solve a Rubik's cube. We switch things this way and that, only to find that something important gets pushed out of the way. When I work with teachers on scheduling, one of the things I tell them is that it's helpful to look at their schedules across a week rather than on a daily basis. When we look across a week, we should make sure that our balanced literacy framework is indeed balanced. We should account for several sessions of shared reading, interactive writing, daily word study, and daily reading and writing workshops, which include small-group instruction.

In an ideal world, everything important happens every day. In reality, however, the only parts of my schedule that are non-negotiable are the daily reading, writing, and math workshops as well as a time when I read aloud to my students. There are days when I might switch shared reading for interactive writing, or I might condense the time allotted to a workshop or two because of a field trip or assembly. Also, one day per week our administration provides each first-grade class with an extra 20 minutes of recess, in addition to the daily recess that preceded lunch. On my bonus recess day, I have to make necessary schedule adjustments.

I realize that it may be difficult for readers to lay this schedule alongside their own because they most likely have completely different school cultures, sets of district mandates, or value systems about what to spend time on. However we schedule, I want to suggest that we don't forget our students. I'm reminded of an important lesson about children and scheduling that I learned from Hannah Schneewind, a colleague at P.S. 321. A couple of times a week Hannah scheduled math in the morning and writing workshop after lunch. When I asked her about this, she said she scheduled that way for children who struggle with literacy. Hannah helped me realize that it must feel really overwhelming for students who struggle with reading and writing to arrive at school each day and face only literacy tasks until lunchtime. Hannah scheduled math (or science, social studies, inquiry, or choice time) in the mornings a couple of times a week out of consideration for those children. When I made this adjustment to my schedule, I saw immediate effects. Herbert and other students like him would light up when they checked the schedule upon arrival and saw that we were going to have math in the morning. Herbert would pump his fist and exclaim, "Yes! Morning math!"

Balance is a good thing. We strive for balance in our lives, our diets, our checkbooks, and our teaching. As I work with young children, I've come to realize that teaching within a balanced literacy framework provides many points of entry into the club of readers and writers (Smith 1987).

This chapter has described components of the literacy day with a particular emphasis on the independent reading workshop. In the chapters that follow, I suggest ways to plan for a balanced curriculum within the independent reading workshop that produces well-rounded readers who decode words proficiently, comprehend texts deeply, and pursue reading joyfully in their lives inside and outside of our classrooms.

Units of Study in a Primary Reading Workshop

Chapter 3

IMAGE IT'S EARLY AUGUST. It's a warm summer day, and you're at the beach. You're standing in line to buy lemonade at the concession stand. You brush sand from the backs of your legs as you anticipate how refreshing that cold drink will be. The sun is bright, the sky is blue, and you are really only beginning to feel the serenity of summer vacation. Just then a couple of people join the line behind you.

The sounds of the waves and seagulls and laughing children fade out as you overhear one of these people say, "Well, we've been working with Kayla all summer, you know, nothing too intense—just a tutor and some computer reading games. She's really freaked out about school. She's scared she won't learn to read."

"Well, this is the big year for her, first grade. Just pray that her teacher is good," the other says.

All of a sudden this conversation you're eavesdropping on transports you from a relaxing day at the beach to the hectic beginning of school. Your stomach starts to tighten. You pay for your lemonade and walk back to your beach chair as if you were wearing a backpack heavy with plan books, professional literature, and math manipulatives. Your mind races as you think about setting up your classroom, planning your year, and buying supplies.

Suddenly, your day at the beach becomes just another off-site school day. There's no way you're going to be able to get your mind back into your fluffy novel. Instead, you take out a pen and any scrap of paper you can find in your beach bag and start jotting down some to-do notes. Doesn't summertime provide many moments where total bliss turns to utter madness as we think so hard about how to make the upcoming school year better than any that have come before it?

On those hundreds of occasions when my own summer bliss turns into frantic worrying about school, I can calm myself by pretending that the school year is a story and that I already know the ending. I know that in the end I'll want all my students to read words with fluency and accuracy, to understand a variety of texts, and to love reading. I'll want my readers to go forth into the next grade and beyond feeling joyful about books and confident about their reading.

In this story of a school year, I must create an ever-evolving setting that will support my beginning readers in September as they grow into the fluent and independent readers I envision. This story has many different characters—the students and their families—whom I need to get to know quickly. My teaching drives the plot, so I must find a realistic, effective way to get young characters in this story to change from being early readers to fluent and confident readers. There are no special effects in this story, no magic, no sleight-of-hand. At times, this story will be a drama, and at other times, more like a comedy.

The units of study I teach in reading are the chapters in this story of a school year. Each one lays the groundwork and sets the scene for the next. They carry a sense of continuity and consistency, and bring the students and me to the ending we all hope for: a classroom full of strong readers who love to read, children who are ready for the work of next year and beyond.

Units of Study: The Chapters of Our Teaching

For some, the phrase "unit of study" connotes a scope- and sequence-driven curriculum developed by a textbook company somewhere far away that has no real connection with the human beings in the classroom. Others might imagine pre-tests and post-tests, teacher's manuals and worksheets. Rest assured—the units of study I describe in this book offer different ideas than these.

Before I go on to describe the units of study that have become my reading curriculum, I must reveal that I didn't always focus my teaching of reading through units of study. But once I began to plan my curriculum for the independent reading workshop in units of study, my teaching had a makeover. Just as with the makeovers we see on television or in magazines, my "before" needed some work. In the days before I planned for units of study, I knew what I needed to teach my students about reading, but I didn't really have a clearly devised, long-term instructional plan. My teaching was more like a constantly revised to-do list than like a well-planned curriculum.

To fuel my to-do list curriculum, I listened carefully to more experienced teachers during grade meetings and school-based staff development. I read professional books and participated in study groups and workshops to learn from other educators. This pursuit of teaching ideas and my desire to meet every need in my classroom created what has been called popcorn teaching: my teaching popped and scattered all over the place. It was hard to project the direction of my lessons from week to week or day to day.

My old reading conference notes and plan books offer evidence of the gentle frenzy of my teaching at that time. I remember sitting beside Emerson as he read *Little Bear* slowly and laboriously yet accurately. I worked with him on fluency and phrasing in the reading conference, and jotted down a note to do a whole-class mini-lesson on the topic. Next, I moved over to Tireq, who was sitting leaning against a bookshelf, deeply involved in his latest Cam Jansen book. After conferring with him, I noted he needed some comprehension strategies to help him hold on to the story in longer chapter books. I added, "mini-lesson on rereading as comp. strat." to my to-do list. Next, I crossed the classroom to confer with Kate. Once again she was reading comfort books, books that were much too familiar and easy for her. And once again I noted that I needed to work with the class on book choice. These three conferences alone showed me so many things I could teach my whole class in reading workshop mini-lessons. And in my valiant effort to teach it all, I felt as if I wasn't teaching anything in a way that made a lasting impression on the children.

Looking back on this time, I can imagine my teaching as a tour bus. We'd cover a lot of ground, but the stops were quick and superficial. I've come to believe that having so many places to go is one of the hardest things about planning our mini-lessons for the independent reading workshop. We keep moving, and we expend lots of energy, but over time our teaching may be forgettable.

There are probably lots of teachers like I was then, teachers who've noticed their own gentle frenzy in their classrooms. We need to realize that in all the other content areas we do teach in units. For example, in math we'll spend a few weeks focusing on geometry rather than jumping day to day from geometry to addition to patterns. The same goes for science, social studies, and writing workshop. So, then, in the independent reading workshop, too, we ought to spend a couple of weeks of whole-class instruction focused on one thing rather than flitting day to day from one teaching point to another. In individual and small-group work we can attend to more specific individual needs, but during whole-class teaching during reading workshop we need to have a plan that moves the entire reading community along. Having units of study in the independent reading workshop will help us plan for our teaching in a way that moves the group along while supporting individual learners.

The units of study I suggest for independent reading workshop in this book are not exhaustive nor etched in marble. Teaching is always a personal work in progress that changes and grows with our experience, our knowledge, and the standards to which we are held accountable. The stories about teaching in this book come mostly from my own classroom, but the information I share has been developed in study groups and alongside many other educators with whom I've worked at the Teachers College Reading and Writing Project and P.S. 321 in Brooklyn. And, of course, I must acknowledge there is a considerable body of research that these learning communities use as a foundation for the structures and details of practice.

There remains considerable debate among the staff and teachers affiliated with the Teachers College Reading and Writing Project over the details, chronology, and interpretation of the various units of study. My intention here is to explain some of the units of study that have been effective in my own classroom. I hope readers will regard them as models rather than as mandates and use them to help decide which units of study would be most effective in their own classrooms.

For each unit of study I've indicated the time of year I'd most likely teach that unit, but each classroom differs in timing. Some units of study may take a teacher two weeks instead of four; others may require a little bit more than four weeks. So, again, this is a suggested plan:

Units of Study Across the School Year

September	Readers Build Good Habits (Chapter 4)
Late September–October	Readers Use Strategies to Figure Out Words (Chapter 5)
November–December	Readers Think and Talk About Books to Grow Ideas (Chapter 6)
January	Readers Use Word Power to Read and Understand Their Books
February–May	Readers Pursue Their Interests in Books and Other Texts (Chapter 7)
June	Readers Make Plans for Their Reading Lives (Chapter 8)

Readers Build Good Habits

I begin the year in independent reading workshop by teaching children about the expectations and procedures we will follow. I lay the groundwork for the reading work I want children to do throughout the year and beyond by teaching them about the habits of good readers, such as the importance of reading every day, how to work with partners, and how to talk about books. I also use this time to assess the children, to get to know them as readers, which includes much more than simply knowing their reading levels. During this time, I teach children early print strategies and reinforce their knowledge of letter-sound relationships and phonics in other components of balanced literacy, such as shared reading, word study, and interactive writing.

Readers Use Strategies to Figure Out Words

Once I've assessed the children and laid the groundwork for how our work will go in the independent reading workshop, I'm ready to begin teaching them about the strategies and skills they need to read the words on the page. I match children to books by guiding them to the leveled books in the classroom library so that they will be able to choose just-right books to read during independent reading time. As children acquire and become flexible with reading strategies, I turn the focus of lessons to reading with fluency. Throughout I also make sure to constantly reinforce the important work of meaning making alongside word solving.

Readers Think and Talk About Books to Grow Ideas

As children become stronger at reading the words in their books, they tend to talk less about the stories. It's as if they just want to get through the words in their books and move on to the next one. This is the time of year when I want to show them the value of talking about books in ways that support and ensure comprehension. Readers need to think about the stories and have ideas about them as they read. I spend time showing my students the kinds of thinking that strong readers do, and I teach them how to help themselves understand the texts they're reading. Children will have many opportunities to talk with partners about their books. Of course, this move toward comprehension doesn't mean I leave print strategy instruction aside. In small-group instruction, shared reading, writing workshop, interactive writing, and reading conferences, I constantly support students as they continue to learn how to figure out the words in their books.

Readers Use Word Power to Read and Understand Their Books

When children return to school in January many teachers launch a unit of study to tune-up and extend students' use of print and comprehension strategies. As students read more challenging texts at higher levels, the demands on them as word solvers and managers of meaning also increase. They are expected to use a variety of strategies to figure out words, self-correct at the point of error, read with fluency, and understand their stories so their ability to orchestrate semantic, syntactic, and graphophonic sources of information needs to be efficient and effective. Teachers might spend the first week after vacation assessing readers to inform instruction and to make sure children are matched with appropriate texts. I do not provide details for this unit of study, although teachers can use the other units as templates for planning, and they can build on the print and comprehension strategy work already done with their students to create a unit of study on word power that meets the needs of their students.

Readers Pursue Their Interests in Books and Other Texts

In this unit of study I provide opportunities for children to use what they have learned to understand why we read. I show children how reading helps them become learners, thinkers, and inquirers. During these months I launch several mini-units on the subject Readers Pursue Their Interests in Books and Other Texts. The children immerse themselves in reading particular genres, such as nonfiction and poetry. I show them how readers may fall in love with particular authors' books during a whole-class author study. There is also time during this unit for brushing up on any areas of reading vulnerability. I call this unit of study "teacher's choice," that is, a teacher can decide what mini-lessons to teach based on the needs and interests of her students and what they know about strong readers in the world outside school.

Readers Make Plans for Their Reading Lives

By June I've given my students a well-rounded experience with reading. My units of study during independent reading workshop and other literacy components have covered a lot of ground, and readers have changed significantly in skill since the beginning of the year. But soon my students will be beyond the reach of my teaching, so I want to help them make plans for their reading lives that will stay with them after they leave my classroom. Together, we think of ways to stay strong as readers over the summer, and the children set their own goals and make plans for meeting them. We also spend some time reflecting on the year of reading we've just shared.

Teaching Topics Within Units of Study

Unit of Study	Teaching Topics
September Readers build good habits.	Management and procedural expectations Reading identities—who are we as readers in this class? Taking care of books Understanding reading workshop procedures How to stay focused on our reading How to work with reading partners How to have a good talk with our partners
Late September–October Readers use strategies to figure out words.	Getting our minds ready to read Acquisition of print strategies Flexibility with print strategies Reading with fluency Choosing just-right books
November–December Readers think and talk about books to develop ideas.	Book talks with partners Retelling Envisioning, predicting, making connections, having thoughts Strategies for monitoring comprehension Strategies to fix comprehension challenges
February–May Readers pursue their interests in books and other texts.	Genre studies (e.g., nonfiction, poetry, picture books) Author studies Character studies Procedure for working in reading centers Reading projects Determining importance, synthesizing text, inferring
June Readers make plans for their reading lives.	Reflecting on how we've grown as readers Making reading plans for summer (and for life) Setting goals as readers Determining our new reading identities

The table lists each unit of study discussed in this book and what I usually cover in each unit. The chapters that follow explore the units of study and these teaching topics in more detail.

Planning for the Units of Study

The units of study that have been most successful in my classroom are those that were planned in collaboration with colleagues. I was fortunate to work at a school that provided teachers with biweekly grade-level meetings and weekly common prep times so that we could plan curriculum and reflect together on both our teaching and our students' work.

When I sat down with other teachers to plan out a unit of study, our planning time followed a certain routine.

- Backwards planning (goal setting)
- Brainstorming teaching ideas

- Drafting a teaching plan
- Revising when necessary

Backwards Planning (Goal Setting)

Beth Handman, our assistant principal, had taught us how to backwards plan by first stating our goals for the unit of study. The goals are always twofold: goals for what we want to cover and goals for what we want our students to be able to do or know by the end of the study. It helps to refer to the state and district standards when laying out goals. In New York City schools, for example, the end-of-year grade-level standard for first grade is that students should be reading books at Guided Reading Level I (Fountas and Pinnell) with accuracy, fluency, and understanding. Knowing this standard, we can look at the text characteristics and the characteristics of readers of books at level I to figure out the print and comprehension strategies the children will need to control in order to successfully read level I books by the end of the year. This knowledge of grade-level expectations for print and comprehension strategies helps teachers plan the steps to be taken in each unit of study as well as the work to be done in other components of the balanced literacy framework.

In addition to print and comprehension strategies, students need to develop reading habits that will support them in becoming strong, lifelong readers. These habits include reading every day, talking about books with others, making careful book choices, and developing a willingness to read in a variety of genres. Each unit of study provides opportunities to reinforce these habits, so we must consider ways to fit this work on reading habits into our units of study.

In backwards planning, when we know the year-end standards, expectations, and goals for our students, we can then plan the steps to get them there.

Brainstorming Teaching Ideas

Once we have stated our goals for a unit of study and are ready to plan, we need to decide what to teach our students so that they can advance toward the goals. At my school this most often involved working with colleagues to brainstorm all the possible things we might teach within a particular unit of study.

Brainstorming is a messy process, and anything and everything is accepted at first. Later, the items can be sorted, prioritized, or discarded. That's why it's so beneficial to collaborate. When brainstorming with colleagues, I know that Kristen Jordan will always think of something I've forgotten. I can count on Lisa Ripperger to make sure we're keeping the struggling readers in mind, and I depend on Eve Litwack to come up with an innovative way to teach a particular skill or strategy. I know that Jessica Borg Weinberger will help us pay attention to the details and consider the possible challenges or obstacles within each unit.

When we finish brainstorming all the things we could teach within a unit of study, we can take a very close look at the list and sort the items. Sometimes we might decide to combine things that are redundant or naturally go together and to discard things that don't quite fit. After consolidating and tightening, we try to put the items in some sort of sensible sequence so that the topics we teach within a unit of study naturally build upon and segue into one another. This forms the path that our teaching will follow within the unit of study.

Drafting a Teaching Plan

Once the path is determined, we can create a day-to-day teaching plan in more detail. Typically, teachers do this work individually rather than at a collaborative planning meeting because . . . well . . . the custodian wants us out of the building by 10 p.m. So, each teacher will likely develop a slightly different blueprint for the way the unit of study will proceed in his classroom. These differences can be attributed to the strengths and needs of particular classes and to individual teaching styles.

Revising When Necessary

Although each teacher creates a blueprint for her teaching within a unit of study, it's important that she allows for some flexibility based on the needs and strengths of her students. For example, during a unit of study, the teacher may decide to spend more time teaching a particular skill or strategy if her assessments indicate it's necessary. On the other hand, a teacher may decide that a particular concept is best taught in small-group instruction because most of the class has already mastered it. It's important to be well prepared during units of study, but it's also crucial that our teaching is responsive to the needs of the students in our classrooms.

When I do staff development to help teachers plan for what to teach in their units of study, I often ask them to jot down what they think are the most important things to teach their student readers across the year. Almost everything they come up with fits into one of the units of study discussed in this book. Occasionally, a teacher will come up with something that doesn't seem to fall easily into one of these units.

Recently I was stumped when a teacher asked, "What about dictionary skills? Which unit of study would that go in?" She explained that she spends a couple of weeks teaching her first graders how to use a dictionary to look up words they don't understand as they read. My first thought was that this did, in fact, fall under the unit of study Readers Use Strategies to Figure Out Words. Even so, I didn't want to publicly advocate spending a couple of weeks early in the year teaching first graders to interrupt their reading and consult a dictionary every time they got to an unknown word. I believe there are better ways to spend two weeks in the school lives of new first-grade readers.

Besides, I'm sure that only a few kids in most first-grade classrooms would be able to read the types of texts that would have enough tricky vocabulary to warrant a dictionary, especially early in the year. If this were the case in my classroom, I would teach these strong readers how to use the context of a story or passage to figure out a word before teaching them to consult a dictionary. On the other hand, if a teacher feels strongly that her strong readers need dictionary skills, she could take some time either in small-group work or word study to teach them.

I tell this story because even though everything we imagine teaching first graders may fit within the units of study, we need to be thoughtful about what we spend time on in our whole-class mini-lessons. As Lucy Calkins often reminds teachers, a choice *for* something is also a choice *against* something else. Our class time is precious and finite, so we must plan wisely.

Our units of study and the teaching we do in the independent reading workshop do not happen in a vacuum. There are many things we need to consider as we plan for and work through our units of study. To guide my thinking when I plan for the details of a unit of study, I keep a planning chart inside my plan book (see appendix). It's time for a true confession: I have teacher fantasies. In one, I fantasize about being a superhero teacher named UltraOrganizo. I write neatly all the time, my files are always orderly and up-to-date, and I have socks, earrings, and cardigans that go with each holiday, even Presidents' Day and Earth Day. And I would dutifully fill in the planning chart.

When I first began work with planning charts in reading, I would fill in the chart completely. It kept me on track with the details of the units of study while also helping me to maintain a sense of the big picture. Nowadays, instead of actually filling in the chart in great detail, I keep it on hand as I plan for units of study and use it to remind me of what to consider. In the following section I've described the kinds of things that I tend to write in each box on the chart when I do fill it in.

Goals

I list the things I want the children to be able to do by the end of the study. My goals come from four places: the standards, the unit of study itself, my knowledge of the readers in my room, and what I know about the reading process. When goal setting for a unit of study, I try to plan some bottom-line goals that I want all my students to meet and some specific goals for particular readers based on their needs or strengths. For example, in a character study, some bottom-line goals might be for all readers to be able to identify characters, name their character traits, and use text evidence to support their thinking. For readers who are reading more challenging texts, I might expect them to be able to talk about when and why a character changes and what factors contributed to the change.

Bends in the Road

If we think of the plan for a unit of study as a kind of map, we can see that the direction of our teaching shifts within a unit of study. Lucy Calkins and her colleagues call these shifts "bends in the road." For example, in the unit of study Readers Use Strategies to Figure Out Words (see Chapter 5), our teaching has several bends in the road as we head toward the goal of helping children become efficient and flexible word solvers. We begin by teaching them how to get their minds ready to read a book (bend 1) so that they will activate schema to predict and expect the text. Next, we teach a series of lessons on the strategies they can use to figure out what the words say (bend 2). Once students have acquired a variety of print strategies, we teach them how to become flexible with the strategies (bend 3). This naturally leads to work on fluency in reading (bend 4). And last, we might do a series of mini-lessons on how to choose just-right books wisely and independently (bend 5).

Each of these bends in the road might involve a few days to a couple of weeks of teaching. Sometimes these bends are referred to as strings of mini-lessons. A unit of study is composed of several bends in the road. The amount of time we take for each bend depends on the needs of the children.

I plan for the bends in the road of my teaching in sequential and cumulative ways so that what I am teaching today will lead into tomorrow's work, and this week's work will lay the groundwork for next week's challenges. Once I've mapped out the bends in the road, or strings of mini-lessons, I can plan out the daily teaching. Of course, my daily plans need to be flexible. The curricular decision to slow down or move more quickly is based on the ongoing assessments of the readers in my class.

Classroom Library

I think of the classroom library as a marketing tool. In much the same way that bookstores and public libraries change their displays to reflect the seasons and to attract readers to specific books, the library in my classroom changes to reflect the work of the class. In my planning I consider how the classroom library will look and what kind of books I need to support the work the children will be doing. For example, when we're immersed in the print strategy work, the leveled books in our classroom library will be featured in a more prominent position. Later in the year, if we're doing a nonfiction study, the nonfiction books will be plentiful and prominently featured. In addition to the books the children will need to do the work in the unit of study, I also want to make sure I have all the read-aloud books, Big Books, and other texts on hand that I plan to use during the particular unit of study.

Even though the classroom library changes to support and reflect the work going on in each unit of study, there are some constants. My library has a wide variety of texts available all year. There is a large selection of nonfiction as well as picture books, chapter books, series books, and poetry. There are always books gathered around themes or topics, although these may change throughout the year. For example, we may begin in September with a basket of books on a school theme, then move in October to a "scary book" basket for Halloween. During December and January I pull my Martin Luther King Jr. books out of the biography basket, and we create a specific MLK Jr. basket. One year, Anna noticed we had lots of books throughout the library about baby brothers and sisters, and she gathered them together and created a "baby" basket and a label to go with it.

A considerable portion of the books in the classroom library is leveled. Our leveled-book baskets reflect the range of readers in the classroom in terms of the levels represented and the number of books in each basket. In September and October, for example, the early-level-book baskets will have lots of books, and we may not even put out our higher-level-book baskets unless we have readers who are ready for them. Leveled books are indicated in some way, for example, by a dot on the cover that corresponds to a dot on the basket. Each leveled basket needs to have a variety of kinds of books. The baskets might include nonfiction, trade books for which we've determined a level, and small copies of Big Books, if available. The leveled library is described in more detail in Chapter 5. Suggestions for professional literature that helps teachers level classroom libraries are given in the appendix.

Materials and Resources

When planning units of study, we need to consider the materials our students will need to do the work of a particular unit of study. When we are doing comprehension work in the unit of study Readers Think and Talk About Books to Grow Ideas (see Chapter 6), I introduce sticky notes as a way to hold thinking as we read. I not only provide sticky notes in my classroom but also teach children how to use them in a way that supports their thinking instead of distracting them. Late in the year, when we're doing the unit of study Readers Make Plans for Their Reading Lives (see Chapter 8), I may invite guests to talk to the students about their plans for reading over the summer. Besides inviting guests and providing materials, I consider how I'll use class charts and rubrics to support our work. Other considerations for materials and resources are gathering and preparing assessment tools, reflection sheets, bookmarks, reading logs, and so on that are needed in a particular unit of study.

Workshop Structures

Just as the classroom library changes to reflect the work of a particular unit of study, I think about the structure of the independent reading workshop and consider how it can support the work the students are doing. Will students have private reading time and partner reading time, or just one or the other? Will partnerships be ability-based or interest-based? What will small-group work comprise—guided reading groups or strategy lessons? Will there be reading centers?

The ways partnerships are created for the independent reading workshop change throughout the year. During the first unit of study, Readers Build Good Habits, partnerships tend to be random as I get to know the readers in my classroom. When we move on to the next unit of study, Readers Use Strategies to Figure Out Words, partnerships will be more long-term and ability-based. Later in the year, when we immerse ourselves in nonfiction reading, partnerships may be more interest-based, which means that children who share an interest can get together even if they are reading at diverse levels. In each of the chapters that follow, the issue of reading partnerships is explored.

Additional Planning Considerations

Other Literacy Components

We can't teach reading through the independent reading workshop alone. We need to consider how the other parts of our balanced literacy framework will support readers and how we can synchronize the components for maximum effectiveness. For example, during our print strategies unit of study, Readers Use Strategies to Figure Out Words, my conferring work in writing workshop will offer letter-sound support. When we're working on comprehension strategies, I consider how can I use read-aloud books to reinforce our work. I also consider what word study should consist of during a particular unit of study.

Sometimes it may be true that all the components do not work in sync, and that is fine. For example, the thinking and talking we do around read-aloud books tends to be more advanced than what we observe children doing independently early in the year. What we are doing in read-aloud then is planting the seeds for what we want their future book talks to be. Or, we might find that the small-group work with the most struggling readers seems to be in a holding pattern; for example, even after we've worked on fluency with the whole class, we might be still working on fluency with particular readers during strategy lessons or guided reading.

When planning units of study, I always consider the ways that the other components of balanced literacy, including shared reading and interactive writing, can enhance, support, complement, or lead the work we're doing in the units of study in independent reading workshop.

Work Students Are Doing

If anyone were to look into my classroom during a particular unit of study, what would they see? Would children be reading by themselves or with a partner? Would some children be jotting on sticky notes? Would children be reading nonfiction or poetry? Would readers be sitting at tables or in cozy spots around the room?

For each unit of study, it helps me to visualize how independent reading workshop will look and sound. I know that during our whole-class nonfiction study, the prime shelf space in the classroom library will be occupied by nonfiction book baskets. I can imagine children sitting side by side at tables with their reading partners and their nonfiction book basket. Their baskets will have several books on topics of their choosing. They'll have sticky notes to jot their thoughts, and the workshop will have an energetic buzz as children read and talk about their research topics.

I also want children to understand exactly what we're doing and learning as readers. If the person looking into the classroom were to ask Kadeem and Jonathan what they are doing during the nonfiction study, I'd want them to be able to say, for instance, "We're researching whether all sharks are dangerous or if there are some nice ones." During the print strategies unit of study, if the visitor asked Deanna what she was doing, I hope she'd be able to say something like, "I'm reading, and I'm being really brave with the tricky words."

Support for Struggling Readers and Strong Readers

I have similar concerns about struggling readers and strong readers: I worry about teaching to the middle of the class most of the time. I have to make a special effort to think about the content of my mini-lessons to make sure I teach to both ends of the continuum of readers. Either through the materials I use or the examples I share in mini-lessons, I try to make sure that my mini-lessons reach all the students. I also consider how I can give the range of readers in my class small-group or individual attention.

I begin by asking, What are my goals for struggling/strong readers in this unit of study, and how can my teaching help them meet these goals? During the unit of study Readers Build Good Habits, for example, I might meet with the five most struggling readers in a small-group setting to teach them how readers settle down with a book. For strong readers like Eliza, who reads speedily and voraciously, I might need to teach them in reading conferences to slow down and take a moment to think about what's going on in their stories.

I use my ongoing assessments to tailor my teaching toward the strong or struggling readers, and I most often do this teaching in small-group settings or individual conferences.

Home/School

At the beginning of each unit of study, I send a letter to families that explains what we'll be working on together in class and includes ways they can support their children at home. When I'm reading aloud a chapter book to the class, I might send a copy home for a child who has been absent so that an adult could read it aloud and bring the child up-to-date.

I also plan for reading homework during a unit of study because I want my students to connect the reading they do in school with the reading they do at home. Every night my students take a classroom library book home, and at the very least, they indicate the title and the author on the homework sheet or in a reading log. During a particular unit of study, I might have the children do a little extra. For example, when we're immersed in a character study in the spring, I might ask children to jot a few sentences about the main character in their books, using text evidence to support their thinking.

Assessment

For each unit of study, I carefully set goals and plan my teaching, so I also have to make sure that the assessments are appropriate and reflect our work. Although running records offer much information, for some units of study they are not the only way to measure children's progress. For example, when we're working on retelling, I develop a rubric for retelling and use that as my assessment. When children finish a book, I'll meet with them and ask them to retell the story to me while I fill in the rubric.

I try to find or create assessments that are aligned with the content and goals of the unit of study. I also consider ways that students can self-assess. Assessment is ongoing, of course, but there are times I need a more formal assessment. Also, during each unit of study, I consider whether there are school, district, or state assessments that are required at particular times and I plan for them accordingly.

Celebrations

In writing workshop we usually end a unit of study with some kind of celebration, and it's easy to do so because there's a clear product—a piece of writing—to celebrate. In reading, the product is not so tangible. In spite of this, I think it's important to be creative and think of ways to celebrate the new learning that has gone on throughout a unit of study. For example, when children are working on print strategies and fluency, I might schedule a celebration to which we invite fifth-grade reading buddies so that they can listen to their first-grade partners read aloud to them.

I plan my celebrations at the start of a unit of study because then we have a set date by which we need to finish our work in that study. It helps keep my teaching moving.

Standards That Are Addressed

Because we are accountable for seeing that our students meet mandated standards, it's helpful to list the specific standards that are addressed in each unit of study. I always try to have a copy of the standards available when I am planning for the work we'll do.

In the following chapters, I take readers on a tour of each unit of study as it has played out in my classroom or the classrooms of teachers with whom I've worked. I lay out ways of launching particular units of study and discuss the bends in the road of our teaching. My hope is that readers will adapt the information in this book to the needs of their own classes.

I began this chapter by imagining it was early August. Now, let's imagine it's early June. It's 5:30 p.m. You're still at school going through all that you've accumulated throughout the year. The song of the ice cream truck plays its optimistic tune outside the classroom window. You look back over your students' early writing and see the hundreds of ways it has changed. Chelsea is finally spelling *was,* not *wos.* Adrian is no longer writing only about his baby brother falling out of the high chair and bleeding all over Adrian's new sneakers. Jesse is finally taking risks with personal narrative instead of the fantasy stories he stubbornly wrote for the first several months of school. They've all grown so much.

You find some of your early record-keeping and see just how your students have developed as readers. You think about Sulianne, who started first grade as a very strong, yet rigid, reader. You remember when she announced in the first week of school, "I only read chapter books, hard chapter books." You look through her file and see how she's broadened her reading life. She has grown to love poetry and has spent the last month searching for poems by the poets she loves, and for poems about grandmas so that she can give her own grandmother a personalized poetry anthology for her fiftieth birthday.

You look at Jennifer's reading log and still wonder what exactly she needs. She has struggled all year, at home and in school. Although she's able to read slightly harder books now, her reading has not improved enough. You've worried all year, and you will think of her often throughout the summer, still wondering and worrying. And then you remember how Jennifer pulled you aside at dismissal one day a few weeks ago because she needed to talk to you "in privates." She asked if she could take three books home that night, instead of just one.

"Three books? What's your plan?" you asked her.

"Well, I'm tryin' to be better at reading, and I can practice the books first and then read them to my baby sister." You think about that interaction with Jennifer and know that she has indeed learned. She's learned that reading is important enough to care about. She's learned that you can work hard and get stronger at reading, and that reading is a special thing to share with someone else. Jennifer has learned a lot this year, and so have you.

Setting the Tone and the Bottom Lines

Starting from the first day of school I want to ensure that our classroom will be a hotbed of reading activity throughout the year. To do this, I need to rally my students into sharing my enthusiasm and love for reading. I want them to be thrilled when they find new books in the library. I want them to be eager to share their thoughts about their reading. I want them to look forward to independent reading workshop in the same way they are excited for recess.

These earliest days of the school year are crucial for setting the tone and a sense of expectation, and establishing the management procedures we will rely on throughout the year. Alice Ressner, a friend and second-grade teacher at P.S. 321, is masterful at laying this groundwork. When I was a new teacher,

struggling in the typical new teacher ways, she kindly recommended two things: slow down and be consistent. I always remember this important advice. In fact, I would consider these words to be part of a tattoo, if I were going to get one.

The advice to slow down may feel counterintuitive at the beginning of school. After the summer we're eager to get going because we know how much work there is to be done to get our students from where they begin to where they need to end up. Also, I always suffer nostalgia for my previous class during those first few weeks of school. I know, of course, that I'll grow to love and enjoy my new class just as much as any other class that I've taught before, yet I always wish this new group of students and I could just hit the ground running. But, as Alice wisely says, it pays to slow down at first.

Slowing down means that we temporarily suspend our worries about getting to print strategies and reading levels. If we rush too quickly to these concerns without first laying a solid foundation for our independent reading workshop, we'll forever be dealing with management issues.

Here's my cautionary tale. It was springtime. I was still dealing with a problematic noise level during reading workshop, and many of my reading conferences were still management conferences. "Lily and Tashia, what is something that partners can do to make plans together?" I asked two children who were stubbornly refusing to get to work because they were arguing about whose book to read first. Meanwhile, I had Alex and Stephanie standing near me saying, "Ms. Collins, we got a question," over and over as I was trying to have a reading conference with Daniel. This was late April. I was frustrated because I knew that the too-high noise level, the lack of cooperation among partners, and the continual reading conference interruptions should have been things of the past.

"With this class, I feel like I'm driving an 18-wheeler full of bowling balls down an incline and I need to make a sharp right-hand turn," I told a colleague, describing my pessimism about changing the tone of the class. "It's as if their course is set, and all I can do is make minor changes in steering."

When I reflected on what had gone wrong that year, I knew I had jumped right in to the nitty-gritty reading work in September and had spent minimal time teaching my class the routines and procedures that would make the work go smoothly. Thus, in the spring I was still dealing with management issues that should have been taken care of much earlier in the year.

Because we'll have independent reading workshop every day, I need to teach my students how we'll work during this time. I must make very clear my expectations for noise level and work habits during reading time. My teaching at this time ranges from the small details of how to make the physical transition from mini-lessons to independent work time to the larger issues of how to work and talk with reading partners.

I also make sure that I provide a variety of reading opportunities throughout each day, from the independent reading workshop itself to the little pockets of bonus time for reading that sometimes arise, so that my students are, in fact, reading every day and having time to practice how to be good readers. I also begin my work in the other components of the balanced literacy framework, such as shared reading and interactive read-aloud, so that my expectations for how we work and learn together will carry over into these other times of day.

I have learned to invest time during the first couple of weeks teaching my students about the management and procedures of reading workshop. I do this by getting to know my students as readers and as people, and by making clear the expectations I have for the tone, work ethic, and behavior in my classroom.

To establish a successful independent reading workshop, I consider some reading habits to be bottom-line habits, just as brushing our teeth before bed and washing our hands after going to the bathroom are. These four habits are essential for our reading work together:

- Strong readers read every day.
- Strong readers talk and think about books with other people.
- Strong readers read everything in sight.
- Strong readers take care of books and protect their reading time.

These reading habits are the first thing I work on in my classroom. As these habits become internalized and consistent, the children can begin to acquire the strategies that will help them become powerful readers.

❖ *Strong readers read every day.* It doesn't take a district mandate to tell us that it's important to make time for reading every day. It's common sense that in order to get strong at something, we need to practice, practice, practice. I want my students to know that a strong reader is no different from, say, a strong baseball player. Both need lots of practice to get really good.

I tell my students that each day we will meet for a reading lesson and then they'll have time to read books that they've selected from the classroom library: "When we read every day, we build the muscles that we need to read words and to understand stories, just as a baseball player builds the muscles he needs to throw and bat and run fast when he practices every day."

Right from the first day of school I also make it clear that reading every day means more than just reading at school. On the first homework assignment, I ask children to sketch and label a picture of the best place in their homes for them to read. We talk about how it's important to read in school every day so that I can help them and also important to read at home so that they can help themselves get better at it. Also, in the first couple of weeks of school, I put a system in place so that each student takes home a book from our classroom every day.

❖ *Strong readers talk and think about books with other people.* We spend a great deal of time in the early grades reading and talking about books. I want my students to get to know each other as readers and friends so that social networks around reading may develop. We spend a few of these early days discovering (or creating) our reading identities and deciding on what we need in our classroom to support each of us as readers. We also do some early partnership work at this time to lay a foundation for the kinds of conversations that will develop later in the year within partnerships. In Chapter 4, I describe specific ways to help children share their reading identities and work in partnerships during reading time.

I also begin right away by reading aloud a variety of books throughout the day and providing time to talk about the stories. These first stories are often about the beginning of the school year and about making friends. I set up these early interactive read-alouds by saying to my class, "I've been waiting to read this book to you so that we can talk about it together. I can't wait to hear what you think." Even though part of my objective during these early interactive read-alouds is to plant seeds for accountable talk, I also teach children my expectations for behavior and participation during read-aloud and whole-group book talks. It's crucial that students understand how to be helpful and contributing members of our community of readers.

And, of course, like any other class, we work in these early days of school on being good talkers and listeners (to the teacher *and* to each other) and being good friends.

❧ *Strong readers read everything in sight.* Taylor was a voracious reader. When I conferred with her during writing or reading workshop, she would look over my conference notes to see what I was writing about, even though she couldn't read my cursive. When I passed out the school medical record cards to students before their annual eye and ear exams, Taylor tried to figure out what her medical record card said. "What's MMR mean?" she asked as she pointed to the vaccination checklist. In short, Taylor noticed text everywhere and tried to make sense of it all. I describe her to my students every year as an example of someone who tries to read everything in sight.

I want all the readers in my classroom to realize that they can read, whether or not they can read the words in books. I want them to read the world. I tell them that when I'm on the subway, if I don't have my own book or newspaper, I read the subway signs and take sneak peeks at other people's newspapers. "It's like I have to read anything I can get my eyes on," I say. "I even try to read advertisements that are in different languages."

I urge them to do this everywhere: "Try to be the kind of reader who reads everything he can get his eyes on in the world." I support students as they learn to read the environmental print around our classroom, our school, and our neighborhood. We also learn some short shared texts together so that there is print in our room that everyone can read right away.

❧ *Strong readers take care of books and protect their reading time.* The schools, and teachers themselves, spend lots of money on classroom supplies and books. Those books need to last year after year, so we depend on children to take good care of them. One of my pet peeves is when children walk over or around a book that is lying on the floor. This irritates me because someone carelessly left the book on the floor and someone else ignored it as if it were a piece of litter. I want my students to handle books with care and reverence.

So, during these first weeks of school, I make a big deal out of examples of children taking good care of books or being careless with them. It's not unusual for me to interrupt reading workshop to say, "Oh, no, there's a book on the floor! Watch what I do to take care of this situation." I dramatize picking up the book and putting it back in a book basket. "I hope you readers will do the same thing if you ever find one of our books on the floor." It is crucial that children understand the value of books and treat them accordingly. After all, the library takes up the best real estate in the classroom, and taking care of our books is one way we can show how much we value reading.

Another way we want children to show how they value reading is to be sure they're working hard during reading workshop. We must convey the idea that reading time is incredibly important, so we will all work hard every moment. I help children imagine ways that they can eliminate distractions by teaching them how to politely ask other children to lower their voices or to get back to work. I tell the students that I can't be the only one who takes care of our reading time; they also need to take some responsibility for it.

Taking care of books and protecting our reading time are community issues. I want children to learn very early in the year how to make good decisions for themselves as readers, as reading partners, and as members of the community in our classroom.

Readers Build Good Habits

Chapter 4

I CONFESS I USE A LOT OF MENTAL MANIPULATION in my teaching. Don't worry though. It's not diabolical, I don't profit monetarily, and nobody gets hurt. It's just a teaching tool that I use to help things go my way in the classroom. Here's an example of what I mean. During the morning meeting on the first day of school, I look around at the fresh haircuts, bright new sneakers, and sweet faces, and say, "Do you realize that you guys have a great job this year? Yep. It's a great job. You are first graders, and you are so lucky to have such a great job." It's actually the old "these are the best days of your lives" speech miniaturized for six-year-olds.

The students usually look a bit confused or uninterested, so I go on to explain, "My job here is to be a first-grade *teacher,* and your job is to be first-grade *students.* I love my job because I get to work with kids and use the paper cutter and have lots of birthday cupcakes, but I have to say that you guys definitely have a very cool job, too. Talk to someone sitting next to you about the cool stuff you can do on your job as first graders." I listen in as the students turn to someone sitting next to them and predictably list recess, block building during choice time, bathroom passes, and eating lunch in the big-kid cafeteria as some cool things about being in first grade.

After a few minutes, I pull the class back together: "I listened in as you guys talked about some great things about being first graders like recess and blocks and lunch, but you know what I think is the best part of being a first grader? I think the best part is that you'll get time to read *every day.* Imagine that. Reading time is built into your job, *every day,* and you are so lucky. Not many jobs in the world have reading time built right into them every day."

Now, of course, I realize that to consider daily reading time a great boon may be a stretch for some children, particularly those who already feel like struggling readers or who have other kinds of anxiety about reading. And in spite of our most private teacher fantasies, we need to admit that there are children who begin first grade just not very interested in picking up a book.

For these reasons, I begin my year by talking about reading in a way that is enthusiastic, genuine, and comforting. I essentially launch a public relations campaign about the joy of reading. I want to make reading something to love, not just something to learn. We teachers exert a lot of power over the tone of our classes and the attitudes of our students, and when we are excited about something, our students become excited about it, too. I call this phenomenon the contagious enthusiasm principle, which, I suppose, sounds better than calling it mental manipulation.

Goals and Bends in the Road

These first few weeks of school are precious, and the teaching opportunities are fleeting. When I hear teachers say, "Oh, I don't get any teaching done at the beginning of the year, it's all procedures and management," I want to tell them that spending time on procedures and management in the beginning is, in fact, good teaching and a good time investment. As I've said before, when we slow down and spend time early in the year establishing a solid foundation for our reading work, we don't have to spend time throughout the year working on management issues. And doing a few lessons on acceptable noise level in September isn't nearly as frustrating as needing to do those same lessons over and over again in November, December, March, April. . . .

During the first few weeks of school my teaching goals are to establish the solid foundation necessary for children to work independently and effectively during independent reading workshop and to instill the essential habits (see planning chart). In *Reading with Meaning* (2002), Debbie Miller writes that the work we do in September is "less about teaching children how to read and more about modeling and teaching children what it is that good readers do, setting the tone for the workshop, and establishing its expectation and procedures, and engaging and motivating children to want to learn to read."

In this first unit of study, or any unit for that matter, our teaching does not follow a straight and linear path to meet our goals. Instead, there are bends in the road that we take in our teaching so that we can reach our goals. At each bend in the road we teach a string of mini-lessons to help children move along toward the goals we have set.

The bends in the road of my teaching during this first unit of study are

- Readers have reading identities and share them with each other.
- Readers take care of books and the classroom library.
- Readers understand the reading workshop procedures so that all readers can do their best work.
- Readers stay focused on their reading.
- Readers think and talk about books with others.

Each bend in the road has a series of mini-lessons to go with it. The mini-lessons originate from three sources: the goals for our work together, the teacher's knowledge of the reading process, and the needs of our students. Of course, each teaching situation is different, so my bends in the road may be different from other teachers' or occur in a different sequence.

In the sections that follow, I describe the work that I and other teachers have done during this unit of study, Readers Build Good Habits.

Reading Identities: "Wait! I'm Only Six!"

In the early days of the school year, we all scramble to get to know our students. Like many teachers, I send home a first-day letter that includes a brief questionnaire for parents. One question is always the same: "Please tell me anything about your child that you think would be helpful for me to know." The responses, ranging from none to long biographies of the child's short life, are helpful, but I often find that they give me more information about the parents or families than about the child.

I can always turn to my students' kindergarten teachers, who provide important academic and social information about the children. I find, however, that each child reacts differently in every classroom setting. Every year the new teacher, the new classroom space, and the new classmates create

	Planning Chart
Unit of Study:	**Readers Build Good Habits**
	Dates:

Goals	• Students will understand the expectations for independent reading workshop time. • Students will know how to take care of books. • Students will learn strategies for working with and talking to a reading partner. • Students will learn the bottom-line habits for reading work. • Students will learn the system for taking books home and bringing them back. • Teacher will assess all readers to determine reading levels.
Bends in the Road	• Readers have reading identities and share them to build community. • Readers take care of books and the classroom library. • Readers understand reading workshop procedures so everyone can do their best work. • Readers stay focused on books even if they aren't yet reading all the words. • Readers think and talk about books with others.
Classroom Library	• A variety of baskets labeled with contents, such as books on a topic, books by an author, books of a genre (e.g., poetry), books in a series, ABC books, "Books We've Read Together" (books teacher has read aloud). • Leveled books are not featured prominently at this point. • The library is used only during the free reading time after children do their morning jobs and before morning meeting.
Materials and Resources	• Big Books with story lines for shared reading. • Charts to match Bends in the Road. • Table-top baskets with a variety of books from the library. • Picture books to read aloud about beginning school, making friends. • Large bookmark for each child with name on it (may be decorated during free time or as morning job).
Workshop Structures	• Mini-lesson, work time, share time. • Private reading time, partner reading time with conferring. • Partners are not long-term or ability-based; students tend to partner with others sitting nearby.
Other Literacy Components	
Work Students Are Doing	• Students choose books to read from table-top baskets. • Students use bookmarks to save place for next day. • Students read privately or with partners. • Students may or may not be reading conventionally.
Support for Struggling Readers	• Frequent support through individual conferences. • Assess early to identify challenged readers and understand their challenges to guide instruction. • Teach strategies for focusing and staying with books during small-group lessons.
Support for Strong Readers	• Students assessed as already reading conventionally are guide to just-right books in the leveled library. • Teach strategies for print and comprehension in individual conferences.
Home/School	• Send home letter describing take-home book system. • Invite parents to celebration. • Ask students to bring in a beloved book from home.
Assessment	• Do quick assessments to determine reading levels in preparation for the next unit of study. • Assess/create rubric for how reading workshop time is going and report back to students. • Note other characteristics of readers in addition to reading levels.
Celebrations	• Parents as reading partners: "Come see how well we're reading during reading time." • Reading workshop contract signing party. • Read-a-thon, invite buddy class or families.
Standards That Are Addressed	

an opportunity for even our youngest students to reinvent themselves. Also, my "what a sweetie" take on a particular child can be another teacher's "what a headache" perspective.

So, although I take into careful consideration the information I receive from families and previous teachers, I know that my most important early work is to get to know the children myself. I need to assess not only where they are as readers but also who they are as readers. Even at this young age, our students have reading identities to reveal.

I do this work of discovering reading identities in a couple of ways. For homework on one of the first days of school, I ask children to bring in their favorite book from home. In a note attached to the homework, I assure families that the books will be well taken care of and that they will be returned after a week or two. I know that some children won't bring in a favorite book because they might not have books at home. In these situations I privately invite the child to go to our classroom library and pick out a book: "You might even find a book you remember from kindergarten."

On the day when the children bring in their favorite books (or find one in the classroom library), we assemble in a circle at the meeting area, and the children lay their books in front of them so that everyone can see what they've brought to share. I explain to them that just as bookstores set up a shelf for staff favorites, we're going to devote a shelf in our room to class favorites.

I start by asking, "So, what do you notice about our favorites?" At first, the students tend to just look around the circle at the books everyone has brought in. One year, after what felt like a long silence, Julian raised his hand and said, "Well, we all brought in our favorite books."

I told myself to think fast and make something of Julian's statement of the obvious. "Yes, that's true, Julian, we all brought in favorite books. We all have books we absolutely love, just as grown-up readers do. But would everyone take a good look around at each other's books? What do you notice about the books we've brought in? Take a good look at people's picks."

As the class looked around at each other's books, I got the conversation started by saying something that I noticed.

"Gee, a couple of people have brought in books about animals. That tells me that some of you really like animals, am I right?" The children agreed and then began to notice other similarities among people's favorites.

"Look, both me and Afiya brought in Rugrats books," Sarah said. Although I may not have wanted to acknowledge the abundance of books that were movie or TV show adaptations, I knew this wasn't the time to present a lecture on "Ms. Collins's Ideas About Quality Children's Literature."

"I see that, Sarah, and I'm thinking that maybe you and Afiya could get together and talk about your books with each other." Afiya and Sarah nodded and smiled at each other. In my response, I tried to take attention away from the topic of Rugrats and focus instead on the reading habit of talking about books with other readers.

"Look at how old Reina's book is," Alex snickered, as everyone's attention was drawn to a tattered paperback copy of *Goodnight Moon*. Reina slowly slid the book into her lap, embarrassed as some of the kids laughed along with Alex. My instinct was to admonish Alex for the mocking tone in his voice. Instead, at this moment, I thought there was more to be gained by celebrating Reina's book. That way, Reina would feel better about her choice, and Alex would see by example that we don't mock other people in our community. Besides, I could always take Alex aside after circle time and have a little chat with him, which I did.

"Wow, Reina, may I see your book again?" I asked enthusiastically.

She hesitantly showed it without looking up. "Reina, is that one of your favorite books from when you were a little kid?" I asked.

She nodded.

"It looks like you've read it a million times. I have tons of books that look like that. Tell us about it," I said. "I think it's so cool that you have a favorite from when you were very little."

"My mom used to read this to me every night when I was little and I loved it," she said softly.

"Isn't that so cool?" I said as I looked around at the rest of the class. Just then Natasha said, "I still have a book from when I was a baby. I loved it, but some of its pages fell out."

"You know, I still have some books from when I was little, too, and they are still special to me even though they look a little raggedy. Reina, your book has made us all think of some great memories. I'm so glad you brought that one in."

Just then Anna blurted out, "Reina, you better take good care of it so that you still have it when you're a grown-up."

Reina put the book back out in front of her again.

After this kind of sharing and talking about the books children brought in, which took no more than 10 minutes, I asked the students to put their books on our slanted bookshelf, labeled "Check out our class favorites." When we had a free moment over the next few days, I asked the rest of the children to show their books to the class and to share why they were favorites.

One day we had an extra 5 minutes before lunch. I asked Vivian to get her book from the shelf and bring it to the meeting area. She stood in front of the class and said, "I love this book because my mom went away for work but she gave me this book. She wrote me a note inside. My dad reads it to me before bed when my mom isn't home," Vivian said as she hugged a copy of *Guess How Much I Love You.*

"Oh, that sounds so nice, and it's kind of like Reina's, isn't it? It's kind of a special bedtime book. How many of you brought bedtime books like Vivian and Reina did?" I was always looking for connections between children, so they could see, from early in the year, that they were not alone in this world of readers.

Next, I chose Patrick, who had brought in a book that seemed very different from Vivian's or anyone else's. Patrick walked to the class favorites shelf and lifted off a thick book that looked a little unwieldy for a six-year-old. "Patrick, your book looks so big and heavy . . . let me see the cover. Wow, it's a book on battleships. That looks like a serious information book. Tell us about it."

Patrick looked around and shyly told the class, "I went with my grandpa and my dad to the *Intrepid* museum. The *Intrepid* is a really big, huge battleship, and my grandpa was in the war, so I'm learning about battleships."

"Patrick, you're reading a book about stuff you're interested in . . . that is so grown-up. I wonder if anyone else is like Patrick and has brought in a book about something that they're interested in or want to learn more about." Again, I was looking for connections between children. In this case, Alex raised his hand and walked over to get his book, the Disney adaptation of *Hercules*. Sometimes my connections have to stretch rather far.

"Alex, are you like Patrick? Did you bring in a book that's going to teach you about something?" Secretly, I was scrambling for a way to connect a cartoon Hercules book to a nonfiction tome on battleships.

Alex said, "I liked this movie 'cause it was cool."

"Alex, are you saying that after you saw the movie, you wanted to read the book because you were interested in learning more about Hercules?" Alex nodded, and smiled at Patrick.

"That is so cool," I said. "You know, Alex, I think I've even got a book somewhere on Greek mythology, and I bet there's information on Hercules. I'll try to find it. You know what, first graders? Doesn't it seem like lots of readers in this class read books that teach them something, like Patrick and battleships and Alex and Hercules?"

Whew! That was a stretch, but we primary-grade teachers get pretty limber, don't we?

The thing to remember when leading conversations about reading identities is that we're working on a few different levels. On the surface, learning about the kinds of books our children like informs us about what might make sense to put into the classroom library. If we notice that a few children have chosen nonfiction books on animals as their favorites, we'll want to make sure some nonfiction books on animals are represented in the library early in the year. If we notice many children bringing in books like Alex—cartoon movie adaptations or scratch-and-sniff pop-up books—we know we need to expose students to a wide range of other kinds of texts.

On another level, the books that children bring to school and the stories they tell about why they chose particular books also reveal information about their reading lives at home. I learned that Vivian and Reina listen to bedtime stories and Patrick listens to oral stories from his grandpa. When Jennifer told me she didn't have a book from home to bring in, I knew I'd have to make sure that she took a book home every day. There are stories behind the books children name as their favorites, and we need to listen closely to find them.

Asking children to share their favorite books from home also helps build connections among children, and I want to show my class the social aspects of reading early in the year. When two children brought in Eric Carle books, I took the opportunity to tell them they should start an Eric Carle book club. Of course, four other children will then want to join when they discover their latent love for Eric Carle's books or perhaps their desire to be in a book club. When Patrick showed his battleship book, I asked the class if anyone else was interested in battleships. When children raised their hands, I suggested that they get together with Patrick before morning meeting to read about battleships together.

In the meantime, I'm always trying to listen for the children's life interests because I want our classroom library to reflect them as much as possible. When I eavesdropped on a conversation and learned that Cassidy was trying to talk his family into getting a dog, I gathered a few dog books and showed Cassidy where they were in the classroom library. As our line made its way to the cafeteria, I overheard Erik and Molly debating the pros and cons of picking scabs. I told them I had a great human body book that might answer the age-old question to pick or not to pick.

I busily forage for students' interests in the early days of the school year. I know I'll find interests that may be real and long-term, like Cassidy and dogs, or short-lived and small, like Molly, Erik, and scabs. Both types of interests can be represented and pursued in the classroom library.

Another way we can uncover the reading identities of our students is to have them sketch their favorite reading memories. Teachers may wonder whether it's possible to pull reading memories from the minds of six-year-olds. The trick to this is to have lots of talk around reading memories before sending the students off to sketch their own. To help them do this, I gathered my class at the meeting area in front of my easel and taught the following mini-lesson.

Mini-lesson

Connection

We've been talking a lot about the kinds of books we love to read, but I still want to learn more about what you do as readers. Besides talking about your favorite books, I thought we could talk about our favorite reading memories. I'd like to know about your best-ever reading moments, about the times when reading felt good for you.

One of the things I love to do when I think about memories is to make a quick sketch because sketching really helps me to picture my memory. Today, we're going to think about and share our best reading memory. I want to teach you how you might think about your favorite reading memory and sketch it so you can really picture it and help us to picture it, too. But first, may I show you a sketch of mine?

Of course, the class enthusiastically says yes because they see the marker in my hand and the blank page on the easel, or maybe just to find out if I can draw as well as their kindergarten teacher.

Teaching point and demonstration

Well, I'm going to sketch my best reading memory for you guys.

As I sketch, I hum and talk to myself, trying to get my sketch done as quickly as possible. I hear the children chatting quietly as they try to figure out what

I'm putting on the paper. I might remind them to just watch and not talk because I'm trying to lay the groundwork for what's expected of them during mini-lessons. Sometimes for this lesson I might use a sketch that I have prepared the night before, but I prefer to sketch in front of my students so they can see that sketching moves quickly and is not necessarily precise. I don't want them to be overwhelmed by the idea that they have to draw something incredibly representational. This is not an art lesson, after all.

There, I'm finished. [They see a rudimentary drawing of a time I was reading on the subway.] Did you notice how I sketched this picture quickly? I didn't need it to be perfect because I know I'm going to talk to you about it, too. I sketched myself reading on the subway. I love riding the subway to school because I can get lots of reading done on the long ride. I read different kinds of things, like the newspaper, books, school things, magazines, and anything else I can get my eyes on. I just love to read on the subway because I don't get interrupted at all.

Take a second to close your eyes and see if you can picture me reading on the subway. You can think about my sketch and what I told you so that you can make a picture in your minds.

One of the reasons I draw myself on the subway is because I know that for most of my students a subway ride is not a daily event. I want to avoid providing the temptation to copy my drawing. Rather, I want them to think of their own reading memories and draw those.

Okay, so that's my reading memory that you're picturing in your minds, but soon you're going to get a chance to think of your own. Want to know a little secret? It was hard for me to decide to draw this one because I've got lots of great reading memories. Did you see how I decided on this and sketched it quickly? Did you notice how when I sketched it, I really tried to picture in my mind what it looked like when I was reading on the subway so that you guys could picture it, too?

Active engagement *How about you guys, are you ready? I bet you've all got reading memories you can share. I'm going to give you a little time right now to think about a reading memory that you have. Close your eyes and think about it, and then turn and tell the person sitting next to you about your own best-ever reading memory. Okay, go ahead, think about your reading memory. Close your eyes so you can really picture it. [I give them about 10 seconds or so.] Okay, now turn and tell the person sitting next to you about your reading memory.*

I listen in to some partner conversations. After a minute or so, I reconvene the class to report back what I heard.

I heard some great stuff out there. I heard Max say his great reading memory is of reading in a tent with a flashlight. Someone else said they love to read in the puffy chairs at the public library after school. Is there anyone else?

I rarely open up the active engagement to participation in this way because it can tend to either make the mini-lesson last too long or take us off track. Today, because I listened in, I choose Stephanie, a child who can share something that will help our work. The following conversation ensues.

"I read in the car when my mom takes me to school," Stephanie says.

"Really? I'm trying to picture it. Can you say more about what it's like when you read in the car?" My purpose in asking this question is to help Stephanie and others imagine the details in their memories.

"I got books in the pocket in the car seat, and I read them like this." She pretends she has a book on her lap.

"Oh, so you're a car reader who has books in the seat pocket that you read whenever you're in the car. I can picture it, how you hold the book in your lap that way you showed us. Is anyone else like Stephanie?" A few kids nod. "Well, Stephanie, I guess you'll be sketching a picture of yourself in the car reading with a book in your lap. Then we'll all see what it looks like when you're having a great reading time. Who has a completely different kind of reading memory to share?"

"I like to read in bed with my mom," Trevor says.

"Me, too," yells Jonathan, practically lifting himself off the rug. I want to nod in Jonathan's direction, but I'm trying to set a "don't call out" tone for our whole-class meetings and lessons, so I ignore his comment.

Stephanie's sketch of reading in the car.

Trevor's sketch of reading in bed with his mother.

"Trevor, tell us something about what it's like when you and your mom read in bed, so we can really picture it."

"Well, me and my mom get in my bed, and I can pick two books, and she reads them to me before I go to sleep."

"That sounds really special! What a cozy time. Can you imagine how you'd draw that?" He smiles and nods.

"I gotta put my pillows and my light by the bed and my mom and me, and maybe my cat 'cause sometimes she jumps on the bed, too," Trevor says.

"Right now, those of you who have memories of reading in bed with a grown-up, like Trevor, close your eyes and picture your scene because it's going to look different than Trevor's or anyone else's." [I give them about 5 seconds or so to do this.]

Link to ongoing work

I love how you guys have favorite reading memories even though you're only in first grade. It's so important to think about those times because I want our classroom to be the kind of place where each of you can make new reading memories.

Readers, your job now is kind of big. You'll have to really think about your reading memories again and make a quick sketch of them so that the rest of us can picture them, too. Then, when it's time for you to read today, we're going to try to make our classroom the kind of place where you can make new reading memories. But first, let me give you some paper for your sketch.

I pass out half-sheets of paper for their sketches so they are not overwhelmed by too large sheets. Usually, I let students use color pencils and crayons. When most of the children are finished, I tell them to share their pictures with the others at their tables. Then, while they are still at their seats, I say, "Tell me. Did any of your friends surprise you with what they drew? Were there any cool reading memories?"

"Yeah, Julia says she builds a fort and reads there so her baby brother doesn't bother her," answers Gaby.

"How cool! Julia, are you the kind of reader who likes calm and quiet when you read? I'm like that, too," I say. "I guess our reading time in this classroom will have to be calm and quiet for readers like us. Was anyone else surprised by what their friend shared?"

"Theria reads wrestling magazines with her brothers," Jonathan says, laughing with the other kids at the table. Wrestling is one of those hot topics that children seem to know isn't talked about in front of teachers, so they are getting a kick out of the fact that Theria has been outed.

"Theria, do you love wrestling?" I ask. She nods and looks embarrassed.

"Yeah," she says quietly.

"She reads them in her dad's store because they have wrestling magazines. Her brother does, too," Jonathan adds.

"Hmm. You know what, Theria? That tells me that you're the kind of reader who reads about things you love. How many of you try to find books and magazines about things you love?" Hands go up. "Theria, you've discovered one of the big secrets about reading—that you can read about stuff you love. If you guys let me know what you love, we can try to get books about it in our class."

"Even wrestling?" Jonathan asks, giggling again.

"Well, maybe not everything," I say with a smile.

In the conversation we have about the students' sketches, I try to relate what they say about themselves to how our class reading workshop should be. In other words, I use their stories to help us all imagine what reading time will be like in our class.

For example, when students share stories and pictures about reading with other people, I connect it to our class work by saying that we, too, will have partners in reading. When they tell the class a story about reading alone, I use that to tell them that we'll have private reading time. If they share how they like to read in a quiet, private place, I say that we need to have a quiet reading class, too.

Drawing Themes and Connections to Class

Reading with someone else (sibling, parent)

"We'll have to make time for you to read with others, like partners."

"We'll have to make sure that we have time to listen to great books together. I'll read aloud to you a lot."

Reading in places other than home (car, train, vacation)

"We'll have to be sure to read every day, wherever and whenever we can, just as you do."

Reading alone or in a private setting

"We'll have to make sure our class is calm and quiet."

Reading well-loved books

"We'll have to make sure our library is full of books you love."

It's worth adding that children's sketches of their favorite reading memories also make great bulletin board items for those early days of school when the empty walls are just waiting for children's work.

The work of discovering reading identity can be done throughout the day for the first few days. I know teachers who discuss it at their morning meetings and others who talk about it in the afternoon before the students leave for the day. I usually start it during reading workshop but then bring it up a few other times, like the 5 minutes before leaving for lunch. The timing itself is not as important as making time for everyone to be heard.

While we explore reading identities over a few days, we can begin independent reading workshop by doing a mini-lesson or leading a discussion about reading identities. Then we send our children back to their seats to read from baskets of books that we've put on their table-tops. These baskets contain a variety of texts in terms of genre, topic, author, and level of difficulty.

When I send my students off to read after these lessons on reading identity, I might say, "Find a book that you really love, and read like Reina does,"

Taylor's sketch of reading alone.

or "Look for a book about something you want to learn so you can read like Patrick does," or "Today, let's make sure our voices are calm and quiet so readers like Julia and I can concentrate on our work."

As the children read, some may look at books with a buddy while others may prefer to look at books by themselves. In these first few days I don't overly manage this time beyond making sure people are focused and using quiet voices. As I confer with children, I try to figure out their reading levels and other information about them and their relationship to reading (see the Assessment section later in this chapter).

Other Mini-lessons

I list here some summaries of ideas for other mini-lessons for this part of the unit of study.

❧ *Who am I as a reader?* We all have tastes as readers, just as we have tastes with food. One way readers can learn about themselves is to think about what kinds of books they like. We can think about the kinds of books we love to read. Today, when you read, notice what kinds of books you're really interested in, and after reading time, we'll talk about them.

❧ *What do I need to read well?* There are things I need to have so that I can teach well. I need kids, I need supplies, and I need plans. There are things that readers need to read well, too. I'm the kind of reader who needs quiet so that I can concentrate on my book. Today, when you read, I want you to think about what you need as a reader so you can do your best reading work.

❖ *Readers have books that are special.* Do you have a special toy or stuffed animal? Those are things that many kids have. Readers also have books that are really special to them for one reason or another. I want you to notice if any books feel special to you.

❖ *What are my goals for reading this year?* Wow, first grade! You're going to change so much this year. You're going to get taller, lose some teeth, learn to write well, do hard math problems, and become really strong readers. Because this is a brand new year, it's kind of like New Year's when people make resolutions or goals for what they want to do in the new year. Well, we can make resolutions as readers, too. One of my own resolutions this year is to read some books about early American history, especially about our first presidents. I also want to get better at reading poetry. I love poetry, but I'm not as strong at reading it as I am at reading nonfiction or chapter books. I'm wondering what goals you have as readers this year. Think about it as you read today, and we'll share at the end.

Readers Take Care of Books and the Classroom Library

When I was a child and went to the public library, I remember, there were ominous signs placed on the bookshelves: "A misplaced book is a lost book!!!" I don't know what it was about these signs that made them so scary; maybe it was the triple exclamation points, the bold font, or the finality of the message. Anyway, I was always so careful when I pulled a book off the shelf because I wanted to be sure I put it back into its correct place.

If I think back to when I went to bookstores as a child, I don't remember being so careful there. I'd sit up against a bookshelf in the children's section with a small pile of books and never concern myself with putting them back in the right place. Why did I treat the library books with more respect than the bookstore books? My answer to this question has helped me teach my students how to treat our classroom library.

In the public library I had a stronger sense that people shared books. I felt that I was accountable to all the other people who visited the library and to the workers whom I regularly saw pushing around book carts as they returned books to the shelves. I had to be careful with the books because other people needed me to be so. And then there was the head librarian. Her presence was known and clear; she often talked to library patrons about what they liked to read and whether they had enjoyed the books they were returning. In the bookstore I didn't have the same sense of community. I had no connection to the people who restocked the shelves, nor did I feel there was a system to the books. In the public library, however, the card catalogs with their drawers as long as my arms, the Dewey decimal system, and the book jackets with complex call numbers taped onto the spines indicated to me that there was a lot of work done behind the scenes to enable me to feed my reading habit. I didn't want to mess it up.

Also, the library was quiet and peaceful. Even my little brother knew he should whisper when we were there. It was so quiet that if you paid close attention, you could hear the librarian stamping the due date on the library cards of people who were checking out books. In the bookstore the sounds of the public address announcements and the normal conversation levels among customers made it feel like I could have been in any store, anywhere.

In my classroom I want to create an aura around the library and the books that is similar to the one I remember in my hometown public library. I make sure my children know right away how precious the books are to our community. I don't just tell them this but show them as well. If I find a book on the floor, which inevitably I do, I stop the class and say, "Boys and girls, eyes this way! Look what I just found on the floor! A book! Let me make sure it's not ruined!" I then flip through it dramatically and pretend I'm examining it closely before putting it back. "If you *ever* see a book on the floor, please, please take care of it and put it back. These books are like treasures, and we need to take care of each one of them."

An unfortunate by-product of this dramatic episode is that for the next few days children run to me breathless if they find a book on the floor. "Look, Ms. Collins, this precious book was on the floor!" Theria said one day, with one hand on her hip as she handed the book over to me. "Thank goodness you found it," I responded. "Can you put it away?" Eventually, though, the novelty of running to me with wayward books wears off, and children just pick them up and put them back.

Putting books back into the right place can be tricky early in the year, so for one reading lesson we might go on a "field trip" into the classroom library. During this time I show my students the various baskets of books and read the labels, and we talk about what we might find in the baskets. I go on to say, "If you ever find a book and are not sure where it goes exactly, something you can do is look at the other books in the basket to see if it goes with them." Then I model doing this. In other classrooms teachers have a basket labeled Out-of-Place Books so that children can put the book somewhere safe until the teacher or class librarians put it in the correct basket.

Some teachers make being class librarian a prestigious and coveted classroom job. When I've had class librarians, I learned that it's important to rotate the job every three weeks or so. Having more children take direct responsibility for the library helps everyone take better care of it over time.

It's also important to hype the class librarian position so that children take it seriously. I usually have a training period for the new monitors, which is one lunch period during the librarian transition. The new librarians, the children they are replacing, and I eat lunch together in the classroom, which is, strangely enough, a huge treat for first graders. After we've finished eating, the former librarians and I give the new librarians a brief overview and run-through of their responsibilities. It takes only 15 minutes or so, but the children get excited about the job.

The class librarians' responsibilities can be vast or small. Here are some examples of things class librarians have been responsible for:

- Making sure the baskets don't have any misplaced books in them
- Fixing the books that need to be taped or repaired
- Making sure children return their take-home books to the classroom
- Announcing new book arrivals to the class
- Being the teacher's helper during reading lessons
- Making basket labels for new categories of books

During this bend in the road about taking care of books and the library, the teaching topic may seem small or inconsequential. In the grand scheme of all the things we need to teach our students about reading, how important is it to teach them to put books away carefully? How necessary is it to take our limited time to teach children how to put books back in the baskets right side up? In my opinion, very important and very necessary. Lessons such as these teach children more than procedures; they teach them about our values and community standards. Here is a mini-lesson that many teachers do to teach children about putting the books away carefully.

Mini-lesson

Connection

First graders, I've got something very important to tell you. I've been noticing that during reading time, you have been busy and focused on your reading, and that's great. But I've noticed one small problem, too. When you're putting books back into the baskets, you're putting them back any which way. Check out this basket with me. I took it off one of the tables to show you what I mean.

I hold the basket on my lap and flip through the books, some of which are upside down or backwards. I even show two books with pages intermeshed for dramatic effect.

Do you notice how these books are kind of messy? Some are upside down, and some are backwards, and some are even kind of stuck together? When this happens, it causes problems for readers because they can't find what they are looking for. It also causes problems for the books because they can get ruined when they are just thrown back into the baskets. We have to take care of our books, even when we're finished reading them, and today I'm going to teach you how. You need to put books back into the baskets when you're finished reading them.

Teaching point and demonstration

I'm going to pretend I just finished reading this book. Watch how carefully I put the book away. [I demonstrate.] Did you notice how I made sure it was put back carefully, right side up with the cover showing? Did you see how I made sure it didn't get stuck with another book? Well, that's just how I want you to put books away every time. Before I give you a chance to try, will you watch me again? This time, I might need your help.

In this demonstration I offer a bad example by tossing the book into the basket carelessly.

Thumbs up if you noticed a problem. [Everyone's thumbs go up.] Tell your neighbor what the problem is and how I can fix it.

I listen for less than half a minute to catch what a few children are saying.

Oh, you guys have eagle eyes. You noticed I wasn't too careful. I heard one of you say that I just about threw the book into the basket. Someone else saw that it was upside down. If I were sitting at your table and did this, you could remind me, in a nice voice, of course, to put the book back more carefully. Do that now. All of you say, "Ms. Collins, would you put your book back more carefully?" [The class says it.] Okay, thanks for reminding me so nicely. [I fix the book.]

Active engagement

Okay, now you try. Move into a circle. I'm going to pass out a book to each of you, and I want you to put it back into this basket very carefully so it's not backwards or upside down.

I pass out books randomly and then move around the circle with the basket so children can put them back the right way.

Wow, you guys have been so careful. None of the books is backwards or upside down. I think you're ready to go read.

Link to ongoing work

Readers, we need to remember that it's important to read, of course, but it's also important to take care of our books all the time. Make sure you remember to put your books back into the baskets carefully, as I showed you, and if someone at your table forgets, you can kindly remind them by saying, "Could you put your book back more carefully?" That's going to really help our class with reading and help our books last all year long.

Teachers reading through this lesson may be wondering if this is really important enough to spend a whole-class lesson on. I would say yes, because teaching children how to put books away carefully is more than a procedural detail. It is teaching about readers' values.

Other Mini-lessons

Here are summaries of ideas for other mini-lessons for this part of the unit of study.

❖ *Readers know what's in the library and how to take care of it.* This month, during reading time, you guys are reading books from the table-top baskets. Soon you'll be picking books from the classroom library. It's important that we learn about taking care of books so that we can take care of our library. Let me show you what kinds of books we have in the library because in the mornings, when you first come in, I'm going to give you time to read anything you want from the library. But first I want to teach you about what kinds of book baskets we have in the library so you'll know where to find books you love.

❖ *Readers borrow and return books carefully.* Readers, everyone has pet peeves. Pet peeves are things that bother us a lot. For example, I have a friend whose pet peeve is when people cut in line. It drives her crazy. Last year I had a student whose pet peeve was when kids would leave tissues on the floor. She would get so mad! Well, I'm going to tell you about my pet peeve. My pet peeve is when people aren't careful about putting books back in the library and put them back in the wrong place. I want to teach you how readers pay attention to where their books come from so they can put them back in the right place.

❖ *All readers are responsible for library housekeeping.* This morning, after you had free reading time in the library, it looked like a mess. I didn't fix anything up. Take a look around. What problems do you see? [Children turn to a partner and name problems such as upside down or backwards books, books in the wrong baskets, books on the floor.] How will we solve the problem? We have to solve it quickly so that you guys can begin to shop in the classroom library.

❖ *Readers follow the system for taking books home and bringing them back.* Guess what, readers? Many of you told me that you want to borrow books from school to take home so that you can show your families the cool stuff you're learning to do. I decided that taking books home is a great idea, so I want to teach you our system for taking home books.

Understanding Reading Workshop Procedures

After we've had these talks about reading identities and taking care of books at reading workshop time, I send the children off to read. For the first few days of school, there is a basket on each table with books representing different levels, topics, and genres. I want the baskets to reflect the wide variety of choices available in our library. After the mini-lessons the children go to their seats to choose books to read from the table-top baskets. This is very simple and very contrived. There is no milling around or searching for books in the classroom library. The children learn to leave the meeting area and quickly get to work at their tables.

Remembering the advice to slow down, I use these days to teach some of the most basic procedures of reading workshop, such as the transition from mini-lessons in the meeting area to work spaces for independent reading time. We work on achieving and maintaining a comfortable noise level, staying focused during work time, and putting books back into the right place.

In an ideal world we'd send children off to read, and they would find the perfect book in which to lose themselves. We would go from child to child to confer and have engaging and informative reading conferences that move the readers along to greater reading glory. And then, when it's time for reading to end, the children would join in a collective sigh as they reluctantly put their books away.

In the early days of first grade, however, reality looks a little different. Here are some predictable things students do during the first few days of school:

- Children sample the books in the table-top basket and declare that they are finished reading after a nanosecond. We can teach these children how to slow down and spend more time with one book rather than racing through everything in the basket. This is an opportunity to teach children how to engage themselves at reading time and how to stay with a book.
- Most children can't help but share a book with a child they are sitting next to. They may talk about pictures, "read" the story (especially if it's familiar), or read the text if they are able to do so. We can note some of the things children are doing for ideas for future mini-lessons on partner reading time.
- Children will play around and do things we wish we hadn't seen, like sliding books back and forth as if they were playing table hockey, showing off their new cartoon character watch to anyone who's interested, and leaning way back in their chairs to reach that critical balance point. In these cases, we can approach them with surprise: "I am so shocked, Jeremy. It's reading time, but you're not reading! Oh, no, you're wasting the precious time. It's such a shame because you don't have much time left for reading today. So you need to get focused right away."

Rather than fretting about such behavior, we can take a close look at what students are doing (or not doing) and let this guide mini-lessons for the next week or so in this bend in the road on building a productive reading community.

Students need firm support as they begin to take the plunge as readers. Although they may not be very proficient at reading words yet, there are reading behaviors that they can learn. So, it's important to slow down and deal with the nitty-gritty of an independent reading workshop: the noise level, traffic patterns, and interruptions during conferences.

Dealing with Noise Level as a Community

When the children are reading at their tables during these first couple of weeks, it's inevitable that the noise level rises as they read together and share things they notice about the books they're reading. I want the talk and sharing to happen, of course, but I don't want my class to sound like the cafeteria when it's full of children sharing fruit roll-ups and talking about loose teeth and cool lunch boxes.

I strive to differentiate clearly between library voices, regular voices, and outdoor voices, and I let my students know that I expect them to use library voices during reading time. I also emphasize that fooling around is usually loud and that library voices are always soft. We talk about considerate ways for children to let other people know they are talking too loud during reading time so that I don't have to be the sole noise police. I want my students to be able to solve these issues before they come running to me to take care of problems.

If the noise level rises to unacceptable levels, I stop the class. I don't want them to get used to working loudly because I know I'm setting a standard in these early days. It will just get louder as the year progresses if we begin with an elevated noise level. Some teachers play classical music at a low volume and use that as the indicator for the class noise level: if you can't hear the music, the classroom is too loud.

I try to help my students develop an internal sense of appropriate noise levels so that they can begin to monitor the noise themselves. During reading workshop, when the noise rises, I stop them and whisper, "Boys and girls, it's getting too loud to think in here. Let's start again but quieter this time." By whispering myself, I am inviting them to use low voices. It usually works, at least for a few minutes.

If, after a few days, the noise level is still unacceptable, I pose the problem to the class: "Readers, there's a problem here. Reading time is too loud, and many of you are having a hard time getting your best work done in the noise. People keep forgetting, so I need your help. What can we do?" I take a couple of suggestions from the students, and depending on their practicality, we implement them. Their suggestions have ranged from having a noise monitor at each table (kind of practical), to banning any kind of talk (impractical), to collecting money to buy me ear plugs (nice idea, but no dice).

I know teachers who have dealt with noise levels by having a couple of minutes of silent reading time at the beginning of reading workshop. After the silent time, the children are more likely to speak to each other quietly because they've had quiet as they've settled in. Other teachers let children spread out throughout the room during reading time so that the chatter is more dispersed. They feel that this is quieter than having all the children concentrated at tables. Yet other teachers, from the first day of school, begin work time with private reading so that children look at books silently by themselves. Then they move the class toward partner reading time so that children can talk about their books. Some teachers feel their students need this very unambiguous differentiation right from the start. These teaching decisions, like any others, are up to individual teachers based on their own teaching styles and their students' strengths and needs.

Traffic Patterns and Reading Spots

A basic management procedure I tended to overlook at first was the way classroom traffic moved. I'd have logjams in the writing area, bottlenecks near the sink, and mob scenes at the coat closets before dismissal. From watching veteran teachers around me, I learned how to tame the traffic in my classroom.

I concentrated on children's movements during transitions. I need transitions in my classroom to happen quickly and with focus. To help this occur, I learned to spend time during the first weeks of school having the children practice what it means to take a direct route from tables to meeting area, from meeting area to tables, and to and from the closets during dismissal.

It's easy to teach children how to physically move from one thing to another without tears or bloodshed, but it's harder to teach them the "mind work" of transition or how to move with intention. So often when a six-year-old leaves the meeting area to get to work on something, he gets distracted along the way by the work-in-progress in the block area, by the new addition to the turtle tank, or by a conversation about recess plans with his best buddy.

When children get off track and let go of intention, we run into problems. Transitions take longer and longer, and our voices get louder and louder as we exhort students to get ready for the next thing. We need to help our students think, What am I about to do, and what do I need to do it? as they get ready for independent reading or any other work they are about to do.

We all have different levels of tolerance for transition noise and chaos. I know one teacher who spends lots of time teaching her children how to pick up their chairs when they push them in to the tables. "I just can't bear the sound of chair legs dragging on the floor," she explained when I marveled at how quiet her room was during transitions from tables to the meeting area. I've also been in rooms where the bottom of every chair leg and desk leg has a neon green tennis ball fitted onto it. Besides adding lots of color to the classroom, the tennis balls muffle the noise of moving furniture.

We have decisions to make once children have transitioned into work time. For reading workshop, we decide if children will read at their tables or in reading spots around the room. The teachers I work with seem to be split evenly on this issue. Teachers who have children read at their seats find that it's easier to do a visual scan of the room during conferring. For some children, sitting at a desk helps them stay focused on their work. On the other hand, teachers who let children choose reading spots around the room say that children stay focused on their work because they don't want to lose the privilege of having a reading spot. One teacher said, "We spend time talking about our favorite places to read, so I feel that I should let them find these kind of places in class." This teacher lets children pick reading spots biweekly so that there aren't daily battles for the most desirable places.

In my classroom I find it more manageable for children to sit at desks when they read. I can easily see everyone at a glance. As the year progresses and children have internalized expectations for reading workshop, I begin to let children read in other places. I treat these reading spots as a privilege, not a right, and if a child isn't getting her work done, I quickly move her back to a desk during reading time.

Having said that, I need to also say that I love the idea of beginning the year with cozy reading spots around the room, and I know many teachers for whom that works very well. These teachers design their classrooms with little nooks and crannies, and they often have big floor pillows and rug swatches for comfort in these reading spots. Many teachers who let their children spread out into reading spots will say that their children focus better during reading time because they don't have other children right nearby to distract them, which can happen when children are all reading at their table seats.

No matter which way we decide to let children work during reading time, we need to make the expectations clear for how they need to work.

Getting Rid of Interruptions During Conferences

Another important procedure I work on from the beginning of school is making sure my students understand that they are not allowed to interrupt me when I'm conferring with a child. This training takes consistency and time. It helps to confer with students during reading, writing, math, and other times so that the idea of not interrupting conferences is reinforced throughout the day.

Everyone in the community must understand the sanctity of conference time. Some teachers wear a special necklace or hat during conferences to signal that they are not to be interrupted. Simply telling first graders not to interrupt conferences is usually ineffective. We need to help them figure out ways to help themselves. I usually do a mini-lesson or two about my expectations for reading conferences.

Mini-lesson	
Connection	*Every day when you are all reading, you'll notice that I move around to talk to kids about their reading. I take notes on this clipboard I have with me. I am busy learning about you guys so I can help you get better as readers. That's why, when I'm working with a reader during a reading conference, it's important that we don't get interrupted. Today, I want to teach you about the jobs we have in conferences so that you can really understand why it's so important not to interrupt them.*
Teaching point and demonstration	*Let me show you what I mean.* I ask a volunteer to sit at a table and pretend to read. I sit down next to the reader as the class watches. *Watch closely what I'm doing and what Sophia is doing.* I whisper this loudly to the rest of the class, and Sophia and I dramatize a reading conference. After a minute or so, I ask the students what they noticed. *Turn and tell your neighbor what you noticed.*

I listen in as the students talk. They usually say things like, "She was sitting right near Sophia," or "She was writing down stuff," or "She was watching Sophia read," or "Sophia was reading and then she had to talk to Ms. Collins."

You guys are absolutely right. I sat near Sophia, watched her closely, wrote stuff down, and talked to Sophia about her reading. My job is to teach Sophia something that will help her become a stronger reader. Sophia also had a challenging job because she was doing reading work and then talking to me about it. This is called a reading conference, and it's important for teachers and kids to have this time together. But I need all of your help. When I'm conferring with someone, it's important that the rest of you don't interrupt. That means not coming up to me when I'm working with someone. It's a very important rule in class—no interrupting during reading conferences because we all have challenging jobs to do in conferences.

Active engagement

Right now, I want you to turn to your neighbor and remind her about the jobs that I do and that you do when we are having a reading conference together. Right now, turn to your neighbor and list the things out on your fingers. I hope you get to four fingers, at least.

As they turn and talk, I listen in and then report back the things they said, while listing them on my fingers.

Link to ongoing work

Today during reading time, and any day for that matter, I'm going to have a few conferences, and you guys are going to try really hard not to interrupt me and the student I'm conferring with because you understand what important work we're doing in a conference.

I send the readers off to read, and of course, I am interrupted during the conferences even after doing that lesson. I try to be very consistent in my responses to the interruptions. Some teachers put up their hands, shake their heads as if to say "not now," or simply ignore the interruption as much as possible. When my students interrupt me after this lesson, I know that in tomorrow's mini-lesson I'll talk about the interruptions, and we'll figure out other ways to help ourselves besides approaching the teacher during a reading conference. In a few of my classes, we've created charts about this.

Helping Ourselves Not to Interrupt Conferences
"Can I go to the bathroom/get a drink/get a tissue?"
    "Take care of your business before work time."
"Someone is bothering me."
    "Tell them to stop because it's reading time. If it doesn't get better, wait
    till I finish the conference and tell me then."
"I'm stuck on a hard part."
    "Work more on the hard part. Ask a friend to help."

It also helps to be consistent with conferring during all the content areas. In other words, have the same standards, procedures, and expectations for math conferences and writing conferences as you do for reading conferences.

Just like the early work in any content area, many of my early reading conferences concern the procedural issues of independent reading time. I help my students understand and meet the class expectations for noise, movement, and work habits. I call these types of conferences management conferences, and my goal is to have fewer and fewer of these as the days go by. The less time I need to spend in management conferences, the more time I can spend conferring with students about their reading.

Other Mini-lessons

I've listed summaries of ideas for other mini-lessons for this part of the unit of study.

❖ *Noise levels that are good for all readers.* You guys, when we talked about our best reading memories, many of us shared times when we were reading in a cozy place, all quiet and calm. That's how our classroom needs to be during reading time so that we can all do our best work. Today, I'm going to teach you how to make your voice a library voice because that will help to keep our classroom quiet for all readers.

❖ *Kind reminders for noisy or distracting behavior.* Readers, I have some good news and some bad news. First, the bad news. Yesterday I was having a conference with someone, and I could hear a reader at the next table fooling around and talking kind of loud. That was bad news. But here's the good news. Just as I was about to go over to the table and talk to the noisy reader, I heard a kid say, "Excuse me . . . can you keep your voice quiet so I can concentrate on my reading?" You know why that is good news? It's good news because it was such a nice way to ask someone to be quiet. "Excuse me . . . can you keep your voice quiet so I can concentrate on my reading?" That sounds so much better than, "Hey, be quiet!" or "I'm telling the teacher how noisy you are."

For the rest of the lesson, the children can generate other nice ways of addressing each other.

❖ *Be considerate to other readers.* Yesterday, I saw some more good news. Terrance and Miranda both wanted to read a *Biscuit* book at reading time. They grabbed the book at the same time. I thought, Oh, no . . . it looks like trouble! But Terrance and Miranda did something so cool. Terrance said, "Miranda, you can read it first if you let me read it when you're done." Wasn't that a good move? Terrance decided to be patient and wait until Miranda was finished. I loved that. Today, I want to teach you how readers can take turns with books so both people get what they want.

❖ *Move smoothly and quickly.* First graders, one of the things we don't have enough of in this class is time. It feels like we need to have school until nighttime just to get everything done. Because we have lots of working and playing to do in school, we have to be sure that we're making time for it all. One of the ways we can make the time is by moving quickly but safely back to our seats from the meeting area. Let me show you what that looks like.

❧ *Learners stay focused.* You know what I noticed? When I say it's time to go to your reading spots, sometimes you take the long way around the room. It's like you're taking a little tour or something. When you do this, you lose some of your precious reading time. Today, I want to teach you how to stay focused so that when you move from one thing to another, you can do it quickly. Something I do to help me stay focused is remind myself what I'm doing. So if my teacher said, "Boys and girls, get your reading bins and begin reading," I might say to myself, "Get your reading bin, get your reading bin" to help me stay focused on what I need to do.

❧ *Readers don't interrupt reading conferences.* We've learned about the important jobs the teacher and the student have to do during reading conference, but I notice I'm still getting interrupted as I confer with readers. Today I want to teach you again what it looks like when I confer so that when you see me conferring with a reader, you will remember not to interrupt.

Staying Focused on Reading

In the first couple of weeks of school, when many first graders may not be reading the words in their books, our mini-lessons and reading conferences support their approximations and their exploration in books. Although what they are doing may not feel like serious reading work, we can, through our conferences and mini-lessons, make what they're doing important and readerly.

Adrian and Emily were sitting side by side reading a stack of books from the basket on their desk. They had a few early reading books mixed in with some picture books and a Seymour Simon book on snakes. They were giggling together, and at first glance, it seemed like reading was the last thing they were thinking about. I was of two minds: one told me to put an end to their giggling and get them back on task; the other told me to find out what they were doing before reacting. Fortunately, I had some patience that day.

"I saw that you guys are laughing while you're reading. Is your book funny?" I asked, noticing they were looking through an early reader with one line of text on the page, probably not the funniest book in the room. At first they seemed embarrassed and hesitant to tell me what was going on. I think they thought they were in trouble.

"I asked that question about whether your book is funny because I love funny books. I love to laugh while I'm reading."

"We were laughing because of this page," Emily said, as she flipped through to find the funny part. She stopped at a page with a photograph of a little boy sitting in a bathtub. Emily looked at Adrian, and they both smiled, trying hard not to laugh in front of me.

"What about it made you laugh?" I asked, smiling back at them.

"It looks like Michael," Adrian said, as they both giggled and looked over at Michael, another student in our class.

"You know, you're kind of right. I can see how it reminds you of Michael," I said in genuine agreement. At this point, I knew I needed to make something bigger out of this moment. It had to be about more than finding a resemblance to Michael and bathtub pictures.

Like most reading conferences, this one could have gone several different ways. I chose this: "It's cool that you guys looked so closely at this picture and it reminded you of someone. That happens a lot when you read. The book makes you think of someone else. Last night, I was reading, and my book had a character that reminded me of my grandma. That happens all the time to readers. May I tell the rest of the class about it during share time?" They nodded enthusiastically.

Some of the work our students will do in the first couple of weeks of independent reading may seem far from conventional reading. We need to find the ways it approximates and encourages reading, so we can connect it to the work we will soon be expecting of them. When we face a class full of children who are not yet reading conventionally, our job is to observe them to see what they can already do, and then explicitly teach them the other things they need to do to grow into strong and independent readers.

I list here some ideas for mini-lessons for this part of the unit of study. Instead of writing the text for actual mini-lessons I might do, I provide a rationale for these mini-lessons. Although each could be the topic of a single session, some might be teaching points over a few days or so, depending on the needs of the students.

❧ *Strong readers read the pictures.* Because some students aren't yet reading words, I take a day or two and model for them how to spend time *really* reading the pictures. I show them how to notice details in the pictures, how to tell the story of the book through the pictures, how to find what they think is the most important picture in the book, and how to talk about the pictures with a partner. These mini-lessons help children learn to stick with a book for a longer time instead of simply flipping through it and going straight to the next book. These lessons teach children to look more closely at books and to notice details, discrepancies, and surprises, as well as the value of slowing down.

❧ *Strong readers read the story.* Even if the words are too hard and the text is too long, I share with children how they can "read" familiar picture books. I often demonstrate with a book that I've already read aloud a few times. I show them how to read it by using the pictures, the literary language of the text, and their sense of the story. This kind of mini-lesson helps children see the value of revisiting familiar books and helps to build their sense of story.

❧ *Strong readers act out the story.* We talk about how characters might sound and how to use our voices in different ways when we read. We might think about how to tell a story in a sad voice or an excited voice or a creepy voice.

These mini-lessons help children understand some of the enjoyable things to do with books and offer a beginning look at character, fluency, and reading with expression.

✿ *Strong readers notice details or new things when they reread their books.* I want my class to value rereading familiar books, so I spend time celebrating new discoveries in old books. We talk about how we might notice new things in the illustrations, or we might think new thoughts when we read a book again. Mini-lessons on rereading are helpful for getting children to linger with and revisit familiar texts.

✿ *Strong readers are reminded of things when they read.* This is a time to whet the students' appetites for the variety of connections they can make when they read. I may touch lightly on text-to-self and text-to-text connections (Keene and Zimmermann 1997), knowing that this will be something we continually return to throughout the year. These mini-lessons help children realize that readers have thoughts as they're reading, even if some of them aren't yet reading conventionally.

Readers Think and Talk About Books with Others

It was a crisp October day in Buffalo, and no, it wasn't snowing yet. I was about to do a demonstration lesson in René Brown-Baugh and Nancy Kalinowski's kindergarten classroom at Westminster Community School. I was planning to do one of the early "how to be a great reading partner" lessons, and I was curious to see what the students had in mind about partnerships already. While the thirty-eight kindergartners began settling in the meeting area for the mini-lesson, I struck up a quick conversation with the first bunch of kids who arrived and sat nearest me.

"You guys, may I ask you a quick question? I'm wondering, What do you know already about being good reading partners?" Several of the children raised their hands, and I looked toward a little girl with a shy smile and lots of braids.

"You shouldn't cut your partner's hair," she said confidently.

"Yeah, and don't say the f-curse to your partner 'cause that can hurt his feelings," added the boy next to her.

"You guys are so right! We shouldn't cut our partner's hair, and we shouldn't say curse words, either. I'm so glad you mentioned those things because it shows me you know a lot already about being partners. I'm glad because today I'm going to teach you something else about being great reading partners. I can tell that you're ready to learn this stuff."

For the demonstration lesson that followed this short conversation, I taught the students how good reading partners sit side by side and hold the book in the middle so both readers can see it. After the lesson, the children went off to their reading spots to read with their partners. Thankfully, there were no incidents involving scissors or swear words.

When I shared the children's prelesson comments with the teachers at our follow-up meeting, René and Nancy laughed and said that, sure enough, there had been a hair-cutting incident and an improper exchange of curse words between some seat partners in the last few days. Clearly, these teachers had already had some teachable moments about partnerships in their kindergarten classroom.

When I teach about partnerships during this first unit of study, my goal is to lay a solid foundation for all the partner work that will follow throughout the year. Even though one of my biggest goals is for students to have compelling conversations about books with their partners, I first need to make sure that they know the nuts-and-bolts of reading partnerships, even if that might include such seemingly obvious things like partners don't cut each other's hair and don't curse at each other.

During these first few weeks of school, my mini-lessons about partnerships focus primarily on cooperation and the ways that good partners can read together, and I try to appeal to children's sense of civility and community. Instead of just teaching them to hold the book in the middle and to sit side by side, I make sure they understand that good partners do these things so that both partners can see the book. We sit close and put the book in the middle because it's the fair way to do it.

It feels natural to work on partnerships during these first weeks of school because most young readers tend to want to read with someone else. I've found that even if I send students off to read with the explicit understanding that it's time for them to read alone, in the early days of the school year, children seem to inevitably gravitate toward each other to ask questions about their stories, to show parts of their books, and to share ideas.

Usually around the third week of school, after I've done the work of the first several bends in the road of this unit of study, I feel ready to turn the spotlight on partnerships for several days. At first, my students will simply partner with their seatmate. Then, after a couple of days, I switch the partners around so that children get opportunities to work with other people. I assign these partners because I don't want to take class time for children to make these choices. Also, when we let children publicly pick partners, whether it's for reading or for gym class, it's inevitable that feelings will be hurt and the seeds of drama planted.

In the next unit of study (Chapter 5), I describe partnerships in greater detail because at that time we use our early assessments to create ability-based partnerships that will last for longer than a week or two.

Mini-lessons

Some ideas for mini-lessons for this part of the unit of study follow.

❖ *Partners sit side by side and read with the book in the middle.* Boys and girls, when you and your partner read together, there are some things to know that will help each of you read the book well. Today I want to teach you how partners sit side by side and put the book right in the middle so they both can read it.

- ❉ *Partners plan ways to read together.* Yesterday I saw lots of cool things that partners were doing. I listened in and saw how nicely you were reading together. Today, and for the next couple of days, I want to show you different ways you and your partner can read together. Today, I'm going to teach you how partners can read like a chorus, how to read and make both your voices sound like one voice. It's like singing a song together. Your voices match.

   Other possibilities: Partners can echo read—I read, you read; partners can take turns reading—you read it first and then I'll read it; partners can help each other notice details on the pages.

- ❉ *Partners take turns making decisions.* It's only fair if both partners can make decisions. There is no boss in a partnership. Today I want to teach you that partners take turns making decisions, and one of the most important decisions partners make is deciding which book to read. Let me show you how you can be fair when you make the decision.

- ❉ *Partners talk about their books.* One of the coolest things about having a reading partner is that you have someone to talk with about your book. Partners have millions of things to talk about, but today I'm going to teach you about one thing that you can talk about—readers can talk about their favorite pages in their books.

   Other possibilities: funny parts, sad parts, weird parts, confusing parts.

- ❉ *Partners solve their own problems.* I notice that sometimes partners get in a hole and have a hard time climbing out. They fall into the hole when they don't agree on something, or when they get too silly and have trouble concentrating on their reading. When this happens, it often interrupts my reading conferences because I have to remind partners to get to work. Today, I want to teach you one way to help yourselves when you run into trouble making decisions. This is something you know from when you were really little, but let me remind you. It's fair when people take turns. So, if you've already picked one book that you and your partner have read, it isn't too fair if you choose the next one. What *is* fair is to say, "It's your turn to pick the book now because I already picked the last one."

Assessment: Getting a Read on Your Readers

My assessment plan for the first couple of weeks of school is to get an educated first impression of each child. Because I will be creating ability-based partnerships by the end of September, I need to determine the reading levels for each child. I also want to learn not only what they can read but what they like to read. I want my classroom library to reflect the strengths, needs, and interests of the readers in the class.

In order to do these assessments quickly yet accurately, I carry around an assessment kit along with my conferring clipboard during the first unit of study. My kit is simply an accordion file containing several books representing a range of reading levels as well as copies of typed text from each of the books.

At P.S. 321, the first-grade teachers work together to create a set of assessment texts. The chosen texts do not circulate in the classroom libraries because we want them to be fresh reads for the assessments. We choose books that represent a range of reading levels, with two assessment books for each level. We type up the text (double-spaced so we have room to record our running records) and leave space to jot other observations made during the assessment, such as notes on fluency, comprehension, and attitude.

Of course, we didn't have to create our own assessment materials. Many premade assessment kits are available to teachers, but these kits are expensive, and we found they weren't especially fine-tuned to our needs. We divided the labor among the first-grade teachers to create something more in line with our needs.

So, I'm ready to assess my students in an efficient and accurate manner. I gather and organize my assessment materials even before the first day of school, making sure all the books and assessment sheets are at hand, along with a class list so that I can note the date and level of everyone's assessment, in a sturdy plastic accordion file. The appendix provides an assessment template.

It's challenging to find assessment time in the first few weeks of school. I do some of the assessments during reading workshop but don't use the whole work time to assess. I make sure that I confer with a few people or partners, as well as assess, during reading time because I want my students to become familiar with reading conferences. I also assess a student or two in the morning before the class meeting while the rest of the class is working on morning jobs.

In the past, I've tried to race through my assessments to get them all finished as quickly as possible, but I've found that I give up some quality of life when I do this. If I focus too heavily on assessing, I'm not able to focus as well on managing and getting to know my class, which are both crucial in these early weeks of school.

My next task is to organize the assessing. A strategy that has worked well for me is to loosely group the children based on information I've received from their kindergarten teachers so that I'm assessing children who are similar as readers around the same time. For example, I might find three children who ended kindergarten reading early chapter books, so I would plan to assess those children one after another.

It's very informative to watch how these three readers approach and work on the same text. When I assess them in succession, it's easier to see the subtle differences among them, even if they are at the same reading level. If I had spread out their assessments across the weeks, I might not have noticed their similarities and differences as much.

Let's imagine now that I'm assessing Nicole. I asked her to meet me at the meeting area, and I laid some books out in front of her. I choose the books to lay out based on what I know from her kindergarten end-of-year assessment. I usually put out books that are below the assessed level as well as at that level. I begin low to account for possible loss of reading skills over the summer break. Also, it's important that this first assessment be comfortable and nonthreatening for the child. I start with easy texts rather than something too challenging so the child can be successful and confident right away.

"Nicole, please choose a book that you'd like to read with me." I purposely say "read with me" rather than "read to me" because I don't want to make this a scary occasion for the students in these early days of school.

I like to watch and note how children pick a book. Some children seem to choose any book without much intention, whereas others take time to look at and comment on the covers before selecting one. Some children flip through the pages of a couple of the books and make their choices based on what they notice inside. The way that children approach the books is important information to note because it tells us something about what they already know and think about reading.

A child who picks a book passively or tentatively may not realize that the cover and the inside of the book offer information about the story. She may not know that she could pick a book based on what interests her. She may not feel enthusiastic or confident about reading. She may not be used to choice.

A child who picks a book with more intention, perhaps after looking at the covers, knows that he can choose based on what looks good or interesting. A child who looks inside the books probably knows to check if the words look hard or easy. I make sure I note how a child chooses and what he says while making his decision.

Nicole scanned the books, and she didn't touch any of them. She pointed at *Max's Box* and looked at me. "Oh, you want to read that one?" I asked. She nodded, and I told her she could pick it up and flip through it.

After the child makes a choice, I ask how she decided on the book, and I note the response.

"Nicole, why did you pick this one?" I asked.

Nicole shrugged and said, "I don't know."

I note my observations and the response on the assessment sheet. Although I may have an idea or theory about the child as a reader already, I need to be sure that I keep an open mind because she may simply be shy or nervous. After all, this is one of the first times that she's really sat one-on-one with me and been asked to read.

"Nicole, you picked *Max's Box*. What do you notice about the cover?"

"There's a boy sitting in a box," Nicole said.

"Hmm, you're right. The title is *Max's Box,* so I wonder if he's Max," I said.

"Yeah, he's Max," Nicole said with certainty.

I usually tell the child the title and begin a little conversation about the cover before the reading begins. I try to have a standard way of doing this for each book so that the children all get the same start. Sometimes I make adjustments based on my sense of the child.

"It's time to read. What do you usually do before you start reading?" I asked Nicole.

Nicole shrugged and said quietly, "I read." She opened to the first page. I ask this question because I want to find out if the child flips through the book at all or if the child opens immediately to the first page. I also pay attention to how the child approaches the text as she begins reading. Does she appear confident, enthusiastic, hesitant, timid?

I usually wait to see how the child works on the first page. Often, however, especially if he is a very early reader or seems tentative, I say, "Oh, may I read the first page? Then you can read the rest." I note on the assessment sheet that I read the first page to the child.

If the book is clearly too easy for the child, I let him read through it and then suggest another book for him to read. Or, if the text is obviously too difficult, I say, "Oh, this one seems a little tricky today. How about picking another one to read?" Then I pull out an easier book, and we follow the same procedure.

I used to ask, "Do you think this book is too hard?" but I found that is a tricky question to answer. If the child thinks she is supposed to be able to read it, she may say it isn't too hard and keep trying to read it. Then it becomes a prolonged struggle for the child, and I feel as if I'm losing precious time from accurate assessment.

After the child reads the book and I note the running record, I move on to ask, "Tell me, what was that about?" or "If you were going to tell your mom about the book, what would you tell her it was about?" As the child responds, I try to write down exactly what she says. I usually don't ask follow-up questions, but I've come to realize that some children comprehend a text but have difficulty putting their understanding into words. If I detect that this is the case for a particular child, I might ask a few questions about the book. Again, I jot down the questions and responses.

When we ask children what a book was about after they've read it, the range of responses, even for the same book, is usually wide. Some children easily summarize and say, "This is about a kid who has this box, and he likes to make pretend with it." Other children retell by saying, "This book is about a kid named Max who makes his box into a rocket, a boat. . . ." Other children might fix on one page: "Max makes his box into a rocket." Others might say something vague or misguided like, "It's about an astronaut," or "The boy likes boats." It's important to note these responses because they inform us about what kind of reading comprehension work we need to do in our mini-lessons, shared reading, read-aloud with accountable talk, and during small-group work instruction.

Before filing away the assessment, I make sure I take some time to analyze it for more information. I compute the accuracy rate and self-correction ratio and do miscue analysis (Clay 2000), which will inform my teaching in the next unit of study on print strategies. In general, if a child reads a text with at least 90–95 percent accuracy, and with fluency and comprehension, I consider that text to be at the child's independent reading level. If a child reads with high accuracy but is unable to talk about the book in a way that indicates comprehension, I will not consider that book to be at her independent reading level.

After assessing the class, I put the assessment sheets in piles by various reading levels so that I can create ability-based partnerships for the next unit of study. It's important, however, that we take time to consider more than reading level alone. Two children who share a reading level might still have very different strengths and needs as readers. We need to consider these issues along with the level. Also, if a child is on the verge of being able to read books at the next level, I match him with a child at that higher level if it would be mutually beneficial to these children. Overall, I want to make sure the ability-based partnerships are compatible in a number of ways. I consider personalities, work habits, and social dynamics in addition to reading levels.

Besides these more formal reading assessments, I use my anecdotal notes from across the day as well as information from families and last year's teachers to get a more complete picture of the readers in my class. I pay attention to how children do during the other components of balanced literacy by noting their level of participation and enthusiasm, their strengths and struggles. All these sources of information in combination with the reading assessments help me to work with individual readers, create reading partnerships, and plan curriculum.

It's important that we don't become so focused on our early assessments that we use them to reduce our view of children to their reading level. I've heard teachers talk about children as if reading level was their primary way of identifying them: "Oh, Brian, he's an E," one teacher told me when I asked her about a student I was going to confer with during a reading conference demonstration. When I asked what exactly she meant, she told me that Brian reads level E books. Of course, knowing the level at which a child reads with accuracy, fluency, and comprehension provides valuable information if we are very familiar with the leveling system. Even though I was familiar with this school's leveling system, and I did have an idea of what level E readers could do, I still wanted more information about Brian. I guess I was looking for specific and personal information about who he was as a reader and a person.

"Can you tell me something else about Brian?" I asked.

At this point, the teacher said, "Oh, well, he loves to read. He knows lots of sight words, and he's eager to take on challenges. Sometimes, though, he reads really fast and he gets mixed up on the easiest words." This additional information was helpful, so I went into my conference with Brian with a bit more understanding. Reading levels tell us something, but they don't tell us everything about the children we teach.

In order to get a more complete picture of the children in our classes, some other aspects of literacy we can investigate and assess are

- What are the child's attitudes toward reading? Is the child eager, hesitant, or resistant during independent reading workshop, shared reading, read-aloud with accountable talk, or writing workshop? Does the child participate often?
- Toward what kinds of books does the child gravitate during reading workshop or the other reading times? Is there a regular author, topic, or genre he prefers?
- What is the level of participation during book talks, either whole-class or in partnerships?

- How does the child take on challenges? with frustration or resourcefulness? tentatively or with a "dive right in" approach?

Celebrations

At the end of this unit of study, it's time for our students to show the world who they are as readers and how they value independent reading time. I've gathered ideas for several different options for celebrations that enable children to share their enthusiasm for reading, to show off their good reading habits, to tell who they are as readers, and of course, to enjoy snacks together.

Parents as Reading Partners

At P.S. 321, the first 50 minutes of the first Friday morning of each month is designated as "parents as reading partners" time. Parents or other important adults in the children's lives accompany the students to class and read to and with the children. Fathers, mothers, grandparents, babysitters, big sisters and brothers, aunts, and uncles squish into the children's chairs or sit on the carpet with groups of children. The grown-ups read with their own child and usually pull in other children to join them.

For the first such celebration, there are a few different things to consider doing to make the morning celebratory:

- Children interview adults to find out about their reading identities.
- Children give adults tours of the classroom with a focus on the library.
- Children and adults sketch and color pictures of themselves reading for a display.
- Children pick a favorite book and read to or with an adult.

Reading Workshop Contract Signing Party

After the children have had several consecutive and productive reading workshops, the teacher could, with great fanfare, tell them they are ready to sign a reading workshop contract. The contract isn't full of rules and regulations. Rather, it is more like a mission statement for independent reading. It can be rolled up like a scroll for an extra dramatic touch or written on a piece of posterboard to be posted (and referred to) throughout the year. I know teachers who've brought in special glitzy pens with metallic gold and silver ink for the children to use when they sign the contract.

After the signing, someone could take a photograph of the whole class standing around the contract. Then, of course, out come the celebratory snacks.

Read-a-thon

After the first month, when routines and procedures are in place, the class can have an invitation-only read-a-thon. Children invite family members or members of the school community to bring in a book and join them for a 30-minute read-a-thon.

During the read-a-thon, the teacher recreates a reading workshop by starting with a mini-lesson for everyone, moving to independent reading time, partner reading time, and then share time. Of course, the mini-lesson is simply an opportunity to let the children shine: "Readers, we've got so many important people here for such an important time in our day, independent reading workshop. Can you think of the big things our guests need to know about independent reading so that they can do a good job like you do?"

The first reading celebration of the year is over; there are reminders everywhere: the sticky pink spots on the tables from the spilled fruit punch, the doughnut crumbs crushed into the carpet. Cleaning up after school, I think about the celebration and how the families seemed charmed by the way the children proudly showed off the class library and talked about their reading.

Soon it will be October, and I've finally begun to settle in with this new class. I know they have lots of baby sisters and brothers in their families. I learned that a couple of them are coping with their parents' divorces. There's a silly little clique that needs gentle harnessing to stay focused. I've slowed down, I've been consistent, and I have fallen in love with this energetic bunch of students. I've taken great care launching the reading workshop, and now we're ready to enjoy the journey ahead.

Behind-the-Scenes Work

When any unit of study comes to a close, I like to take a few days to get my students, our classroom, and myself ready for the next unit of study. I call these my buffer days because they give me time to wrap up loose ends and make preparations for our upcoming work.

During these buffer days, I usually assess readers during reading conference time so that I can make whole-group, small-group, and individual instructional plans that align with both the children's needs and our next unit of study. My mini-lessons during the buffer days are often of three kinds:

- *Refresher mini-lesson.* I teach a particular skill or strategy that I've previously covered in order to remind students to use it during independent reading time. I try to use a different connection, demonstration, or active engagement activity to make the lesson feel new to students. Most of my refresher mini-lessons tend to be about

reading with fluency, the comprehension strategies that good readers use as they read, or reminders about word-solving strategies.

- *Discussion/inquiry mini-lesson.* I facilitate a class discussion about something to do with the upcoming unit of study. I might say, "Readers, for the next couple of weeks, we're going to learn about the kinds of things that readers do as they read that help them to figure out the words in their books. I'm wondering what you know about that already." I ask the children to turn and talk about this as I listen in to gather comments to share with the class. At the end of this lesson, I might say, "You know, you have a head start for our next study because we're going to learn a lot about figuring out words, but you already know some things that will help you. Today, I want you to pay attention to the smart things you do to figure out words. At the end of reading time we'll see what you noticed."

  The class discussion might also be about our changing reading identities, how readers can build stamina, ways readers extend focus and concentration as they read, or the qualities of good reading.

- *Management mini-lesson.* Buffer days are good days to work on classroom management and procedures. We can revisit noise level, book choice, taking care of books, partner work, or anything else necessary to help the children do their best work during reading time.

When the first unit of study comes to a close, I make sure I schedule three to five buffer days so that I can get ready for the unit of study Readers Use Strategies to Figure Out Words. During these days, I do the first seasonal rearrangement of the classroom library so that our library features leveled book baskets. Children will begin working in ability-based reading partnerships, which are based on my September reading assessments. This is also the time when children receive their own independent reading book bins, which will soon contain a selection of just-right books for each reader.

The Ever-Changing Classroom Library

The classroom library needs to reflect the reading work the class is doing, so it is time to change the library into one that will best support young readers. At this point in late September or early October, the books in the table-top book bins have been reintegrated into the classroom library. The leveled book baskets are now featured more prominently in the library. Of course, there are other baskets of books on a range of topics and in a variety of genres for the children to continue to explore. Although the emphasis of our reading work in October will be on print strategies and reading just-right books, I never want to limit the world of reading for my students. I believe children benefit from exposure and access to many different kinds of books, although at this time of year I make sure most of their reading time in class is spent reading just-right books, which are books at their independent reading levels. Many teachers define a book at a child's independent reading level as a text the child can read fluently with at least 90–95 percent accuracy and comprehension.

The Leveled Library

There are many different systems and methods that teachers can use to level their classroom libraries. It's certainly not necessary to reinvent the wheel because there are many published leveling systems that we can use to guide us. I've relied heavily on the leveled library section of *The Art of Teaching Reading* (Calkins 2001) and on *Matching Books to Readers* (Fountas and Pinnell 1999) to help me level particular texts.

Without getting into the details of leveling books, I'd like to share some ideas I've found helpful in my attempts to level books and to build a comprehensive leveled library.

It helps to have a schoolwide leveling system in place that is consistent across grades and includes a system for how the level will be indicated, such as putting a colored dot, letter, or number on the covers of the texts. When leveling is schoolwide and consistent from one classroom to another, it makes it easy for teachers to exchange texts and reorganize their leveled libraries if they change grades. Also, it's beneficial for children to know that a book with a yellow dot on the cover in second grade will be similar to the yellow dot books they read in first grade.

When teachers get new books and want to put them into the leveled library, it's helpful to have a handy list of the characteristics of the texts at each level as a quick reference. Although a variety of professional literature describes text characteristics across levels, it may feel cumbersome or time-consuming to flip through one of those books when we just need to level our books quickly. For this reason, several of my colleagues have made guide sheets that list the text characteristics for each level. On a one-page sheet each text level is indicated, and below that, a bulleted list with the characteristics of the texts for that level.

It also helps to have a couple of benchmark books at each level that a teacher knows well. Teachers can use these benchmark or prototype texts to compare with other books they are trying to level. For example, if a teacher knows that *Frog and Toad* books are representative of a particular level, they can use a *Frog and Toad* book as a standard for that level when trying to figure out the levels of other texts.

Based on my September assessments, I tailor my leveled library to the needs of the class. If I find I have lots of readers who read books at the earliest levels, I make sure my leveled library is full of easier books, of course. In most classrooms, teachers do need many easier books because children can read several during one independent reading session. On the other hand, if there are a large number of proficient readers, I make sure my baskets at the higher levels have enough texts to support these stronger readers.

Unfortunately, many teachers who want to have independent reading workshop in their classrooms may not have enough books at appropriate levels for their students. To deal with this problem, the teachers at the Westminster Community School in Buffalo set up a buddy system to exchange leveled books between grades. Each teacher had buddies at the grades above and below with whom they exchanged books. By exchanging books with a specific teacher, they felt more secure that they'd get the books back. Therefore, they were more willing to share them.

The buddy system works this way. In early fall the first-grade teachers would hold on to the easiest titles and in winter pass them back to their kindergarten buddies. At that point, most first graders were beyond those early levels and the kindergartners were ready to tackle print work. Then, at the end of the year, the kindergarten teachers would pass the books back up to first grade so that first-grade readers would have them again in the fall.

The appendix suggests some professional resources to guide teachers about leveling a portion of the classroom library.

Teaching Students About the Changing Classroom Library

Rather than take up reading workshop time to explain the leveled library and the ways the library has changed, I usually talk about this during one of our morning meetings during the buffer days before the next unit of study. I gather my class in the meeting area and ask the children to look around at the library and notice what looks different. They see the obvious changes and say, "You put baskets with dots on the top shelf," or "There's a basket of Halloween books now."

"Good observations," I say. "Yesterday, I dug out my Halloween books and made a basket for them. I love reading those books at this time, and I figured you guys would probably want to get in the spirit of the season, too. And, yes, I did put those dot baskets on the top shelf. I did that because we'll be shopping for books from those baskets and I wanted to make them easy for you to reach. I made these changes because our reading work is going to change. I wanted to make sure we have the books we need to do this new reading work. Let me tell you a little bit about the books with dots on them."

I go on to discuss the leveled library with my class. Although every teacher has a different way of explaining how the leveled library works, I think it's important to talk about it in terms of books, not in terms of readers. In other words, I explain how the baskets work instead of saying, "If you're the kind of reader who can read really hard books, this orange dot basket is for you. And if you read easy books, this blue dot basket is a great basket for you." Comments like these can set up a high-pressure dynamic because in most early-grade classrooms, there's a lot of status around reading "hard" books.

To focus on books rather than reading levels, I say, "During the next few weeks we'll be finding our just-right books from these baskets with dots on them. First, let me show you how these dot baskets work. All these books with yellow dots in this yellow dot basket are kind of the same. Let's take a look at a few of them." I flip through a few so the class can see they all have a few lines of text with very supportive pictures. "If a yellow dot book is the kind of book that feels right when you read it, this would be the perfect basket for you to find other just-right books. I just know that each of us will find a special basket full of books that feel right for us as readers. I just know that not everyone will find their just-right books in the same baskets, and that's okay because we're all different kinds of readers. We all need different things as readers, and these baskets are where you will look to find your just-right books, which are just what you need as a reader. I'll help you find your special basket."

To show the children where they'll find their just-right books, I meet with small groups of children during the buffer days in the pocket of time between morning arrival and morning meeting. I gather a group of children who, based on my assessments, are reading independently at the same level. So, for example, I gather six children who I've determined ought to be able to read at a particular level. Suppose I pull together the children who are able to read blue dot books independently. I ask them to meet me in the classroom library, and I show them the blue dot basket. In the blue dot basket, each book has a blue dot on the cover, and the harder ones have a + written on the dot.

"Readers," I say, "I want to show you a basket of books that I think you'll really love." I slide the blue dot basket to the middle of our circle. "I've been getting to know all of you as readers, and I think this blue dot basket is full of books that will help readers like you become stronger. I've noticed that you are really great at using pictures to help you figure out words, and these books have great pictures. I think you're ready for the challenge of having more than a couple of words on the page, and you'll see that these books actually have lots of words that you know and some words that you don't." I show them a few blue dot books and flip through the pages. Then I read some titles of the other books in the basket and spread them out on the floor. "Look at all the different stuff in this blue dot basket," I say enthusiastically, knowing that I'm marketing these books to them.

I end our meeting by saying, "Right now, I want each of you to pick about eight blue dot books that you'll keep in your reading bin for the week. Then, next Monday, when it's time to shop again for your just-right books, I want you to head straight to this blue dot basket. You'll be sure to find some good stuff in here. These books are good, and good for you." This little talk takes not much more than 5 minutes, so I can often meet with two or three groups of children in a morning and introduce them to their leveled book baskets. While I meet with a group of students during this time in the library area, the other children are working on their morning jobs.

At this point in the year, late September or early October, I am very direct and clear with students about where they will shop for their just-right books. I tell each child which dot basket she will go to when she shops for just-right books, and I tell her how many to borrow for the week.

Barbara Pinto, a first-grade teacher at P.S. 6 in Manhattan, even puts an index card indicating the dot color of the just-right book basket in each child's book bin. This helps children remember exactly where to shop for just-right books without having to tug at Barbara's sleeves for a reminder.

Of course, we need to remember that children move at different rates through the levels, so we have to be vigilant about nudging children to the next level when they are ready. In other words, there's no such thing as a blue dot graduation day when all the blue dot readers move on to the next level.

This movement among levels is very individual and fluid, and we must make sure to stay knowledgeable about our children's reading so that each child can move along a gradient of difficulty in a way that is paced appropriately for her.

Places for Just-Right Books

Until this point in the year, children have been selecting books at reading time from communal table-top baskets. Each day, they take books from these baskets and, at the end of reading time, put them back where they found them. This works well to help children become familiar with the range of books in the classroom. However, during this unit of study on print strategies, when the expectation is for children to have books that match them as readers, it's not efficient to send them off every day to hunt for just-right books from the classroom library, which is filled with a variety of texts. I used to have my students do this, and the library area turned into a kiddie cocktail party. My students would hang out and mingle rather than find a book and get to work. I was not alone with this problem, and a wise teacher somewhere realized that children needed a "shopping day" to find their just-right books to alleviate library loitering.

In many classrooms, teachers designate one day in the week to be a shopping day. For example, if Monday were the shopping day, children would get new books for their book bins on Monday during morning arrival or as their morning job. On Friday, the students would return books to the library that they had finished during the week, so the library baskets would be replenished in advance of Monday's shopping. As the year goes on, and as children grow more independent, many teachers begin to loosen up the shopping day and let children shop whenever they need a book.

At first, many teachers, myself included, had children keep their independent reading books in their desks. Predictably, some children began to accidentally hoard books in the black hole that is a first-grader's desk. I remember looking inside Andy's desk after school one day and finding three *Frog and Toad* books, twelve Little Red Readers, which must have been there since October, a very overdue public library book, and a long lost book on gerbils that John had brought from home.

Another drawback of children's keeping books in their desks is that it's difficult for the teacher to quickly account for what children are reading without having to bend over and search inside the students' desks to find their books. To solve these logistical problems that result from children's storing books in their desks, another wise teacher came up with the idea of individual book bins.

In many classrooms teachers buy plastic magazine holders for each student to use as his book bin. These last from year to year, and they can hold both small and larger-sized books. Some teachers use brightly decorated cardboard magazine holders, which look beautiful. Other teachers use plastic bags, fabric bags, plastic baskets, or expandable file folders. Whatever type of container, we should keep in mind that it will be used daily by young readers, moved around the room, and filled with books throughout the year, so durability is key.

There are many different ways teachers store the book bins. This can be tricky, especially in a small classroom with many children. Finding a place for twenty-seven book bins can be a feng shui nightmare! Each year I worked hard to try to figure out more efficient and space-saving systems for storage in my classroom. Some years, I had children keep their book bins on the floor beside their seats or on top of the tables. These storage spots were fine, but the downside was the visual clutter of having bins on and under tables. Some children would spend time aligning their book bins on the tables like the Great Wall of China to separate their work spaces from others'. As one might expect, building the wall of book bins would often turn into a distraction from their work. Also, because the bins were constantly accessible to the children, they would fill them with pencils, scraps of paper, discarded Band-Aids, remnants of food, and other little things that had nothing to do with reading.

One year Jessica, my teaching partner, and I noticed that there were lots of fruit flies in our classroom. We couldn't figure out why we had this problem until one day during reading workshop. We watched a tableful of kids nonchalantly swatting fruit flies away from their heads as they read. We went over to this particularly infested table and discovered an old apple core in the bottom of Stephanie's book bin. "I had it in my pocket and wanted to throw it away, but we're not supposed to get up when it's work time, so I put it in my book bin," she said. It was then that we realized that we needed to find a better place for book bins than on top of the tables. Also, I made a note to myself: mention the importance of putting only inorganic material in book bins.

Jessica and I found that it worked best for us to have a few places in the room where clusters of children could store their bins. We assigned spots for students to put their book bins so that they didn't need to spend precious reading workshop time looking around the room to find where they had put their bins yesterday. Having a few book bin storage locations around the room made it easier for us to quickly look through children's bins to see what books they had got and what they needed. These storage places were easily accessible so that if children were done with their math work, for example, they could take a book from their bin to read quietly until others finished.

A number of teachers prefer to call individual book containers by other names because "book bins" sounds too cold and far removed from reading. Some teachers call them nightstands, bookshelves, or book files, for example, because those words feel more authentic and connected to reading. I recommend that teachers use whatever term feels comfortable and use it consistently. Decisions about what to call book bins, what kinds of bins to use, and where to store them are left to individual teacher choice because there are so many options, teaching styles, and aesthetic sensibilities among us.

When my students begin using book bins, I like to make the distribution of the book bins as ceremonial as possible without hiring a caterer and sending out invitations. I want the children to feel that these empty book bins will soon become special places for them to hold their reading work. On the first day I give out book bins, we gather in the meeting area for a mini-lesson on book bin care; I even cover minute details like how they should hold the bin from the bottom so that it lasts all year. We talk about how to put books in it and what tools readers may need to keep inside.

One year my class decided they needed bookmarks, so for a week one of the offerings during choice time was bookmark making. By the end of the week every child had made a watercolor bookmark, which I laminated. They kept those all year. Other tools that may go into the book bin throughout the year are sticky notes, reading logs, reading folders, and other things particular to the reading work in the classroom.

Although the book bins offer teachers a great tool for managing the classroom library traffic and book choice, the real purpose of books bins is to be the place for children to hold on to the books they are reading. In general, children keep from two to ten just-right books in their book bins each week. Children who are reading the easiest texts might need to have eight to ten books to sustain them, whereas children who are reading early chapter books might need to shop for only one or two books for the week. As mentioned earlier, children shop for their just-right books from the leveled portion of the library, and each child is directed to his appropriate leveled basket.

Many teachers, myself included, also let children pick one or two books of interest from anywhere in the classroom library to keep in the book bin. We let them do this because we believe it's important that children are aware of the wider world of texts, beyond the dots and leveled baskets. We want them to know that they can find books about their interests and that they can develop interests by reading books. We want them to know the feeling of getting lost in a story, whether or not they are reading the words conventionally. Some teachers call these books look books or study books to differentiate them from just-right books. The main difference between these study books and just-right books is the expectation that children read their just-right books conventionally and that they read study books in the best way they can, which may or may not mean they are reading the words conventionally.

It's important to emphasize again that during independent reading workshop children are expected to read their just-right books exclusively, even if they've chosen a study book on mummies that they are just dying to read. I provide a separate time at the end of independent reading workshop or at another time of the day for children to read their study books. It's important to say very clearly and consistently to our students that reading workshop is a time to read just-right books because children, particularly those who struggle with reading, often try to read their study books covertly during independent reading workshop. This means that they aren't spending enough time reading appropriate leveled texts, which is precisely what they need to do to grow as readers.

For students who have difficulty managing their time between just-right books and study books, it works to store their study books separately from their just-right books so that they aren't distracted during reading workshop.

Some teachers ask children to keep their just-right books in a bag within the book bin so that during independent reading time they can just lift out the bag full of just-right books.

Questions About Shopping for Books and Book Choice

How can I organize shopping for books?

Designating a shopping day helps to cut down on chaos. In many classrooms, children return books to the classroom library on Friday afternoons and shop for new ones on Monday mornings before the meeting. On Monday mornings, the children might have a job to do at their seats while the teacher calls a table of students at a time over to the library to shop. The teacher hovers around the library to guide children toward appropriate books, if necessary.

Other teachers let a portion of the class shop each day. Each table or set of students has a particular shopping day. No matter what system we choose, it's important to teach children exactly what we expect to happen during shopping time. Some bottom-line expectations might be

- Readers put books back in the right place.
- Readers choose a certain number of just-right books for their book bins.
- Readers choose one or two other kinds of books.
- Readers focus on shopping for books during shopping time.

How many books should children have in their book bins?

As a general rule, children should have enough books to keep them reading for the week but not so many that they jump from book to book in an attempt to read them all. Many first-grade teachers invite the stronger readers, the children who are reading early chapter books, to pick one or two appropriately leveled books for their book bins. In my experience, when these strong readers have more than a couple of books, they never finish any of them. Instead, they start them all and jump from book to book. When we limit the number of books, they are more likely to finish those they have in their bins. If a child reads through the two books and can talk about them in a way that shows understanding, I often let that child pick new books even if it's not a shopping day. For beginning readers, it makes sense to shop for more books, perhaps eight to ten appropriately leveled books, so that they have enough to keep them reading for the week.

In addition to just-right books, my students pick one or two books that they are interested in from the nonleveled part of the classroom library. Often this choice is a nonfiction book or a compelling picture book. During reading workshop—private and partner reading time—my students read just-right books exclusively. I provide other times in the day when they can read the other books in their book bins, such as the settling down time after lunch, arrival time in the morning, or even after successful reading workshop time.

Some children constantly take books that are too hard even though I've been very specific about finding just-right books. How can I stop them from taking the wrong kinds of books?

First of all, I wouldn't want to say they're taking the wrong kinds of books. Underneath their misguided choices we can find insights into their beliefs and attitudes toward reading. I think students are making a positive statement when they choose hard books. They are saying, "I want to be challenged," or "I want to be the kind of reader who reads this kind of book." Unfortunately, these choices might originate from family pressure to read harder books or from social pressure from their best friend, who can read harder books. When children continually choose books that are too hard, I confer with them and ask why they are making these choices. After we talk, I say, "I love how you're trying to challenge yourself as a reader, so let's make a deal. I'll let you take this challenging book if you find other books that are just right for you. You can read the challenging book when you have free time, or you could take it home and read it with a grown-up. But during reading time we're trying to get stronger as readers, and your just-right books will help you with that. Deal?" The child will always agree to the deal, and I might find it necessary to send a quick note home to the family about my conversation with the child.

Some children always try to fill their bins with books that you know are too easy for them. Again, I confer with the child to find out his motivation, and strike a deal in the same way. He can have his one comfort book to go along with the just-right books.

During reading workshop some students read picture books or nonfiction books that are too hard for them instead of just-right books. How can I change this?

This is a typical problem. I'm thinking of Lucas. Early in the year, he had the obligatory ten just-right books, with text such as, "I am jumping. I am running. I am sleeping" in his book bin. Alongside these ten books, he'd have a book on insects filled with photographs and gore. It's easy to see why Lucas would tend to want to read about insects. I used to remind children, "It's time for your just-right books," but that was an inefficient use of conferring time. Here are a couple of ways that I've learned to deal with this problem:

- *Bags in the bin.* The just-right books are stored in a bag in the book bin. During reading workshop, children take out the bags of just-right books rather than their whole bin. Then they're not distracted by other books because they've only got their just-right books in front of them. At the end of private and partner reading time (with just-right books), I always provide at least 5 minutes for students to read anything they want from their bins.
- *Free reading time.* Some teachers don't have children shop for books that are not just-right books so that children will not be distracted by them during reading time. These teachers simply provide time in the day for children to read anything they want from the classroom library. In my class, I have free reading time first thing in the morning after my

students finish their morning jobs and before the morning meeting. They know that at this time they can read anything they want with or without a partner.

How do I know when children are ready to move to the next reading level? In some cases, we just know. In other cases, we'll want to assess to see in a more precise way whether children are ready for the next level. In many schools teachers have designated a couple of typical books at each level that are used for assessment purposes. One of these assessment books may be representative of the easier books at a particular level, and the other may be representative of the more challenging books at a particular level. These assessment books don't circulate in the classroom library. The teacher has them set aside for assessment purposes only.

When deciding whether a child is ready to move on to the next level, we might ask the child to read the easier of the two assessment books at the next level to see how she does, or we might assess her with the more challenging assessment book at her current level. If she reads with at least 90–95 percent accuracy and fluency, and if she can retell the book with evidence of understanding, it's appropriate to move her to the next level.

When children first move to the next level, it's important that they have some transitional books in their book bins. So, if a yellow dot reader is ready to move to green dot books, he should still have yellow dot books in his bin as well as a couple of the more challenging green dot books.

As the child makes the transition into the new level, I'd support him with a few guided reading sessions.

Ability-Based, Long-Term Partnerships

Teachers who have ability-based reading partnerships value the power of children's reading books and talking about them together, and find it especially beneficial for the youngest readers. Of course, we also provide ample time for children to read by themselves. Many teachers I work with call this time private reading time. Partner reading time is not instead of private reading time, but rather in addition to it.

It used to be a frequent practice to pair a stronger reader with an emergent one. The conventional wisdom was that the stronger reader would support the emergent reader so that he could take on more challenging work. The benefit for the stronger reader was that she would solidify her skills and thinking about reading by demonstrating for and supporting another child. What we found, however, was that most of these partnerships tended to reinforce the children's initial roles and identities as readers. For example, the stronger reader would have difficulty teaching her partner: when the partner got stuck on a word or was struggling with the text, the more proficient reader would become impatient and immediately tell the partner the word or give unhelpful hints. For example, if a child was stuck on the word *puppy*, the stronger partner might say, "It's a baby dog . . . it's cute and cuddly." This clue only helps with that particular word rather than providing reading strategy support that works across words and texts. As for the weaker reader, a passive stance toward reading seemed to be reinforced: "Oh, my partner will tell me the word, so I don't have to give it a try."

So we turned to ability-based partnerships in an attempt to balance the workload between the pair of students. There were some misgivings at first. Some teachers thought that struggling readers would reinforce each other's weak habits and strong readers would never get to "share their wealth." There were thoughts that the reading community would turn into a virtual class system, with reading ability the valued currency, if partnerships were ability-based. At first I was one of those teachers with misgivings.

Then I began to think about partnerships outside of school. At the time, I was training for a marathon, and I went to hear a speech by an elite runner. The runner spoke to us about physical training, psychological readiness, and running philosophy, and I left there with two lines of thinking. On the one hand, I was highly motivated to begin methodically adding to my weekend long runs, as the speaker had suggested, and I was determined to start a stretching program. On the other hand, I was slightly deflated because I didn't have many hours in the week to dedicate to my training, nor did I have a corporate sponsor who could subsidize a single-minded running focus, as the speaker did. Also, I was not a tiny wisp of a woman who could glide with the wind, as I imagined the speaker could. Even if it were a possibility, this woman could never be my running partner. I would always be running behind, both literally and figuratively.

My actual running partner was more of an ability-based partner. Aaron Spina, my roommate at the time, and I were training together. It was his first marathon and my third. He and I would gather running tips from friends and magazines, and share them. He was faster than I, and he helped me to gain some speed. I had more endurance, and I helped him to build up his long runs. We complemented each other because we were working within each other's zone of proximal development (Vygotsky 1962). We had different strengths and weaknesses, but we were able to support each other toward our goal of marathon fame and fortune. Actually, we simply hoped to finish in an upright position before nightfall. And we did.

I share this story to show how I came to value ability-based partners, both inside and outside of school. I watched as Deanna and Reina, two beginning readers, read together. Deanna worked on the text, while Reina read along and offered support. Deanna got to the word *climbs* and said, "cuh luh, cuh luh, cuh luh" as she tried to figure it out. While Deanna was doing this, Reina studied the picture of a monkey going up a tree. Reina pointed at the picture and then gave the word a try herself: "/cl/ /cl/ /cl/? Clim clim? That doesn't make sense." Deanna moved right in and said, "*Climb*, let's try *climb*." Together, Deanna and Reina went back and read the sentence from the start: "The monkey climbs the tree." Now, if Deanna had been reading with Anna, a very precocious reader, Anna would have said, "It's *climb*, Deanna. *Climb*, okay?" Anna may not have slowed down enough to model how to make the sounds of the first letters of the word or to remind Deanna to check the picture. Reina naturally did these things because that is exactly where she was as a reader, just like Deanna.

In addition to ability-based partnerships, the teachers I work with have also grown to value long-term partnerships, even for the youngest readers. Again, this is an idea that evolved over time. Many teachers used to let the kids select new partners weekly. Mondays would be predictable in that the children would "shop" for partners who would last just the week. There were problems with partner shopping. It could take a long time, and it could turn into a popularity contest, even in the most nurturing, cohesive communities.

When the idea arose to have teacher-assigned long-term partnerships, some teachers hesitated. In classrooms such as ours, where we provide opportunities for children to make choices, it seemed so top-heavy to assign partners. Also, teachers wondered whether long-term partnerships would turn stale quickly and become management problems. Again, I was one of the teachers with these concerns.

Then, again, I made connections to life outside of school. I thought about professional development workshops I'd attended and led. Asked to choose a partner for an activity, I always found it easier to partner with a colleague I knew well. When I partner with someone I don't know well, there are certain startup costs. We have to make small talk about the traffic or the weather in order to warm up to each other. We don't have the shorthand communication characteristic of familiar relationships. I don't invest in the work in the same way as I would with a colleague. When I partner with someone whom I know well, we can get started right away and communicate better right away. I suggest the same holds true for our students. If they have a long-term partner, they will develop ways of working well together and invest more in the partnership.

When we first introduce students to the idea of partner reading in early September, we let them work with different partners often. We want to build community and connection among the children by giving them plenty of opportunities to interact with each other. Also, we are still assessing readers during this time, so we are unable to make ability-based partnerships. After a few weeks, we have our early reading assessments finished and also have a better idea of the social dynamics in the classroom. Knowing our children both as readers and as human beings is crucial in setting up long-term partnerships. Although reading ability is the primary criterion for a reading partnership, we must take into consideration positive social arrangements and classroom dynamics as well.

In a first-grade classroom a long-term reading partnership does not necessarily mean an October-to-June commitment. Occasionally, a teacher may find that a few partnerships are thriving and decide to keep them together. Usually, the partnerships I launch in October stay together until the holiday vacation, and in January, I make changes. If one of the readers is surging ahead and is no longer at a similar level with her partner, I will want to find a better fit for her. I want to emphasize here that there are no hard-and-fast rules regarding partnerships. It's important for us to use the information we glean from our students as we establish partnerships in our classrooms.

Questions About Reading Partnerships

How do I make partnerships if I have an odd number of children?

We can make one of our partnerships into a threesome, although this presents its own difficulties. When I set up a threesome, I say, "You know what? I'm trying to figure out how to make a three-way partnership work. Every year I have threesomes, and they typically seem to have problems. I'm wondering if you three can make your threesome work and then teach me what you do. I have a feeling that you'll find some great ways to solve any problems that come up." The threesome is buoyed by the expectation that it will work out and that they will be teaching their teacher something. Or, we may find that we have some very strong readers who can sustain their own reading. I often put these children into threesomes to meet and talk about books during partner reading time. It's easier to talk about books in a threesome than to read one book in a threesome. Also, I find that an odd number of children rarely poses a problem because there are often children who are absent. In that case, I let the partner of the absent child work either alone or with an unmatched child.

I have a student who has a very hard time working with others. I wonder about making someone have to work with this child every day. Any solutions?

This is a common problem and worthy of a whole other book. The first thing I'd try to do is diagnose the problem. What makes it hard for this child to work with others? I'd observe her closely throughout the day to see where and with whom she successfully cooperates and use this information to help me think about her reading partner arrangements. I'd also talk to her honestly about the situation. I might say, "I've noticed it's hard for you to work with a partner during reading time. I'd love to help you out, so will you tell me what makes it hard for you?" I've also met with children who struggle in partnerships and their partners, and have given them very specific instructions about their work for reading time that day. I might meet with them at the beginning of partner time and say, "Today, Paul will choose the book you'll read together first, and then you'll read Jesse's choice. Now we need to think of a plan. Will you take turns on pages, or will you each read it through?" After they respond, I restate their plan in very clear, concrete language, and stay for a moment as they get started.

Some children want to change partners all the time. It's getting hard to resist their complaining. What can I do?

Ideally, we want these partnerships to be long-lasting, but that's not always possible. I would really try not to change partners on a case-by-case basis because that just teaches children that they don't have to work hard in partnerships. They won't feel that they need to make an investment and work out difficulties because their partnerships are fleeting. My rule of thumb is that when I see restlessness in *many* partnerships in the room, I might keep the partnerships for a few weeks and then make an across-the-board switch (although some partnerships might stay together if they are working very well). Knowing that the partnerships will change offers some comfort and hope for children, yet it also reinforces the idea that in the meantime partners can't just give up on each other. They need to work out their difficulties. If just one or two partnerships are struggling, I meet with them and help them to make goals for working well together.

I have a partnership that is perfectly matched for ability, and they work well together, but they fool around all the time. What can I do?

There need to be consequences when children don't meet behavioral expectations. In this case, a consequence could be that the partnership is suspended for a day or two. I'd say, "I know you two can work well together and that you have lots of fun, but lately it seems as if you're not really getting any reading work done. I hate to do this, but I think you need to give your partnership a break for today. I know that's disappointing, but I think you both need some time to think about how you're going to make this work again. Today, you'll read by yourselves, and I want you to think about how to be good partners and doing your work. Tomorrow we'll talk and see if you're ready to get back together." My tone would suggest that they've lost the privilege of their partnership and that they need to earn it again.

So, we've assigned ability-based partners, reorganized the classroom library to feature leveled book baskets, and distributed the book bins to students. During reading time, we've assessed the children and know their independent reading levels. Now, we're ready to launch the next unit of study, Readers Use Strategies to Figure Out Words.

Readers Use Strategies to Figure Out Words

Chapter 5

RECENTLY, I WAS WORKING AS A STAFF DEVELOPER with first-grade teachers at a large school. One of the things the teachers wanted to work on was planning more effective mini-lessons. On this day, which was the first in our cycle of work together, I was going to do a demonstration mini-lesson in Hillary's classroom.

Before the demonstration, the teachers and I met briefly to talk about and plan the lesson I would soon demonstrate. "Hillary, what have you been working on in reading these days?" I asked. I wanted to model a mini-lesson that would be aligned with the teaching that Hillary had been doing lately.

"I've been teaching print strategies. That's the unit of study we're in," Hillary said.

"Great. What lesson were you planning to do today?"

She flipped through her plan book, each page full of beautifully handwritten notes and layers of sticky notes. "Let's see . . . I was planning to do a lesson on the /oi/ sound," she said.

"Can you say more?"

"Well, yesterday I was reading with Jean-Pierre, and he got stuck on the word *disappointed*. We had just done the /oi/ sound in phonics, so I was surprised that he couldn't read the word *disappointed*. I think I need to go over the /oi/ sound again."

I commended Hillary on using what she observed during reading conferences to help her plan for mini-lessons but gently questioned whether teaching the /oi/ sound would be the best use of her mini-lesson time. That lesson would be very particular to what Jean-Pierre needed yesterday. Perhaps the whole-class lesson should teach a more widely applicable skill or strategy to support more readers. If some students need extra help with the /oi/ sound, I suggested that Hillary could teach it to them in a small group, or she could revisit the /oi/ sound during word study or shared reading.

"When I plan a mini-lesson based on what I observe a child doing in a reading conference, sometimes my lesson can end up being too specific to that child and not helpful enough for the class," I told the teachers. "When this happens, I back up and try to figure out the bigger issue from that conference so that other children can benefit from the lesson, too. It sometimes helps if I say, 'Readers need to. . . .' When I start like that, it leads me to think of broader issues rather than child-specific or print-specific ones." After a brief discussion, these are the ideas the teachers had about the broader issues:

- Readers need to use what they know to read through unfamiliar words.
- Readers need to chunk words to get through the hard parts.
- Readers need to think about what would make sense and use meaning and context to help them.

I asked Hillary which of these suggested lessons would be most helpful for her class, and she said, "I think what would benefit the most children right now would be 'readers need to use what they know about words to help them figure out other words.' Sometimes I'll notice lots of kids hesitating on big words even though the big words have parts they already know."

"Great," I said. "Let's plan together how that lesson might go. We can use what happened in Jean-Pierre's conference for the connection part of our mini-lesson."

I share this story because it was so instructive for me. When we are teaching children strategies for decoding print in this unit of study, we understandably feel like Hillary, that we have to cover all possible aspects of decoding in our mini-lessons, from pointing under the words to reading through the words, from the letter-sound relationships to chunking word parts, and everything else in between.

In my attempts to cover it all, I used to have a list of print strategies taped inside my planning notebook. I would use this list to help me plan my mini-lessons, and I'd check off the print strategies after I had taught each one. I'd feel such a sense of accomplishment when I got through the list. Unfortunately, my teaching was based more on this list of print strategies, which I had copied out of a professional book, than on my knowledge of the needs of my own students. What I later learned to do was to keep this list of print strategies as a reference in my teaching repertoire but to use what I knew about the children's needs to determine which strategies I would focus on in my mini-lessons.

Another thing I learned is that when we're teaching print strategies during independent reading workshop, we need to strike a balance. In addition to teaching some specific strategies for word solving, we need to teach our students about the larger reading issues, such as what it means to be a resourceful reader or how to read with fluency.

It's usually more effective to teach specific print strategies in small-group settings, such as guided reading groups or strategy lessons. After all, when we pull together a small group of children, we can tailor our teaching of print strategies to their specific needs. But when we're teaching a mini-lesson to the whole class during independent reading workshop, we're facing readers with a wide range of competencies and needs. This fact makes it difficult to teach a print strategy mini-lesson that will fit the needs of many students at the same time.

Joe Yukish, a colleague at the Reading and Writing Project, helped me to understand that whole-class mini-lessons offer some children opportunities for acquisition learning while providing maintenance learning for other children. In other words, if more than half of my class needs a particular skill or strategy, like attending to the first letters of a word to figure it out, I can justify teaching it in a mini-lesson. Through the lesson some students will newly acquire the strategy, and students who have control of the strategy already will gain reinforcement. When a small number of children need a particular skill or strategy, as with the /oi/ sound in Hillary's class, it makes sense to teach it during small-group instruction or in a reading conference.

Because we face such a diverse group of readers during mini-lessons, it is important to keep this acquisition learning/maintenance learning factor in mind. And when planning our mini-lessons for this unit of study, we need to balance the teaching of specific print strategies with the teaching of larger issues, such as what it means to be a reader of words.

Bends in the Road

In this unit of study on print strategies, the map of our teaching features several bends in the road (see planning chart on next page). We begin by teaching children how to get their minds ready to read. When they have a sense of expectation for how a book will go or what it will be about, readers are more likely to be able to figure out what the words say. Then we turn our focus toward various print strategies that will help them figure out words.

Sometimes we find that children are familiar with a variety of print strategies but tend to rely on just a couple of them. We want them to be flexible and proactive as they read, so we next emphasize helping children to understand how readers can be resourceful when they get to hard words. One way we are able to tell if they are using strategies with flexibility is by observing their reading fluency. We need to help children read with appropriate fluency, phrasing, and intonation.

Finally, depending on the class, we may decide our students are ready to learn how to choose just-right books. At the beginning of this bend in the road, we guide them toward leveled baskets filled with books at their independent reading levels, but we don't want them to be overly reliant on our leveled book system for choosing appropriate reading material. We want them to have a confident and a realistic sense of what kinds of books are good for them as readers. We want them to be able to choose the right books everywhere, not just in the classroom.

In summary, my whole-class lessons during independent reading workshop are focused on the following bends in the road, which will benefit all my students, no matter what their current reading levels:

- Readers get their minds ready to read (activating schema and expectation).
- Readers have tools to figure out tricky words (acquisition of print strategies).
- Readers are brave and resourceful when they get to hard words (flexibility with print strategies).
- Careful readers read with smooth voices (reading with fluency).
- Careful readers choose books that help them grow stronger at reading (choosing just-right books).

Readers Get Their Minds Ready to Read

Even before they read the first words on the first page of their books, it's important for young readers to get their minds ready to read the books. Having a sense of what a book is about before reading it offers children extra support for figuring out what the text says. When a child has an idea of how a book goes overall as well as what's on the pages before she begins reading, she will be more likely to be able to read the words because she's activated a schema and expectation for the story.

	Planning Chart
Unit of Study:	**Readers Use Strategies to Figure Out Words**
	Dates:

Goals	• Students will know how to use a variety of print strategies and use them with flexibility. • Students will be sure their reading makes sense. • Students will self-correct. • Students will develop an ear for fluent reading and have ways of making their own reading fluent. • Students will know how to choose books that support their work with print.
Bends in the Road	• Acquisition of print strategies: one-to-one, pointing under words, picture clues, getting your mouth ready, looking through the word, meaning clues. • Flexibility with print strategies: being versatile, using more than one strategy at a time, self-correcting when it doesn't sound right or make sense. • Reading with fluency: read like you're talking, use punctuation and meaning clues to read fluently, reread tricky parts so they sound smooth. • Choosing just-right books: importance of reading just-right books, how to find them, criteria to use. • Being brave as a reader: becoming an independent problem solver.
Classroom Library	• Show students how to find books in leveled library. • Show students how to find just-right unleveled books. • Feature leveled book baskets that reflect the range of readers in the classroom.
Materials and Resources	• Big Books to demonstrate print strategies. • Create charts of print strategies. • Introduce independent reading bins. • Make print strategy bookmarks and desk-top charts for readers.
Workshop Structures	• Private reading time, partner reading time with conferring. • Small-group work—strategy lessons and guided reading groups.
Other Literacy Components	
Work Students Are Doing	• Students fill independent reading bins with books according to reading levels. • Students read by themselves and then meet with an ability-based partner to read and talk about their books. • Students work on the strategies they need to read words proficiently. • Students try different strategies to help themselves before asking for assistance.
Support for Struggling Readers	• Frequent support through individual conferences. • Guided reading support, at least three to four times a week. • Print strategy reinforcement during writing workshop. • Recommendation for Project Read after-school program.
Support for Strong Readers	• Strategy lessons on reading for meaning and reading with fluency. • Support for print strategy work on multisyllabic words or unfamiliar vocabulary.
Home/School	• Send home letter describing print strategies to be covered and language used to describe them in class. • Take-home book is a just-right book; child reads with/to parents. • Evening workshop for parents: How to Support Your Young Reader.
Assessment	• Put ability-based partners together based on early assessments. • Use running records to assess students' use of print strategies. • Assess book choices. • Self-assessment: What strategies are easy or hard for students? • Home assessment: Ask families what strategies they see or hear children using at home.
Celebrations	• Read-aloud celebration: Children pick book they can read really well and invite parents or reading buddies to listen to stories.
Standards That Are Addressed	

In guided reading and some strategy lessons the teacher usually begins with a brief book introduction to provide students with a degree of meaning before they read the words. In shared reading, as well, we either do a quick introduction to the text or invite students to get ready to read the story by thinking about the title and cover illustration. In these literacy components, teachers tend to take responsibility for initiating or facilitating the act of "getting our minds ready to read." What we need to do is to teach children how to assume this responsibility during independent reading workshop so that they can get themselves ready to read.

When I think about how I will teach children to do these things, I try to imagine the ways that readers outside of school get their minds ready to read a book. What are the things we typically do before we set out to read something? One day, I went to Community Bookstore, an independently owned bookstore café in Brooklyn, to do some schoolwork. While I sat with my hot cocoa planning out the details of an upcoming social studies unit, I found myself looking at the customers as they browsed books. I noticed that most of them would pick a book off the shelf and look at the covers, both front and back. I imagined they were thinking about the title, looking at the cover illustration (if there was one), and reading the blurb or reviews on the back cover. Then I noticed that most people either put the book back on the shelf immediately or else flipped through the pages and seemed to sample a paragraph or two. I do many of these things, too, when I pick up a book. I realized maybe it's "readers' nature" to take a book walk in this way.

Such things seem to be the most realistic and natural things to teach children to do independently in order to get their minds ready to read. We want them to begin the book with a sense of expectation for what the book will be about and how it goes so that they can read it with confidence.

When we teach children how to take a book walk before they read, we teach them to do the following things:

- Say the title out loud, look closely at the cover illustration, and think, What might this book be about? and What do I expect to see inside this book?
- Check out the author's name and think, Do I know this author? Have I read anything else by this author? If so, what might I expect in this book? This line of thought can also be applied to characters.
- Flip through the pages, look at the illustrations, and think, Do the pictures match or differ from my expectations?
- Flip through the book, sample the text, and think, Do these words look patterned? Do I know some of these words? Are there quotation marks?

When children take a book walk, a teacher can observe whether the child is looking at the cover, saying the title out loud, or flipping through the book to survey the pages. Just reading the title out loud isn't helpful; readers also need to think about what the title says about what's in the book. So when a child reads out the title of a book as, "What Is Round?" we want her to stop and think, Is this book about round stuff? The thinking work of book walks needs to be taught right alongside the observable work. The crucial piece is to show children how to think as they run through the actions. It's the thinking part that helps us get our minds ready to read.

All children need to look closely at a book's cover and think about what they might expect in the story, but we can't take for granted that children know how to do these things. After repeatedly teaching children to pause and think about the cover, I was getting frustrated in conferences when many of them weren't able to tell me the title of their books. In many cases, the problem wasn't that they couldn't decode the title; it was simply that they jumped right in without even paying attention to the title.

What I figured out finally was that many children did not really understand what I meant by "look at and think about the cover" until I showed them. Also, for some children, the titles were too hard to read on their own. When this was the case, I read the title out to them and modeled how it sounds when a reader thinks about what the title tells about a book. When children who need the most support shopped for books, I met with them briefly and read out the titles of their books to give them a head start.

When we model how to get our minds ready to read, we need to *demonstrate the active work*, such as looking closely at the cover and flipping through the pages, and *model the thinking work* by thinking out loud for our students. We need to be as explicit as possible, even when we teach things that may seem obvious and clear to us.

Lisa Ripperger, a first-grade colleague at P.S. 321, taught a lesson to help her students use the cover of the book to get their minds ready to read. Lisa made copies of the covers of several books that were representative of the range of readers in her class. She taught the class, through demonstration, what it means when readers look closely at the cover and think about what to expect from a book. For the active engagement part of the mini-lesson, Lisa passed out the copies of book covers to reading partners and asked them to do together what she had just demonstrated. The benefit of passing out copies of book covers (without the books) is that the children are not distracted by a desire to open the books right then.

I tried Lisa's lesson in my own room, and it worked really well to show my children exactly what it feels like to think about the cover. I made copies of several book covers across a range of levels. Here is the mini-lesson I did, with thanks to Lisa Ripperger.

Mini-lesson

Connection

Boys and girls, we learned yesterday that readers get warmed up before they read, just like soccer players warm up before their games. Remember we talked about how soccer players jog a little bit and stretch so they are warmed up to play? Well, readers warm up, too, although we don't usually have to stretch, do we?

Yesterday I showed you how readers really look closely at the title and the cover and think about what their book might be about. You guys did a good job with that, except I think we forgot one part, the thinking part. Today I want to teach you how readers think when they look closely at the cover and say the title out loud. I want to teach you how to think when you do these things so that you are totally warmed up to read.

Teaching point and demonstration

Watch me as I pretend I'm a first grader and just about to read this book for the first time. [I put Birthdays, *an unfamiliar Big Book, on the easel.] Watch how I get my mind ready to read. [I say the title out loud and name what I notice about the cover illustration.] Hmm, I wonder what this book might be about. [I rub my temple to dramatize thinking.] I bet this book is going to be about people having birthdays. I'm thinking that because the title says "Birthdays," not "Birthday," so maybe it's more than one birthday. I also notice there are lots of kids on the cover.*

Okay, readers, did you see how I looked at the cover closely and read the title out loud? Did you hear me say "Birthdays" because that was the title? Did you notice how I named some things I saw in the cover picture? Did you hear how I did thinking work by asking, "I wonder what this book might be about?" [Again, I rub my temple.] I did that thinking work. That is what careful readers do, and that is what I want you to do when you're reading by yourselves.

Active engagement

Now I'm going to give you a chance to try this thinking work so you can see what it's like. I made copies of the covers of some books, and I'm going to pass out a copy of a cover to you and a partner. You will do this work—read the title out loud, look at the cover picture, and then do the thinking work that is so important by asking yourselves, What might this book be about? [Again, I rub my temple.] I want you to get ready for thinking by practicing asking yourselves, I wonder what this book might be about? Try it. [The children say it and rub their temples.] Okay, side by side with your partner, and I'm going to give you a book cover to think about. I'm going to listen in to hear how it goes for you.

I move around and listen in to Kadeem and Sammy. They have a copy of the cover of *How to Make a Sandwich.* I listen as they say that they think the book will tell what to do to make a sandwich. "They're going to make a peanut butter and jelly sandwich," Kadeem says. When I ask them what makes them think so, Sammy points out that there is a peanut butter jar and a jelly jar on the cover. They notice this even though the word *jelly* is partially hidden. Now, when Kadeem and Sammy read this book for independent reading, they will have it set up in their minds that the book is about making a peanut butter and jelly sandwich. They already have a schema in mind for how the book will go and what it will probably say on the pages.

Okay, readers, let me tell you what good work I noticed. Kadeem and Sammy had this cover. First, they read the title out loud, "How to Make a Sandwich," and then they looked closely at the picture, like this. You know what? They realized that the book must be about making a peanut butter and jelly sand-wich because they saw the jars on the cover. They even knew this was jelly even though they couldn't see the whole word. Kadeem and Sammy thought that their book was going to teach them how to make a peanut butter and jelly sandwich. Then they thought, What might be in the book? They thought that this book would have things like bread, a knife to spread the peanut butter, and stuff you need to make a sandwich. This is how they got their minds ready to read. And everyone can do this same work that careful readers like Kadeem and Sammy do.

Link to ongoing work

Readers, whenever you pick up a book for the first time, remember to get your minds ready to read it. Remember to say the title out loud and look closely at the cover picture. Don't forget, you also need to do the thinking work. You need to think, What might this book be about? Can I hear you guys say that? [The class repeats the line, and many children rub their temples.] Okay, let's see who is ready to read.

Of course, even after doing this mini-lesson, I know I will still need to model "getting your mind ready to read" during shared reading and interactive read-aloud, and enlist the children's help in getting our collective mind ready to read these books. During conferences, too, I'll ask children to show me the cover of their books and tell me how they got their minds ready to read.

Some other mini-lessons that could be taught for this part of the unit of study follow. Instead of providing the text for mini-lessons I might teach, I summarize the ideas for them.

❖ *Readers take a book walk to help them get their minds ready.* Readers often take a book walk through the pages before they read to get their minds ready to figure out the words. In this lesson, we show students what a book walk looks like. As the teacher models the book walk, he says, "Oh, I knew the book would have birthday presents in it because it's called *Birthdays*," or "It looks like there's a pattern in the words, and I know that will help me read them."

❖ *Readers try to get a sense of the story during a book walk.* When readers flip through the pages, they try to get a sense of the story by noticing what's going on in the pictures. It's like they are taking a sneak peek, but they have to wait until they read the words and look at the pictures again to make sure they really know the story. We want to make sure children understand that sometimes their predictions about the text during a book walk might need revising as they read the words. We can demonstrate this by doing an inaccurate book walk and then revising our idea as we read the words.

❖ *Readers remind themselves what the book is about as they read.* The teaching point in this lesson supports children's making meaning and holding themselves accountable for the whole story as they read. Although this isn't strictly a "getting your mind ready to read" lesson, it is an important teaching point to make at any time. It could be taught by showing children that when readers get stuck on a tricky part, they remind themselves what the book is about, and that can help them figure out the tricky part. This lesson could be extended across another day by teaching children to stop at tricky parts to think, What is this book about?

❖ *Readers pay attention to chapter titles and the cover blurb, and sample a page or two.* This is a lesson we can do if most of the students are reading early chapter books or more difficult texts that have less picture support than books at earlier levels. We can model this with an early chapter book and then have children try it with their own books during the lesson. This can also be done in a small-group strategy lesson if only a few children in the class are reading books at this level.

Acquisition of Print Strategies

Teaching print strategies to the whole class in mini-lessons can be difficult because of the wide range of readers we have in front of us. In my own classes I've had children who do not yet know all their letters sitting beside others who are able to read chapter books. A mini-lesson geared toward a child who is still working on one-to-one correspondence is not the mini-lesson that more proficient readers need.

In order to make the mini-lessons useful for all my students, I've learned to spend minimal time teaching each specific print strategy in a whole-class setting. Based on my assessments of the students, I try to figure out which print strategies will affect the most readers. I concentrate on teaching those strategies in mini-lessons to support learning for the children who need to acquire that particular strategy. For others who already use the strategy, these lessons provide an opportunity for maintenance learning.

If less than half the class needs a particular strategy, say, one-to-one matching for the most struggling readers, or using context clues to figure out challenging words for the strongest readers, I might choose not to teach the strategy in a whole-class mini-lesson. Instead, I can teach these strategies to particular readers in small groups, during a guided reading session or strategy lesson. It is at these times that I can pull together the children who share particular needs. So, rather than teaching the whole class a mini-lesson on one-to-one correspondence if only four children need support, I would pull those four children together and teach them in a small group until they acquired the strategy. I know that I can also work on print strategies in the other literacy components, such as word study, shared reading, interactive writing, and writing workshop.

For the independent reading workshop, I turn the bend in the road on the acquisition of print strategies into a mini-inquiry so that there is a sense that the children and I are researching and discovering together the kinds of things readers do to figure out words. I want the children to believe that they all have tools that they can use to figure out the words and that they can share these tools with each other.

To begin this bend in the road, Acquisition of Print Strategies, I gather my class in the meeting area for this mini-lesson.

Mini-lesson

Connection

Readers, can we talk about something? You know we've been learning that readers have to warm up before they read by getting their minds ready for their books, just as soccer players have to warm up before they play a game. Well, I've noticed that you've gotten so good at warming up, you even remind me to warm up before I read books to you.

Now I want to give you more to do as readers because you're so ready. I've been thinking lately that when we read books we're kind of like builders. When we read, it's like we're building a story in our minds. People who build houses or bridges usually carry toolboxes filled with the tools they need to help them do their work. They've got hammers and wrenches and screwdrivers and nails and lots of other stuff that they need to build and fix things.

Well, it's like that for readers, too. We build stories as we read, right? Imagine that we also carry around a toolbox, a reader's toolbox, that has the tools we can use to figure out words. Our tools aren't hammers and nails, though. Our tools are strategies like pointing under the words, checking the picture, thinking about what's happening in the story. For the next week or so, we're going to fill up our reading toolbox with the strategies that we can use to help us read and build the stories in our books. But you know what? I'm thinking that you guys have some strategies or tools that you use already. Today, when you go off to read, I'm going to be looking around and watching to see what kinds of strategies or tools you use as readers to figure out the words to help you build the stories in your books. If you notice that you have a really helpful strategy, let us know about it so we can make sure all of us add it to our reading toolbox.

I use the expressions "reading tools" and "reading strategies" interchangeably in this launching talk and during the mini-lessons that follow. For some children, *strategy* has no context or meaning, so I want to make it more concrete by connecting it to the concept of a tool.

After this lesson, which is actually more of a talk than a typical mini-lesson, I send the children off for private reading time, and I confer with them. The focus of my conferring is to note the print strategies children are already using and to find the ones they need. When the children meet with their reading partners for partner reading time, I focus my observations on the ways that partners prompt each other to use strategies. I try to discover the ways children express their strategy use, so I can use their language in my teaching.

After private and partner reading time, we gather in the meeting area for our teaching share session. "Readers, guess what?" I begin. "I saw you use lots of different strategies or tools to figure out words when you read. It was so cool because I know that we can help each other add strategies or tools to our reading toolboxes. I saw that Stefano and Julian are really great at using the picture to help them. One of their tools is to use picture clues to figure out words, right, guys? Tomorrow, I'll show you how Stefano and Julian didn't just look at the picture but *studied* the picture and thought about what was happening in the story to figure out a word. That's definitely a tool we all need as readers."

In this share session I mention only one thing I noticed, and I do a little preview for tomorrow's mini-lesson. I could have chosen a variety of things to highlight, but using picture clues is something that every reader in the class needs to know how to do, even the children reading early chapter books.

For the next day's mini-lesson, I show the class just what Stefano and Julian did with the picture in their book.

Mini-lesson

Connection

Readers, I told you yesterday how Stefano and Julian used the picture to help them when they got stuck on a word. They didn't just look at the picture but really studied *the picture and thought about what was going on in the story to figure out the hard word. I was thinking that I should show everyone how to do this because it's a really helpful reading strategy or tool. Today, I'm going to teach you how to use the picture and think about the story to help you figure out words, just like Stefano and Julian. Then you can add this tool to your reading toolbox.*

Teaching point and demonstration

Let me show you what they did. Stefano and Julian were reading Hooray for Snail!, *and they got to this page. [I show the page. The text reads, "Snail listens."] They were stuck on this word. [I point under* listens.*] They were looking at the beginning of the word and making the beginning sound /l/, /l/, and they were saying* watched, looked, liked, laughed, *but none of those guesses seemed to work. So this is what they did. Watch this closely. [I dramatize moving my eyes from text to picture.]*

Stefano and Julian looked really closely at the picture, studied it, and thought about what was going on in the story. They were thinking that it was the middle of a baseball game, and the coach was telling Snail to do something. They noticed that the coach was talking and Snail looked like he was listening real hard. Then one of them said, "It's listens! *Snail* listens!*" and that's how Stefano and Julian figured it out. If they hadn't really studied the picture and thought about what was going on in the story, they might still be stuck on that* word. So, readers, when you get stuck on a word, it helps to study the picture and think about what's going on in the story. It's not enough to just look at the picture quickly, like this. [I glance at the picture.] You might have to stop, study the picture, and think about what is really going on in the story, as Stefano and Julian did. This strategy is a great tool for your reading toolbox.

Active engagement

I want you guys to try that right now. I have this Big Book, and I covered up the words on one of the pages because I want you to practice studying the picture and thinking about the story to figure out what the words say. We'll pretend that we got stuck on the words. I'll begin by reading the first couple of pages, and then we'll all get stuck together. We can practice using the strategy or tool of studying the picture and thinking about the story to figure out the words. [I read and get to the page with the covered-up words.] Everyone take a few seconds to study the picture by looking really closely at it, and think about the story so far. Then turn and talk to your partner about what you noticed.

Okay, it sounds like you really studied the picture and thought about what's going on in the story. I saw you really looking closely at the picture, and I could tell that you were really thinking about what's going on. Ready to take a look at the words? I bet they will be easy to read now because we probably have a good idea of what they say. [I show the words, and the class calls them out.]

Link to ongoing work

Whenever you're reading, when you get to tricky parts in your books, I want you to really study the picture and think about what's going on in the story to see if that can help you. Remember, a quick look at the picture is not enough. Study it and think about what's going on in the story. If you do this, and it helps you figure out hard parts, let us know during share time, okay?

That day, after school, I began a chart entitled Readers' Strategies: Tools to Help Us Read Words. Item 1 was "Readers study the pictures and think about the story." We added items to this chart over the next couple of weeks. Notice that in most of the mini-lessons in this bend in the road, we align any strategy for decoding print with the important work of making meaning and thinking about what would make sense in the story. None of these print strategies happens in a vacuum, so we need to make sure that children are holding on to the meaning as they read and using that alongside decoding strategies.

Descriptions of other mini-lessons for this bend in the road follow.

❖ *Readers figure out words by saying the sound of the beginning letters.* During this lesson, the teacher shows children how to locate the beginning letters and what it means to make the sounds in a way that will help them figure out what the word says. As with other print strategies, this strategy doesn't always help when it's done in isolation. The companion strategies to this might be that readers need to reread from the beginning of the sentence and think about what would make sense, or teaching children to ask, What would make sense here?

Also, it's important to teach children to look at the *beginning letters,* not only the *first letter.* If we say, "Look at the first letter," or vaguely, "Look at the beginning of the word," we create problems with reading words with blends at the beginning. We should be sure to say, "Look at the beginning letters."

❧ *Readers figure out words by noticing the ends of the words.* It is advisable to teach this lesson to the whole class if more than half of the students use one-to-one matching when they read, and use the picture clues and the beginning letters to help them figure out words. In this lesson we model by making guesses at tricky words only by focusing on the beginning letters and showing the students how the guess didn't work out until one looks at the end of the word. It can be helpful to revisit a previous lesson or text to make this point. For example, when I taught this lesson, I reminded my class how Stefano and Julian had made several guesses on the "Snail listens" page: "Readers, do you remember how Stefano and Julian said, Snail *looked,* Snail *laughed,* Snail *liked,* and it didn't make sense with the picture? Well, besides studying the picture closely, it would have helped to look closely at the end of the word. Let's try it now. The word couldn't be *looked* because there's no *-ed* at the end. We have to think of a word that starts with /l/ but ends with *-ens.* That's what readers do. They look at both the beginning and the end of a word to figure it out."

❧ *Readers figure out words by moving through the whole word.* In this lesson, we show children how to look across the tricky word (perhaps by running their finger underneath it, from left to right, to help them focus on the whole word). Often teachers prompt by saying, "Look for a word you know within the word," but then the child might be trying to read a word such as *mouse-trap* and identify *use* or *set* inside; or if they're trying to read the word *easy,* they might find *as* inside. In these cases, and many others, the little words inside the larger ones do not help to read the tricky word.

We can teach children to look through the word from left to right to find familiar word parts to help them. They might read *easy* and realize that *ea* is like the start of *ear,* so they pronounce the long *e* sound as they read, which will help them to figure out the whole word. When trying to figure out *mouse-trap,* they might see *ou* and think of *out* to help them, or they'll notice *ouse* and be reminded of the word *house.*

❧ *Readers always think about what makes sense.* This is a lesson that is worth repeating throughout this unit. I add this teaching point to each of my mini-lessons in the print strategies unit of study. We want children to be more than word solvers. We want them to be story builders, so no matter what decoding strategy they use, we want them to check themselves by asking, Does this make sense?

Flexibility with Print Strategies

Emily Swart, a second-grade teacher at Westminster Community School in Buffalo, came to one of our staff development meetings with a frustrating issue on her mind. It was the beginning of the year, and she had noticed that many of her students would stop in their tracks when they got to tricky words. Emily, her colleagues Lynn Hopp and Gayle Irving-White, and I had a discussion about how it seemed that too often children rely on one or two strategies to figure out tricky words. If their strategies work, all is well, but if the strategies don't help, the children either give up or move past the word without working at it.

We checked to make sure the children were in appropriate books, and they were. We checked during conferences to see if they actually had a variety of strategies in their repertoire, and they did. With our prompting, they were able to use other strategies besides their default one.

It almost seems as if children get into little reading ruts. They get very comfortable with a particular strategy or two, say, voicing the beginning sounds of the word and cross-checking with the picture, but if their default strategies don't work, they may not try anything else. We began a line of thinking about how to help children become more flexible with print strategies.

Emily came to our next meeting and shared how she had talked to her children about being brave when they got to a hard word. She had taught them that instead of giving up, they had to be brave and persistent. She told her class that readers have the strategies and the power to figure out tricky words if they don't give up too quickly. For Emily's class, the idea of being brave in the face of tricky words was an effective way of teaching the children to be more flexible with print strategies. In conferences she observed the children trying more than one strategy to figure out the tricky words.

Whether we call it bravery, resourcefulness, or persistence, we need to help children orchestrate the sources of information and use print strategies with flexibility. We need to help them read with a repertoire of strategies rather than getting into a reading rut and relying on only one or two strategies to figure out words. As children move through levels of text difficulty, their print strategies need to change. As they progress, children won't have the safety of patterned text to help them through a book. Soon, the pictures won't support the text with precision. Soon, looking only at beginning letters won't help. Children need to know they can try different things to figure out what the words say.

Here is an example of a mini-lesson I did to help my students understand what it means to be a resourceful reader.

Mini-lesson

Connection

Readers, yesterday something so cool happened. Joe, the custodian, made me think lots about us as readers. This is what happened. He came by after school to fix our sink. You know how it's been dripping for weeks? Well, he came in to fix it, and he brought his toolbox with him, and it reminded me of how we have toolboxes as readers. First, Joe pulled out one wrench, but it wasn't the right kind. He had to go back to his toolbox for another wrench, and luckily he found the one he needed. He could fix our sink because he brought the right tools. I got to thinking, "What if Joe had only brought that one wrench that didn't work? What if he had only brought his hammer? Could he have fixed our sink?" No way! We'd still be listening to that drip, drip, drip if he had only brought a hammer or the one wrench that didn't work.

Well, this made me think of you guys. You know how for the last week or so we've been learning about the strategies or tools that readers can use to help them figure out the tricky parts of their books? You know how we say we have a toolbox full of reading strategies to help us build the stories in our books? Well, we can add to this because Joe taught us a great lesson. Just like Joe, you guys have to make sure you have lots of tools in your reading toolbox so that you can figure out the tricky parts. It's like Joe needs more than a hammer to fix the sink, you need more than studying the picture to figure out the words. For the next few days I'm going to teach you how you can be like Joe, how you can use all your tools as a reader to figure out tricky words.

Teaching point and demonstration

Watch me use my reading tools. I'm going to read this page and get stuck. Notice how I use a couple of different strategies to figure out the word. [I study the picture.] Hmm, the picture isn't really helping me. I'm going to look at the beginning of the word, too. [I say the beginning sound and study the picture.] That's it! Let me check and see if it makes sense. [I say the word.] Yes! Now I know what this says.

Readers, did you notice how I used the picture but it didn't totally help me? Did you see how I didn't give up? Nope, I didn't quit. I tried another strategy. Just like Joe needed to try out different tools when he was fixing our sink, I had to use another tool to help me with the tricky words. Well, you guys can do that, too, when you're reading.

Active engagement

Right now, I want you and your partner to remind each other of all the tools in your reading toolbox that you can use to figure out the tricky parts in your books. I'm going to listen in and see what you guys are saying. [I listen.] Wow, you guys have lots of tools in your toolboxes. I heard you mention lots of different things. [I say a few things I overheard.] Readers, it's so important to bring all of these tools with you to your reading. You've got some really helpful tools or strategies, so you want to make sure that you're using each of them when you need them.

Link to ongoing work

Readers, whenever you get to a tricky part in your books, I want you to remember that you may need to use different strategies to figure it out. You don't have to give up. Try your best by using the strategies that you know. Today I'm going to look for readers who are being flexible and using all of their strategies when they get to tricky parts in their books.

In mini-lessons that follow this one, we want to teach children how to move between strategies. Also, we always combine teaching any strategies with teaching the importance of meaning making: children ask, Does this make sense? Meaning making is the constant companion to any strategies readers use to figure out the words in their books.

❖ *Readers are brave when they get to hard words.* In this lesson we teach students to try a couple of different strategies when they get to a tricky part that they can't figure out right away. Always make sure that one of the strategies you demonstrate is meaning-based, so they ask, Does that make sense?

❖ *Readers always think about what makes sense.* During this lesson we reinforce the idea that even though readers try different things to figure out words, they always have to make sure their reading makes sense. In a lesson like this one, the teacher might get to a tricky word in the teaching demonstration and take a guess that doesn't make sense. He can then say, "Hmm, wait a minute, that can't be right. It doesn't make sense. I'd better try something else."

❖ *Readers ask themselves questions as they read.* This actually comprises a series of lessons in which we teach children to orchestrate the semantic, graphophonic, and syntactic sources of information. As children read or work on tricky words, we want them to be sure their reading and word solving makes sense, looks right, and sounds right. In several lessons, we teach them how to check the sources of information to be sure they are reading hard parts—or any parts—with accuracy. We can also teach children how readers go back and self-correct their miscues on the spot or after they read on for a bit.

❖ *Readers can ask for help.* We can teach our children that sometimes it's okay to ask someone for help, but only if they try their own strategies first, and only if they aren't distracting other readers. We might say, "Readers, sometimes if we get really stuck, we can ask our neighbor or our partner to help us out. That's one of the things that reading friends are for. Of course, we still have to be brave and try things before we ask someone else for help, and of course, we have to make sure we're not distracting other readers from their books by asking for help."

Reading with Fluency

Emery was growing more able and confident as a reader, yet he still sounded like a frightened robot as he read. Nelle, on the other hand, was a strong reader who tended to race through books. She read like an auctioneer, and it almost seemed as if she were skimming her texts rather than reading them. Both children, and most in between, need our support in teaching them to read with appropriate fluency, intonation, and phrasing.

Reading with fluency—with phrasing, intonation, and expression—would seem like one of the most concrete, easiest things to teach young readers. But I often heard myself thinking, I feel like I've taught Emery about reading with fluency dozens of times, yet he still sounds robotic as he reads. Rather than take the low road and blame Emery for his fluency problems, I thought it over and realized that I had probably tried only a couple of different ways to teach him to read fluently and that I had to figure out more ways to teach my students about reading fluency.

One year when Gay Su Pinnell consulted with our study group at the Reading and Writing Project, we went into classrooms to watch her work with guided reading groups. One thing she emphasized, both to the children and to us teachers, was the importance of reading with fluency because fluent reading is a prerequisite for comprehension. When students read too slowly, stop to work out words, and take long pauses, they tend to have difficulty comprehending the text (Fountas and Pinnell 1996) and are more likely to have negative attitudes toward reading.

We have a responsibility to our students to be sure they know how to read with fluency, even at an early age. After all, the voices in which children read out loud will soon become the voices they hear in their heads as they begin to read silently. We need to make sure that their reading voices are not mono-tonal, robotic, mumbly, or lacking the expression, intonation, and phrasing that reflect the meaning of the story.

So, with an appreciation for the importance of children's learning to read with fluency, I decided to begin early in the year with work on fluency. Following is a mini-lesson I teach in this bend in the road.

Mini-lesson

Connection

We've been thinking about reading in smooth voices and how it's important to do that because it helps us understand the stories in our books. When I was meeting with readers yesterday, Joshua said an amazing thing to me. He said that when he's trying to be really careful, he reads slowly, but then it's hard to understand what he's just read. When you read too-slowly-it-can-be-hard-to-follow-the-story. [I say this in a slow, robotic way.] Do you see what I mean? Anyway, I think we can all learn something important from what Joshua said. It's important to read in a smooth talking voice that isn't too slow. Today, I want to teach you how to read in a voice that isn't too slow and that sounds like you're talking normally. It's important that you learn how to read this way because it's going to help you understand what's going on in your story.

Teaching point and demonstration

Watch me as I read this sentence [written on a chart] in a slow voice, and then watch how I fix it up and read it in a faster, talking voice. I-like-to-play-with-my-best-friends-because-we-have–fun-together. Oh, that sounded so slow, like a robot. I'm going to try to read it faster, in a more normal voice, like I'm talking. [Rereads.] Did you notice how it was easier to understand what I was reading when I read it in a normal voice? Thumbs up if you could hear the difference between my robotic too-slow voice and my regular talking voice.

Active engagement

Okay, I want you to practice reading in a regular talking voice. We'll read this sentence together, and then you guys will have some time to practice reading it in a regular talking voice. [Teacher reads and children practice.] I liked how you read it not too slow and not too fast. You read it as if you were talking. It was easy to understand what you were reading when you read it in a smooth talking voice.

Link to ongoing work

Readers, whenever you're reading, whether it's a new book you shopped for or the menu at Two Boots, I want you to remember how important it is to read in a smooth voice that sounds like a talking voice, not in a robot voice. When you read with a talking voice, it's so much easier to understand what you're reading, and understanding what we read is the biggest job of all for readers.

Here are ideas for other mini-lessons to help with reading fluency.

✪ **Readers think about the meaning of the sentence or story.** This lesson most likely should be taught over a couple of days and at different points throughout the year. The teacher reminds students that when they've got the story in their minds, it's easier to read with fluency because they've got expectations for how it will sound. If a child gets stuck on the word *groceries* in a sentence like, "My mom and I went to the store to buy groceries," it should be helpful for the child to go back and reread the sentence from the beginning, thinking about what would make sense at the tricky part. Then, once the tricky part is solved, the reader goes back and rereads the whole sentence with fluency and phrasing, having thought about the meaning first.

✪ **Readers chunk text to make it sound smooth.** In this lesson we show children how some words just kind of go together when we read, like the words "peanut butter and jelly." We don't read those words separately as peanut-butter-and-jelly. We read them as if they are one word, "peanutbutterand-jelly." Putting the words together helps our reading sound smooth.

✪ **Readers use punctuation as a clue to how text sounds.** In this lesson we teach readers that punctuation is a clue the author gives us to help us read the words smoothly. A period tells us to take a quick break and then keep going. Readers' voices change when they see a question mark. And when readers see an exclamation point, their voices sound excited. It makes sense to focus on sentence-ending punctuation if most of your students are reading texts that are easier than early chapter books. Later, when children are encountering a wider variety of punctuation in higher-level texts, they can look for and you can teach them about quotation marks, ellipses, commas, and so on.

✪ **Readers use clues in the text.** In this lesson we teach students that the words in our books themselves help us know how to read them. When we read, we need to think about what's going on in the story because that will help our reading voices. So, for example, reading a book about playing in the snow, we will sound more excited than serious or sad. If children are reading texts with dialogue, we can teach them how the dialogue markers help us read, for example, "she cried" "he shouted," "whispered Mom."

❖ *Readers use a storyteller's voice while reading.* In this lesson I read like a storyteller by suggesting that although the author wrote the story, we are the storytellers when we read it. It's our job to read the story in a way that makes it sound interesting and would make others want to hear it.

Choosing Just-Right Books

It was the two weeks in spring when our school's PTA sets up a book fair in the school lobby. For days, my children had walked by the mobile metal shelves, and they were bursting with excitement when it was finally our class's turn to go shopping for books.

After lunch, instead of trudging straight back up to the classroom, we headed to the school lobby for our scheduled book fair appointment. The children spread out around the maze of metal shelves. Parent volunteers were on hand to help them figure out if they had enough money for the pop-up book on icky sticky insects and the Harry Potter magic wand that doubles as a pencil on one end and a flashlight on the other.

We teachers try valiantly to guide children to our ideas of quality children's literature. Our efforts are often in vain: wonderful books like Valerie Worth's *All the Small Poems* sit alongside something like an anthology of big booger and bathroom poems complete with a page of artfully drawn booger stickers. I'm not often around them when they are choosing books outside the classroom library, so it's always interesting to see what they gravitate toward at the book fair. It's hard to balance my need to control (or, at least, have a say in) children's book choices and their need for independence.

Our time at the book fair was just about over. Almost all my students had finished shopping and were sitting quietly along the wall with their new books and gizmos they had purchased. But Daniel was still walking through the aisles between the metal shelves with nothing in his hands. He looked lost and sad.

"Daniel, did you see anything?" I asked.

"I can't find anything to read," he said.

I was shocked because there were hundreds of books lining the shelves. "Daniel, there's so much here."

"But I can't find anything," he said, on the verge of tears.

Because our time was up, and the fourth graders were swarming in, I took Daniel toward a shelf that had books around his reading level. I told him to quickly pick one of those because we had to get back to class. It was clear that he just picked anything and went to the checkout table.

When we got back to class, I let the children have a few minutes to meet with their partners and share what they had bought at the book fair. I noticed that Daniel showed no enthusiasm or joy about sharing his book with his partner. I felt a load of teacher guilt. I had rushed him into picking something he didn't really want.

Later that night, I couldn't stop thinking about Daniel. I imagined the book fair from his perspective. It must be overwhelming for some children to be let loose amidst a field of books. Daniel was the kind of reader who loved to read but didn't make book choices with purpose and intention. He relied on the leveled library in our classroom to find books to read, and when faced with books without clearly indicated levels, he was overwhelmed. For children like Daniel, it can be a huge task to sort through shelves and shelves of books.

If one of my goals is to make sure children are willing and able to carry on a reading life outside of school, I need to make sure they aren't totally dependent on my leveled library for choosing books. I need to teach them ways to find just-right books on their own.

Although as the year goes on, I let children choose books outside of the leveled portion of the classroom library, I still expect that most of the books chosen on shopping day will be from leveled baskets. During independent reading workshop, my students know that they must read just-right books, so they need to choose books wisely from the other baskets in our library. If children seem to be having trouble choosing just-right books from the other baskets, I guide them back to a leveled basket and tell them to choose all their books from there temporarily.

At this time in the year, I often do a series of mini-lessons to teach children how to make wise choices as they select books that will help them grow as readers. A lesson I might teach to begin this series of mini-lessons on book choice follows.

Mini-lesson

Connection

Readers, last night I was in a bookstore looking for a gift for my nephew. You know my nephew, Georgie, I've told you about him before because he's in first grade, too. Anyway, Georgie goes to another school far away, and he doesn't have the same dots on his books that we do. I wanted to buy him a just-right book so he could have a good time reading it and understanding the story, but I wasn't sure what he could read. So, I called him up and asked him what kinds of books he likes to read and can read. He told me that he loves Biscuit *books, and he said they aren't too hard or too easy. Well, that gave me lots of information because then I could look for books that were like the* Biscuit *books and those would be just-right books for him. I'm going to mail some to him today.*

Anyway, this got me thinking about you guys. You know how to find just-right books in our classroom library because you look at the dots, but our dots are not on books everywhere. When you go to the public library or the bookstore, you're not going to find books with dots, right? So, I need to teach you how to find just-right books when you don't have dots to follow. Today, I want to teach you one way that you can find just-right books in other places besides your dot basket.

Teaching point and demonstration

Watch what I do. I'm going to pretend that I'm a first-grade reader and these are the just-right books in my book bin. What I want to do is look closely at them to see how they go. [I flip through books and note similarities.] Hmm, my just-right books have pictures that kind of go along with the words, but not exactly. My just-right books have one page of words, and the other page has the picture. My just-right books have a couple of tricky words on a page, but I can figure them out when I use my strategies. Hmm. Now, what I need to do is find other books in the library that are like my just-right books.

Did you notice how I looked at my just-right books to see what they have in common? Did you hear how I named some of the things I noticed? Well, you can do that, too, because it will help you find other just-right books.

Active engagement *Now I want you to try it. I asked you to bring two just-right books to the mini-lesson. Look at your books to see what they have in common, and notice what makes them just-right books. Then tell the person sitting next to you what you noticed. I'm going to listen in.*

I move around and listen in as children think about and share what they notice. I need to name their noticing sometimes, by saying, "Hmm, it looks like you're noticing that your just-right books have two lines of words on each page. Good noticing!"

You guys are great at noticing what your just-right books have in common. Some of you noticed that your just-right books have exactly two lines of words on a page. Other people noticed that they have more words than pictures in their books. Some people noticed that their books have chapters, and others noticed that their books have big pictures to help with the words. These things will all help you find other just-right books.

Link to ongoing work *Today, I've put bins of books on your tables. What I want you to do when you go back for reading time is to look through the bins to see if you can find a just-right book, even if it doesn't have a dot on it. You'll want to find a book that matches the just-right books you were looking at. You know, you'll be choosing books for the rest of your lives that don't have dots on them to guide you, so it's really important for you to know what a just-right book looks like for you.*

Some teachers may decide not to teach this bend in the road on book choice so early in the year and instead save it for later. I would agree that if more than half of the children are reading books below the level of early chapter books like *Little Bear* and *Henry and Mudge*, it would make sense to save this series of lessons for later. Children who still need practice in books that support them with the acquisition and orchestration of print strategies (books easier than early chapter book level) most likely need guidance and structure in choosing books. These children may still need to choose their just-right books only from the leveled library.

Here are some mini-lesson ideas for book choice.

❧ *Readers have strategies to tell if a book is just right.* In this lesson or in a few lessons on this topic, we teach children about the strategies readers use to determine whether a book is just right for them, such as checking to make sure there aren't too many tricky words, comparing a book to their other just-right books to see if it's similar, and stopping to think after you've read a bit to check that you understand it.

Another kind of lesson to do around this topic is to provide individual children or partners with a book that's too easy and a book that's too hard. During the active engagement, the children take a few minutes to read the texts so that they have a sense of what it feels like when a book is not quite right for them.

❧ *Readers choose books carefully.* In this lesson we encourage children to put down books that feel too hard for them. We suggest that it's not worth the struggle to read something that's just too tricky, especially when there are so many just-right books. In other words, there are many books that are just right for every reader, so it makes sense to stick with the ones that feel good as one reads.

Assessment

Now that children are reading their just-right books, which are books at their independent reading levels, we need to assess what strategies they use and what strategies they need. The most appropriate and informative assessment for this unit of study is to use running records and miscue analysis so that we can monitor the strategies that children control and those that they still need to acquire. When we administer a running record, we can also assess fluency and comprehension. A resource for teachers who would like to learn more about running records and miscue analysis is Marie Clay's book *Running Records for Classroom Teachers* (2000).

From this unit of study forward, I make sure to take a running record with a miscue analysis on each child at least once a month. I often use my conferring time during the buffer days between units of study to do running record assessments. These assessments go into the child's reading file and allow me to determine whether the child is appropriately matched with books and partners. The assessments inform me about what kind of individual and small-group instruction is necessary to help my students grow as readers.

Celebration

About two weeks before I plan to end this unit of study, I announce to my class that it will soon be time for another reading celebration. "First graders," I say, "I'm amazed at all the great progress you've made as readers. A few weeks ago, many of you were so worried about reading words, but now you're all so brave and ready to take on the hard words in your books. I've been listening in to your reading, and I'm pleased to say that you are really sounding great when you read. Your voices are telling a story, not just reading the words. So, I'm thinking that we need to celebrate how far we've come as readers in such a short time, but I'm wondering how we might celebrate. Can you help me think about what would be a good way to celebrate how we've become such brave, smooth readers?" And then I solicit ideas from the class about how to celebrate our new reading power.

I jot down the ideas children come up with on sticky notes and make executive decisions about which ideas are possible and which are not. For example, a class trip to Chuck E. Cheese might be fun (?!), but I'm sure it's not the best way to celebrate our reading power. So that is vetoed, as are a couple of other suggestions.

The next day we conduct a vote to decide which kind of celebration we'll have. Here are some of the possibilities:

- Invite fourth-grade reading buddies into the room so that first-grade buddies can read to them for a change. Then have snacks.
- Invite families to class so that the first graders can show their reading prowess. Then have snacks.
- Invite kindergartners or other first-grade students, so that first graders can read to them. Then have snacks.
- Have a read-around. The children read to each other in small groups. Then have snacks.
- Take a book home that you learned to read really well and read it to your family. Then have snacks.

My class voted to invite their families to the class so that they could read to them and then have snacks. I set the date to coincide with the schoolwide Parents as Reading Partners session in early November. That would give us a week to get ready. In order to prepare for the celebration, each child chose a book he wanted to read aloud to his family. For the week, I gave them time in the morning before our meeting to practice reading it aloud.

During this period before our celebration, when I read aloud any kind of book, I made sure to model the things the children needed to keep in mind, such as using phrasing, pacing, and appropriate intonation. I emphasized how important it is for readers to use their voice effectively when they read aloud. I revealed the teacher secret for holding a book so everyone can see it. I made sure the children had time to practice reading aloud to each other before the celebration.

On the big day, each child was ready to read aloud to a visitor. Because not all the families were represented, I teamed up children so that all of them had a grown-up who would listen to them read their books. I gave all the grown-ups comment cards so that they could jot a compliment to the student readers. After the celebration, I temporarily collected the comment cards so that I could make copies to keep in each child's reading file folder. The children kept the original cards to share with someone at home.

It's now early November, and we've spent a month or so teaching our classes about strategies for figuring out words and strategies for being active, brave, and resourceful readers. Of course, even though the whole-class mini-lessons on print strategies are over, we still face a class of children with a wide variety of strengths and needs as readers.

In *Becoming Literate* (1991), Marie Clay asks us to "recognize that some children need extra resources and many more supportive interactions with teachers to get them through the necessary transitions of reading acquisition to the stage where they can pick up most of the different kinds of information in print."

With this in mind, it is responsible teaching for us to continue working with our students to support their growing control of reading strategies and behaviors. Even after we celebrate this unit of study on print strategies, we will still work with children on the strategies they need in individual reading conferences and small-group work sessions like strategy lessons and guided reading groups.

And even though the next unit of study focuses our whole-class teaching on strategies for making meaning and monitoring for comprehension, we in no way leave behind the individualized teaching of reading strategies for children who continue to need them. When we provide ongoing strategy instruction and opportunities for children to independently read both familiar texts and new texts at an appropriate level, reading can become "self-managed, self-monitored, self-corrected, and self-extending for most children, even those who initially find transitions into literacy hard and confusing" (Clay 1991).

It is also worth trying this unit of study on word-solving strategies again later in the year. As children read more difficult texts, their word-solving strategies change. To accommodate children's growing needs, we can take time in January or late spring to fit in another unit of study on print strategies, with a focus on higher-level strategy work. These additional units of study focus more on orchestrating strategies, dealing with challenging vocabulary, figuring out polysyllabic words, and other word-solving issues students are likely to face in more difficult texts.

Talk Amongst Yourselves

Before I launch the next unit of study, Readers Think and Talk About Books to Grow Ideas, I like to plan for some buffer days to assess the readers in my room. Because the focus of my teaching will be on strategies for comprehension, I pay particular attention to my students' strengths and needs with regard to comprehension during these assessments. I ask them to talk about their books, retell the stories, and share their thinking as they read so that I can plan for my teaching in this unit of study.

The other important work I do during these buffer days is brush up conversational skills among my children. In this unit of study my students will be talking about their books with partners, so we consider what it means to be a good talker and listener as well as the characteristics of good conversations.

Good Talkers Are Good Listeners, Too

We all know children are not at a loss for talking to each other, but they do struggle at times with listening to each other. When I listen in on first graders' conversations, I'm often reminded of the parallel play of very young children. In the way that two toddlers can play side by side without ever interacting, first graders can engage in conversations with no intersection of ideas or comments. It's often just two children sitting next to each other, each talking to himself and maybe even taking turns nicely. If we want children to become more responsive to each other, we begin by reminding them of what it means to really listen to each other. We need to teach them that listening is more than politely looking toward and nodding at the speaker. Listening is more active; a listener thinks about the speaker's words in a way that enables her to make some kind of connected response.

One Monday morning I asked the children to sit at their table seats before joining me in the meeting area for morning meeting: "Every Monday, you guys rush into class and talk so fast about stuff you did over the weekend. You run up to me and to each other and say, 'Guess what happened?' or 'You know what I did?' I know many of you are dying to talk about stuff you did over the weekend, so I'm going to give you time for that. Just like grown-ups who go to work on Monday mornings and talk about their weekends, you're going to get the same chance. I want you to tell your seat partner about something enjoyable you did over the weekend, and then we'll share. The trick is that when we share, you'll tell us what your partner did, not what you did. You'll have to be a really great listener. Okay, turn and talk to your seat partner and tell him or her what you did over the weekend." The children turned to each other, and the room was abuzz with talk of Chuck E. Cheese, play dates, video games, cousins, and basketball practice. After a few minutes, I stopped them and asked, "Did both partners get a chance to talk?" Heads nodded. "Did you listen to what your partner said?" Again, children nodded. "Okay, who wants to tell me what their partner did? Remember, don't tell what you did; tell what your partner did." Many students were able to give a one-sentence response, such as Joshua, who told the class, "Andrea went to her grandma's house."

"Cool. What did she do there?" I asked, fully expecting that he hadn't found this out. Joshua looked quizzically at Andrea and shrugged. Then, in a stage whisper, I said, "Joshua, ask Andrea, 'Can you say more? What did you do at your grandma's house?' Go ahead, ask her now." Joshua asked Andrea the question exactly as I had suggested, including the stage whisper.

"We had a birthday party for my uncle," Andrea responded, also in a stage whisper.

"So, Joshua, what did Andrea do at her grandma's house?" I asked again.

"She went there for her uncle's birthday party," Joshua responded as he looked at Andrea, who nodded and smiled.

"Joshua, I love how you got more details from Andrea. What a great thing to do, to ask your partner to say more. Good listening!"

Next, Calen raised his hand to share what Violet had done over the weekend. "Violet went to the cinema god," Calen said nonchalantly.

"Huh? What's that?" I asked.

"The cinema god. Um, I don't know, actually," Calen said.

Again, using a stage whisper, I said, "Calen, tell Violet that you don't get it. Say, 'I don't understand. What do you mean, cinema god?'"

Calen turned to Violet and said, "I don't understand. What do you mean, cinema god?"

"I said synagogue. I went to *synagogue,*" Violet said.

"Oh, synagogue," Calen and I and a few other children said simultaneously.

"You guys, see how it's really important for you as a listener to ask your partner what he or she means if you don't understand? Calen, when you said you didn't understand and asked Violet what she meant, it helped us all to get it. Thanks."

I did this "turn and listen to your partner" exercise for a few mornings using different conversational prompts, such as: Tell your partner what you ate for breakfast, Talk to your partner about your favorite animal, Tell your partner about what you did yesterday. I'd have the children tell us what their partner's response was, and if necessary, I'd give them language to ask their partner to elaborate or clarify. This listening practice took only 5 minutes at a time, yet it provided plenty of opportunities for teaching some of the jobs of being a good listener, like stating back what you just heard, asking follow-up questions, and asking for clarification.

The Importance of Understanding in Conversations

When we're working with children, whether in whole-group or individual settings, we also need to be sure that we ask for clarification when we don't understand what they say. Often, during lessons or discussions, it feels easier to just move on after a child makes a comment that we don't quite understand. We'll say, "Okay, anyone else want to add something?" rather than really trying to understand what the first child said. I think that too often we let children say things that are vague, disconnected, or convoluted, and let these comments pass in our attempts to keep the talk or lesson moving. When we let these kinds of comments go by time and time again, we're conveying the message that it doesn't matter if we don't quite understand what the other is saying, and we pass up valuable opportunities to help children improve their oral language skills.

I've learned to press gently for clarification when a child says something that is hard to understand. While I don't want to put a child on the spot in an uncomfortable way, I also don't want to pretend that I understood what she said and move on to another child. Instead, I say, "I'm not sure I understand what you mean. Can you explain that again?" I give the child a chance to try again, and I might say, "Tell me if I got it," or "Are you saying . . . ?" I do this often so that it becomes a norm in our class discourse. I want there to be an expectation that we all need to understand what we're saying to each other, and that if we don't understand, we should ask for help. We can teach even our youngest students the life lesson of the importance of understanding what others are saying and of being understood themselves when they're talking.

Besides these first-thing-in-the-morning talks, we also brush up our listening skills during lessons and in whole-class book talks. I model what it's like when someone is listening (or not), and we practice having the look of listeners. In book talks I stop the class after a few comments to give the students time to think about what their classmates have just said, and then we restart the conversation. We work on the kinds of questions listeners might ask to help themselves really understand what's being said. One year, my class made a chart:

How to Be a Good Listener
Listeners' Bodies
  We look at the speaker.
  We nod, smile, or say "uh-huh" to show we're listening.
Listeners' Minds
  We think about what the speaker is saying.
  We listen hard to try to understand what the speaker is saying.
  We try to picture in our minds what the speaker is saying.
Questions Listeners Ask to Help Them Understand
  We ask the speaker for details: "Can you say more?"
  We ask the speaker to explain what he means: "I'm not sure I understand. Can you explain that?"
  We ask the speaker to repeat what she said: "Could you repeat that so I can understand?"

The Characteristics of Good Conversations

Many teachers with whom I've worked have studied how to have strong conversations with their students. What I learned from these teachers is that there are just a few critical things, some bottom lines, that must be in place in order to strengthen our students' conversations:

- Many voices are heard, and participation is encouraged.
- Good conversations stick with an idea rather than jumping from one thing to another.
- Good conversations about books stick with the book.

Many Voices Are Heard (but One at a Time, Please!)

We've all been in meetings or workshops, at parties or meals, where just a couple of voices dominate the conversation. When I paid close attention to this in my classroom I found that a handful of children did most of the talking during lessons and book talks. In conversations here or there, this is not a terrible thing, but when it happens throughout the day and across the year in a classroom, it is problematic.

I decided to make the issue of class participation into a mini-research project for myself. During book talks and lessons during this week of conversation work, I would quickly jot shorthand notes indicating who participated and what they said. I learned in a concrete way what I had imagined: several children in my class participated much more than anyone else. Because this handful of five children always volunteered to share their thinking, many other children had grown to rely on them to carry the conversational load. The students simply learned to expect that Sela, Laura, Jacob, Harshel, and Kadeem would always raise their hands, so the rest of the class didn't have to. Unfortunately, this allowed the other children to tune out or underinvest in our work. Sure, in order to encourage more participation in discussions, I would say, "Let's hear from some different thinkers," or "I'm going to give 10 seconds for everyone to think about this" before I took responses. These prompts did help to temporarily increase the number of children who participated in a given discussion, but I didn't want the class to rely on my prompting. I wanted all the children to assume more responsibility in conversations.

When I studied participation in my class, I also recognized that there are different conversational styles. Some children were naturally more loquacious and outgoing, and others were more tentative, shy, or reserved, whether we were in the meeting area or on the playground.

Each year I've had students, like Julie, who approach me right after a lesson or a book talk and offer some piece of insight that they didn't volunteer in the whole-class setting. Others, like Shakeem, are more comfortable answering questions with clear right answers, while still others, like Abigail, are at ease pondering an issue that arises during the read-aloud. Although we can't ask children to assume new personalities for the sake of a good book talk, there are some things we can do to invite more widescale participation.

I shared my observations about class participation with my students, and we opened up a whole-class inquiry. We all became more conscientious about sharing the load in conversations. The five usual talkers would try to make room for other voices by not rushing to participate right away, and we all learned to say things like, "Daniel, what would you like to add?" to the children who tended to be more hesitant.

In whole-group book talks during read-aloud times, many teachers have children sit beside an assigned conversation partner. At various points during the read-aloud, the teacher asks the group to "turn and talk" to their partners about something to do with the story. For example, in the midst of reading aloud *Koala Lou,* I might ask something specific like, "Oh, I'm just wondering, given what we know about Koala Lou, what must she be thinking right now? Turn and talk to your partner about it," or "Turn and tell your partner what you're thinking about right now." During this "turn and talk" time, I move around and listen in to several partnerships. Even the most tentative children are expected to have a talk with their partner, and they do, probably because it feels more comfortable to them to talk one-on-one with a partner instead of in front of the whole class.

The teacher can make sure she listens in to the partnerships that include the most hesitant talkers because she may not often hear their voices in whole-group situations. When I listen in to a child who is shy, I'll say, "Daniel, what an important thing to notice about Frog and Toad's friendship! Would you share it with the class when we get back together?" When the class has reconvened, I'll say, "I heard some really interesting thoughts when I listened in to your conversations. Daniel, for example, told his partner that he noticed something about Frog and Toad's friendship. Daniel, can you tell everyone what you told Jonathan about their friendship?" Some children, like Daniel, may need some prodding at first to participate, and then once they get more comfortable using their voices in the whole-class setting, they will begin to volunteer more.

"Turn and talk" time also takes the teacher out of the role of conversation traffic cop. Usually, in whole-class talks, the teacher is the person toward whom comments are directed, and she is the one who determines the flow of the talk. The students grow dependent upon the teacher's reactions to what they say, and they need her to act as a hub for their conversations. When children are allowed to "turn and talk" to each other on a regular basis, and when this talk is valued, it conveys the message to students that their conversations are important whether or not the teacher is listening in. It also helps the community to rely less on the teacher's reactions as the motivating force in conversation.

Another thing we can do to get more voices into our conversations is to teach our students how to invite others to participate in partnerships, small groups and whole-group talks. We can teach them to notice if someone hasn't been heard from and how to ask their partner, "What are you thinking?" or to ask in the whole group, "Would anyone else like to share their thinking?"

All these suggestions work only if there is safety in the conversations. Teachers need to be sensitive to how we respond to comments so that our children believe their contributions will be valued no matter what. This does not mean that each contribution is treated the same, however. It must be okay for the teacher or students to say, "Can you explain more of what you mean?" or simply, "Huh? I don't get what you're saying."

Sticking with an Idea

Several years ago, I was observing in Trish Lyons's first-grade class in Tenafly, New Jersey. Trish was trying to get her class to follow a line of thinking during their book talks. The students tended to jump around in conversation, going from one thing to another. She noticed, at the end of the conversations, that a lot had been said, but no ground had been gained in terms of better understanding or new thinking. In other words, many voices were heard, which was a good thing, but no ideas had been pursued, which was something that needed work.

To encourage longer conversations about one topic, Trish would say, "Who'd like to add on to what Ashley said?" or "Let's stick with John's idea." These prompts would help temporarily, but soon the children would return to saying whatever was on their minds.

Trish decided that her verbal prompts didn't have much staying power in the conversation. They were quickly forgotten amongst all the talking. She realized that she had to approach this issue, getting her children to stick with an idea or line of thinking, in a more concrete way.

"Today, we're going to do something a little different for our mini-lesson," Trish told her class. "We're going to practice what it means to really stick with an idea in our conversations rather than jumping around like rabbits. When we stick with something, we can stretch our thinking, and stretching our thinking is really good for our minds."

"Yeah, it's like exercise," said Brittany.

"Kind of. Today I want each of you to read this short article about a huge earthquake that happened in Kobe, Japan. I found this yesterday and thought it would be interesting because we've been talking about earthquakes lately. As you read it, use sticky notes to jot yourself a note when you have a thought you'd like to think about with the class. After you're done reading the article, we're going to have a talk, and we're going to practice staying with one idea in our conversation."

The article was a *Weekly Reader* type of article and age-appropriate for first grade. It was short, had several photographs and large print, and Trish's class had some background knowledge on earthquakes that they brought to their reading. Trish rarely ever had the whole class read the same text independently, and she knew it would be challenging for a few readers. She invited children to stay with her at the carpet if they wanted to listen to her read it aloud because, after all, the point of this lesson was not to test the children's reading ability but to improve the conversation. About eight children stayed with Trish at the carpet. Some of them needed her to read it aloud because it was too difficult for them to read on their own, and the others just wanted to hear her read it. She read it aloud a couple of times for this small group and provided time for them to jot on sticky notes about their thinking.

After about 10 minutes, the class reconvened. "I see quite a few sticky notes as I look around," said Trish, "and I know that we have lots we could talk about. Today, though, we're going to practice staying with one idea for a while. But first we have to decide what we want to talk about. Any ideas?" Trish wrote some of their ideas on large-size sticky notes and stuck them on chart paper:

How many people died?
I wonder what it feels like to be in an earthquake.
Some buildings didn't fall down. Why not?
My cousin Maddie was in an earthquake in California.
What makes an earthquake happen?

After these five ideas were put forward, Trish stopped the class.

"We've got quite a few things here that would make great conversations. I'm wondering what we want to stick with for a while." She went through the ideas, reading them aloud and modeling her thinking for the class.

"'How many people died?' You know, that's a good question, but it doesn't seem like it will give us lots to talk about because we can just answer it. We reread the article, find the answer, and say something like 'thousands of people' and then we are done with the conversation."

"Yeah, it says right here how many people died," Aidan said, pointing to the article.

"Oh, right! You know, we can answer that question right now, so I guess it won't make the kind of conversation that we can stick with." Trish moved the sticky note off to the side and read aloud the next topic.

"'I wonder what it feels like to be in an earthquake?' That might work for talk because we can find evidence for our thinking from the article, but we can also do some wondering and imagining of our own, so I'll leave that sticky note here."

"'Some buildings didn't fall down. Why not?' Hmm, another one that could work because we could look closely at the photographs and try to figure it out, so I'll leave the sticky note here, too."

Trish read the next sticky note: "'My cousin Maddie was in an earthquake in California.' Oh, that's really sad, but it would be hard to have a conversation about that, I think. It seems like only Jade could really talk about it because it was her cousin, right?" Trish moved the note off to the side.

"'What makes an earthquake happen?' Gee, that's a good science question. We'd probably need another book on earthquakes or an expert to help us though, so maybe it's something to research and talk about later."

"My cousin Maddie is an expert," Jade offered.

"I'm sure she is, but we can't really get hold of her right now, so . . . ," Trish said.

"Yeah, she's in school. Seventh grade," Jade said proudly.

"Okay, class. Let's see. We've got a couple of things we could talk about. What do you think? What do you want to talk about and stick with for a while?" She read the sticky notes again. The class informally voted and chose to discuss what it must feel like to be in an earthquake.

During the talk, the children sometimes went off topic to talk about things like eating with chopsticks, Japanese cartoons, and hurricanes. Trish would say, "Let's save that because right now we're sticking with one idea: what it feels like to be in an earthquake," or "Let's stay with our topic."

After about 7 minutes of conversation, Trish said, "You did a nice job of trying to stay with our topic. It's hard, isn't it? But I loved what happened. We didn't rush through the idea, but instead we really gave it some thought. We reread the article sometimes to find evidence, like what the lady said about her house shaking. We imagined that we were there to really get the feeling. Our talk helped me to really imagine what it must feel like to be in an earthquake, and now I feel like I can understand a little better how those people in Kobe must have felt. I've got new thinking in my head. Thanks! We're going to practice doing this, staying with an idea in our conversations, and I know it will get easier and easier. For today, during private reading time, put sticky notes in places where you get thoughts. And then, when you meet with your partner, do the same thing we just did. You and your partner will choose something to stick with in your conversation. Remember, if one of you gets off the topic, there are things you might say to help the conversation stay. What might you say to your partner to help him or her remember to stick with the topic?"

"You could say, 'Let's stick to the topic,'" offered Charles.

"Charles, that's very clear. Let's all practice saying that together. 'Let's stick to the topic.' Okay, you say it."

The class said it together, and then Trish sent them off to read privately. They each had a couple of sticky notes to mark places in their books that they'd like to talk about with their partner.

The trick to staying with an idea is finding an idea that lends itself to a conversation and is not a dead end. In the example from Trish's class, some of the ideas were actually questions that could be answered quickly from the text (How many people died?) or questions that needed much more information (What makes an earthquake happen?) in order to be a conversation that would last long.

It's easy for us to foresee which ideas will lend themselves to good talk and which would take us to a dead end. We need to help children know the difference, too. A way we can do this is to choose dead-end ideas for conversations and watch the way the talk ends quickly. After doing this a couple of times, we might think with our children about what kinds of thoughts make good conversations and what kinds take us to dead ends. Generally, conversations that start with questions that can be answered quickly from the text are dead ends. Also, we may not hit a dead end, but we can go down a side track when personal connections are superficial or take us too far away from the text. From watching good book talks in other teachers' rooms, I learned that there are some general rules of thumb:

Conversations
Dead ends
Questions that can easily be answered from the text:
    "How many people died in the earthquake?"
Connections and side tracks that take us away from the text:
    "My grandpa was in Japan once; he . . ."
    "I like Japanese food."
Fruitful conversational leads
Questions that can't easily be answered from the text:
    "What did it feel like to be in that earthquake?"
Connections that help us understand the text:
    "When I was little, I lived in California and there was an earthquake . . ."

It's not the worst thing in the world if occasionally our whole-class conversations don't flourish. In the world outside of school, we don't always have memorable conversations, either. I believe there are always teaching opportunities when things don't work out. We can show children when and how to cut the losses on dead-end conversations and move on to something else. We might model this by saying, "Hmm, it feels like we've kind of talked that out. It seems we've hit a dead end. You know how I can tell? I can tell because it feels we have less talk energy, and we're getting kind of repetitive. Why don't we switch gears and talk about something else that's on your minds?"

Staying with a Book

One of the hardest things to do in book talks is to stick with the book. In my book club we'd sometimes realize that after two hours of meeting, we had barely mentioned the book. Of course, all was not lost because we did have enjoyable conversations, but they just were not about the book. We realized that we needed to allow time for some chit-chat as well as our book talk. We tried to begin our book club meetings by talking about anything, and then when the food came, we'd switch over to our book talk. We needed to make a clear transition from chit-chat to book talk and be sure that this transition was consistent and clear. In our classrooms it's important, too, to set boundaries around book talks so that whether children are talking about books in the whole-class setting or within their reading partnerships, they will know when to turn on the book talk and turn off the chit-chat.

In our classrooms, after all, book talks can go off in many directions. Many times a child would make a personal connection during a read-aloud by saying something like, "My sister is a bully just like that!" This personal connection could have helped our conversation if we had used it to help us understand the characters better. Instead, it often seemed that we'd get sucked into the vortex of sibling bully stories, one after the other. My appeals to get back to the book talk didn't always work. What I learned to do in these situations was to say, "It sounds like lots of you have bully stories about your brothers and sisters. Why don't you take just half a minute and tell your partner one of your bully stories. Then we'll get back to the book." In these situations I didn't move around and listen in, but I gave them just enough time to get these stories out of their systems. Sometimes, you can just feel when your class is bubbling over with things to say that may not be the kinds of comments that would strengthen your whole-class conversation about a book. It's these occasions when you might decide not to fight it but to make a little bit of time for it.

You can also teach children to use their personal connections to better understand the text rather than letting them move far from the text. In the example from Trish's class, Jade's offer to talk about her cousin's experience in an earthquake might very well prompt one cousin story after another. You can just imagine how it might go.

Jade shares what she knows about her cousin's experience of living through an earthquake, "My cousin Maddie said that in California her whole house shook and the pictures fell off the shelf. Her Beanie Babies even fell on her bed."

Then Michael says, "My cousin, Jake, has to stay in bed because he has chicken pox, and he looks nasty."

"My sister had chicken pox," adds Lydia.

"Well, my cousin got bitten by a rottweiler and needed stitches on his leg," says Theo.

"My neighbor has two rockwilers but they're nice ones," says Jesse.

"I saw a snake at the zoo," adds Sean. Before you know it, the conversation has gone from earthquakes to childhood viruses to large dogs to snakes and zoo trips. This can happen very quickly in first grade!

There is something we can do before the personal connections take us far away from the book talk. If children make personal connections to the text, as Jade did, I model using these connections to see if they can help us understand what's going on in the story.

I'm reminded of one morning after I had read aloud *Jim's Dog Muffins* by Miriam Cohen, Josh said, "Ms. Collins . . ." and pointed over at Calen, who was hunched over with his face in his hands.

"Calen, you okay?" I asked quietly as Abigail reached over to give his back a pat.

"Yeah, but I'm just thinking about if my dog died," he said without looking up. I had forgotten that Calen's family had just adopted a beloved puppy. For the last couple of weeks, Calen could barely contain himself each day at dismissal time because he was so excited to see his fluffy, energetic little puppy.

"Gee, Calen, this book must have really touched your heart because it reminded you of your own dog and how sad you'd feel if something happened. Calen, may I ask you something, though? I'm wondering if when you think about your dog, does it help you understand how Jim must have felt in this story?"

"Yeah, I would be so sad if my dog died, just like Jim was," Calen said.

"If my dog died, I probably wouldn't have to go to school because I'd be like crying for three days. I'd be so sad," added Laura.

"So you'd handle it differently than Jim. You wouldn't be able to go to school," I said, trying to take Laura's comment back to the text.

"I'd have to go to school, but I'd be like Jim and not talk to anyone," Calen added.

"Jim didn't want to talk to anyone either," Rohan said.

"Hmm. I wonder why," I said.

"When my grandma's dog died, she was kind of like Jim, too. She didn't want to really talk about it with anyone," said Tessa.

"I wonder why that is."

"Well, sometimes if you're so sad if you talk about it, it can make you cry a lot," said Natasha.

"And maybe Jim didn't want to cry a lot in school," said Abigail.

"Some kids mighta laughed at him or something if he cried," said Andy.

It can get tricky to keep conversations focused on the texts, especially when children make deep personal connections, like Calen did. I certainly could have given Calen a chance to vent his feelings about his puppy, and that would have been a fine thing to do. In fact, I did approach him privately right after the book talk to check in and offer some comfort. During the book talk, I felt that if I didn't keep the book front and center, Calen's comment could have just as easily unleashed a torrent of dead pet stories. In this situation, with the whole class gathered for a book talk, I decided to use Calen's comment to remind everyone how personal connections can help us understand the book or characters better. A helpful question to have on tap when children share personal connections is, How does that help you understand the story or the character better?

Readers Think and Talk About Books to Grow Ideas

Chapter 6

I'LL NEVER FORGET MY FIRST BOOK CLUB. I was a graduate student, a late bloomer, I suppose. A book club seemed so fancy and smart. It was pre-Oprah, before book clubs had mass appeal, and I felt kind of honored to be in one, as well as a little intimidated. The founding member of our book club had been in one back home, and she and a couple of the other members had been Ivy Leaguers in undergraduate school. Pretty good company, I thought, feeling slightly out of my league. After all, I had tried to avoid literature courses in college and consequently had spent my whole life up to that point reading by myself. Now I had friends to read and talk about books with, and I wanted to be good at it.

Our first book was an Alice Walker novel, *Possessing the Secret of Joy*. I read it more carefully than I would have if it were just my own private reading. I read as if I were preparing for a pop quiz. I kept track of the details and plot turns. While reading, I tried to anticipate our book club conversation, as if it would be a question-and-answer session like the ones I remember from high school English, where right answers mattered. When the book club meeting date approached, I went back and reread some parts of the book in order to be well prepared. I suppose on some level I was looking for a good grade.

At our meeting, the conversation got off to a swell start. If I remember correctly, we each had something to say as we drank tea and ate cookies. I was having an out-of-body experience as I looked around. "Look at me!" I thought. "I'm living in New York City, talking at a book club meeting with smart people, drinking tea and eating cookies."

It was then that the conversation took a turn. One of the members flipped through her book and said, "There was so much Christian imagery. It's all over the book."

"I was thinking the same thing as I read. Like right in this part," someone else said as she went on to read aloud an excerpt she had highlighted.

I flipped to the page she was reading and felt like I missed something. Christian imagery? I had read right through it. Everyone else had noticed it, and I felt as if I had just failed the pop quiz. As they went around sharing places where they noticed allusions to Christianity and Jesus, I nodded in agreement. Meanwhile, inside, I felt dumb because I had completely overlooked something that appeared so obvious to everyone else.

Two things happened from that experience. First, for the next few books I read, I was seeing Christian imagery everywhere. If the story was about a couple and their child, I thought, "Ah, the holy family." If the setting was in a hot, steamy locale, "Oh, hell symbolism."

The second thing that happened was that I could see concretely and directly just how valuable it is to talk about books. The conversation with my book club opened up my reading to something I had never really thought about or noticed before. In the years since that book club, I've been in other ones, and each time I read and talk with friends about books, my own reading changes and gets better.

I guess you could say that the small-group work of a book club has helped me to become a stronger independent reader. Even when I'm reading something that is not a book club pick, I have the voices of my book club friends in my head as I read. I've begun to pay closer attention to the writer's craft, like Alice Ressner does. I notice the threads of connection throughout a book, like Jacqi McGarry, and I read between the lines more, like Eve Litwack. I try really hard to get to know and understand the characters, like Kristen Jordan does. I've become a better reader because of the company I keep.

In our classrooms, when we provide time for talking about books in partnerships, small groups, and whole-class settings, we are helping readers become stronger. In a very basic example, I know that in September when I read aloud a picture book to the class and Dito calls out, "Hey, that page is just like the cover!" for the very first time, a new line of thinking is opened for everyone. From that point on, all the children will be vigilant about noticing when the cover illustration is also tucked within the pages of the story. Dito showed them something to look for in picture books, in the same way that my book club showed me how Christian imagery is something to be aware of in novels.

One year, when I was reading aloud *Mrs. Piggle-Wiggle* to my class, Emily said, "Every chapter is in a pattern. They go the same way." She explained that the chapters all start with a mother getting annoyed with her child and calling Mrs. Piggle-Wiggle to get some help. I asked the class if we should go back and look for some evidence to support Emily's theory. As we flipped through the previous chapters, we discovered that Emily was right. The chapters did follow a pattern. For the rest of the book, other children added new details to the theory. Max said that Mrs. Piggle-Wiggle's solutions always worked but not until things got really bad for the kid. "I mean, junk growing out of your ears? That's just gross!" he said, using text evidence from the chapter called "The Radish Cure" to make his point.

The idea of books following patterns must have stuck in some children's minds because during independent reading, a few days after Emily's discovery, Silver noticed that some of Miriam Cohen's books follow a pattern, too. "Jim starts out with a problem, like he thinks he won't have friends, but then it gets solved at the end," Silver said. He went on to show me the pages he had marked with sticky notes that supported his theory. This noticing of text patterns, or formulas, throughout chapters and across texts was not taught explicitly by me but learned through whole-class conversation during read-aloud time. The best part was that this whole-class conversation initiated by Emily affected other children's independent reading.

In order to talk well about books readers need to have thoughts and ideas as they read. They have to hold themselves accountable for understanding the text. In this unit of study, we not only teach strategies for comprehension but also show children how to have thoughts and conversations about books. If the print strategies study began to address the question of how to read the words, this unit of study starts to answer the question of how readers think about and understand their texts.

At this time of the school year, first graders have grown much more proficient with the print work of reading. Because we've just worked on the unit of study focused on print strategies and fluency, the children are working with such focus on decoding print that they may be neglecting to think much about the stories when they read independently. This is perfectly illustrated by a comment a student once made during a reading conference. I asked John what he thought of the book he had just finished, and he said, "I didn't really think about it. I was just reading." How true! For many children, once they become proficient decoders, reading is mostly about getting the words, not the story.

Another by-product of the emphasis on print strategies is that we teachers, too, become very print-focused at this time. One year, I realized that all my conferring notes over a few weeks were informal running records. I know that running records provide valuable information, but it's not really necessary to take a running record every time a child picks up a book. It's as if we begin to regard accuracy rates and reading levels as the only revealing details about our young readers.

Alarms go off when I hear teachers say about their students, "Oh she's a DRA 8," or "He's at level F." There is too much emphasis on levels and accuracy rates if the *only* way we describe readers is to talk about the levels of texts they can read. Often the necessary emphasis on print work can come at the expense of teaching other aspects of a successful and satisfying reading experience. I often remind myself that when upper-grade teachers talk about their students' struggles as readers, they list comprehension difficulties and indifferent (or hostile) attitudes toward reading much more often than decoding problems. It is time, then, in first grade to run to the other side of the boat, as Lucy Calkins says, and hold our students accountable for thinking about and understanding their books during independent reading. It's time to impress upon the children that reading is much more than simply getting the words right.

In this unit of study we are trying to do a few things. First, we need to jump-start and strengthen the talks our students are having about books by teaching them to have thoughts as they read. Earlier in the year, our children talked with reading partners about their books, but our expectations for partner talk were more humble than for this unit of study. Earlier in the year, we hoped that partners would say anything about their books. We were pleased if one partner said, "My favorite part is where the dog jumps on the man because it's funny," and then the other partner told her favorite part and why. End of conversation, and on to the next book talk.

At this time of the year, however, we are teaching toward more substantive conversations. As we teach children to go from saying *anything* about the text to saying something substantive, we also teach partners how to talk with one another about their thinking. We do this by teaching children how to have the kinds of conversations that involve an exchange of ideas rather than conversations in which they simply take turns saying some brief thing to each other. We want to help our students add on to each other's thoughts, disagree with civility, pursue a line of thinking, ask for clarification or elaboration, and use text evidence to support their thinking. These things may sound advanced for six-year-olds, but with our support and guidance, they can and do have wonderful talks about books.

In order to talk well about books, it's necessary to have ideas and thoughts as we read. In this unit of study, we teach children about the kinds of thinking strong readers do as they read independently. We already model and demonstrate how to do this in some other components of our literacy work throughout the day. For example, as we read aloud a chapter book or picture book to the class, we think aloud strategically, "I wonder if she's going to win the contest," or "He's not being such a nice friend."

During read-aloud time, we also provide opportunities for our students to turn and talk to a partner about their own thinking, by saying, "Hmm, a lot just happened in this part. Turn and tell your partner what you're thinking right now." Similarly, in shared reading, we can demonstrate how readers do much more than just read the words by showing them ways to think about the story. We might prompt them to make predictions or invite them to make connections with the text. In both the read-aloud with accountable talk and in shared reading, we've been supporting children as they learn to express their thinking and to share ideas about texts. Now is the time during independent reading that we teach them how they, too, can have ideas as they read, by modeling and demonstrating with the kinds of books they have in their book bins.

Finally, during this unit of study, we need to teach our children strategies they can use to check their comprehension and help themselves when they don't understand. I find this to be very tricky to teach new readers. Often children may not even realize when they don't understand a book because they haven't had enough experience with reading to tell the difference between confusion and clarity. We can lay an essential foundation, even now, so that our children expect to understand what they read and have strategies to use when they don't.

During this unit of study we rely heavily on reading partnerships to support the thinking and talking work. We need to provide many opportunities for children to talk and think with each other, sometimes with our guidance and prompting, and other times in more independent situations. During read-aloud our students will sit beside talk partners whom they will think with and talk with about the book. During independent reading children will read privately at first and then meet with their partners for book talks about their just-right books.

We also introduce sticky notes as tools for readers to keep track of their thoughts as they read. As adult readers, many of us jot notes in the page margins or highlight parts of our books where we have ideas or thoughts. These are impractical strategies for use in our classrooms because the books are shared among the community and across the years. Sticky notes offer a temporary yet concrete place for our young readers to hold their thinking so that when they meet with their partners, they are ready to talk.

Although the focus of our whole-class teaching for independent reading shifts to talk and comprehension in this unit of study, we still support our children as they acquire print strategies through small-group work, individual reading conferences, and during shared reading, writing workshop, and interactive writing. In any unit of study we must continue to teach print strategies, especially to our most vulnerable students.

Bends in the Road

After spending a week or so improving the form and content of our conversations (while acknowledging, of course, that this is year-long work in the early grades), it's time to begin the work of this unit of study. We want to help our students have talks about their books, and the easiest way to begin this is to teach them how to retell their stories to another person. I like to begin this unit of study with retelling because we've done some retelling already during read-aloud time, and retelling lends itself to concrete conversation. It always seems easier to start by asking my students to tell their partners what happened in their stories than by expecting them to have grand conversations about the thematic connections with other literature.

Through retelling, we can also make our students aware of the elements of story, particularly character, setting, and plot, which will help them to have other kinds of talks about books. When children retell their books, we can teach them to use text evidence to confirm or revise their thinking, as well. In this first bend in the road, when we teach children to retell, we also teach them the real-life reasons people retell, the variety of ways that people can retell a text, and the qualities of good retelling.

After only a week or two of work on retelling, we are ready to switch direction to teach our children that readers don't just have thoughts after they read a book but while they read the book. We demonstrate some of the different kinds of thinking that careful readers do as they read, and we show them how they can hold their thinking for when they have book talks with their reading partners as well as how they can hold themselves accountable for comprehension.

The word *comprehension* implies thinking, and readers need to have thoughts about the text as they read. In the same way that we respond in conversations with people when we're listening closely and are invested in the interaction, we need to respond as we read books. Careful readers have internal conversations or make running commentary as they read, and we have to show our students what that looks like and sounds like. We want our young readers to hear themselves thinking, "Oh, I didn't get that," or "That's weird," or "I bet she's going to forget the magic key," or "He's acting just like my big brother—ugh!"

We've been modeling this "in-the-book" thinking throughout the year during shared reading and interactive read-aloud, but now we explicitly teach children how they can have thoughts as they read, through our mini-lessons in independent reading workshop.

The next bend in the road is designed to help children check for comprehension and to teach them strategies to help themselves when their comprehension is compromised or lacking altogether. First, we need to make sure they realize that it's vitally important that they understand what they read. Then, we can teach them to be aware when their comprehension is missing or thin. We want our students to be careful readers who will say to themselves, "I didn't get that part," or "This doesn't make sense to me." We can teach our children strategies for helping themselves when they don't understand the text. Just as we gave them tools to figure out tricky words, we give them tools to figure out tricky parts of stories.

In the sections that follow, I detail the bends in the road of this unit of study:

- Readers retell their books to themselves and their partners.
- Readers have thoughts as they read and share their thoughts with their partners.
- Readers have strategies for checking comprehension.

Retelling

Before I had a child of my own, I thought of retelling as a rather bland necessity in the classroom. I felt duty-bound to teach it in deference to the standards. I tried a few different things to make retelling come alive, for my own sake as much as for the sake of my students. After having a son, I found a new appreciation for retelling, and I even wonder if retelling is some sort of social instinct or need.

When Owen was a year old, he began to retell the major events in his life, which primarily concerned the falls and tumbles he took as a new walker in the world. Ian and I noticed that Owen was retelling after he took a few steps and tripped over something. After falling, he got right up and pointed to the spot on the floor where he had stumbled and, in an expressive and exasperated babble retold what had happened and even reenacted it a bit by doing a little stunt-man fall. We respond to these retellings by saying, "And then what happened?" or "Show me where you bonked," or "Wow, Owen, that must have been a big surprise!" Of course, we don't really know what he's saying in response, but it's so clear that he's retelling the event by the way he points and exclaims and dramatizes what has just happened.

At bedtime, we often talk to Owen about the things that we did together that day. "Remember when we went to the park this morning?" I'll say as I get him settled for the night. "First you went on the swings, back and forth, back and forth, higher and higher. You were laughing so hard. Remember? Then after the swings, you pushed your stroller over to the slide. You were working so hard trying to walk up the slide, remember? We decided the steps might be easier, and I helped you up them." Owen contributes to the retelling, too, by gesturing, smiling, and making barking sounds when I say, "And then on our way home, remember we saw Jasper, the big brown doggie?" Then Owen points to his foot to remind me about something. "Oh, that's right, Owen, that silly Jasper kept sniffing your shoe, and then he went bye-bye."

Retelling is not just for babies, and it's not just for students, either. We retell all the time in our lives. For example, when a movie ends and the audience is walking out of the theater, I love listening to the aisle chatter. Many of these conversations involve retelling favorite or confusing parts of the movie. When families gather for holidays or events, we often retell the same stories year after year. Upon our return from a trip or an experience, people often ask us to retell so they can make a picture in their minds of what we did. These and thousands of other examples help us consider some of the real-life purposes for retelling and give us ideas for teaching retelling in our classrooms.

Too often, the only purpose for having children retell in school is to check comprehension. When this is the main purpose, retelling helps the teacher more than it helps the students. However, when we ground our teaching of retelling in real life and teach the characteristics of good retelling, our children will learn to retell in a way that helps them as readers and thinkers as much as it helps us as teachers.

Characteristics of Good Retelling
- Uses characters' names. (Characters)
- Tells where the story is taking place. (Setting)
- Includes the important parts of the story. (Plot)
- Is told in an interesting voice. (Fluency)
- Is checked with book to see if anything was missed. (Text evidence)
- Is checked with book to see if teller understood everything. (Comprehension)

The following is my first mini-lesson on the topic of retelling.

Mini-lesson

Connection

Girls and boys, we've just spent the last month or so becoming strong at reading the words in our books. All of you know where to get your just-right books, and you've been doing a great job at reading with smooth voices. And I can tell you're excited by your reading power because I've noticed that you are just devouring books. You're reading one book after another without even taking any time to breathe!

So I got to thinking that it's time to remind you that there is more to reading than just devouring the words in books. I'm going to spend the next few weeks teaching you how readers don't just read the words but also think and talk about the story. I thought we could start with the kind of thinking and talking readers do when they're done with a book. Instead of going right to the next book, readers think about the one they just finished, and one way they can do this is by retelling the story to themselves or to someone else. Today, I'm going to teach you how to retell your book when you're done with it because I think you're ready to do this big thinking work.

Teaching point and demonstration

Watch me as I retell Birthdays *to you guys. [*Birthdays *is a familiar Big Book.] I'm going to pretend that I just finished it and it's time for me to meet with my reading partner. You guys are going to be my reading partner, okay? Listen really carefully for how I retell this story.*

I retell the Big Book, leaving out a big part. The children clamor to remind me of what I "forgot."

Did you notice how I retold the stuff that happened in the book? When I forgot that one part, you helped me out. Thanks! What a great partner you are! Well, now I want you to try it. I want you to practice retelling to your partner right now because that's going to be your work today during work time.

Active engagement

Right now, turn to your partner. One of you is going to be the reteller and the other is going to be the helper. Decide that now. Okay. The retelling partner will retell Birthdays, *and the helping partner will listen in and help out if necessary, just like you did for me. Okay? Go ahead.*

I listen so that I can share back to the class and get a quick assessment of what their retelling sounds like.

You know, I noticed that you guys did a really good job retelling. I love how you remembered the important parts and included them as you retold the story. That was smart thinking because when you retell, it's important to include the important parts.

Link to ongoing work

So, readers, whenever you finish a book, before you jump right into the next one, take a minute and retell the book to yourselves. Then, when you meet with your reading partners, one of your jobs will be to retell the story to each other. Retelling is something that careful readers do, and we're going to learn how to do it well over the next few days.

In this first lesson on retelling, I'm only teaching my students that retelling is something readers do when they finish a book, and I'm providing an example of what a retelling might sound like. Before I plan out the precise details of my retelling lessons, I want to find out just what the children need to do better. For example, if almost all of them are reading books without well-defined or named characters, I wouldn't need to spend a mini-lesson on how readers use characters' names when they retell. On the other hand, if more than half of my class is reading early chapter books, I would want to teach them how to retell parts or chapters of their books rather than expecting them to wait to retell until they're finished reading the book.

When I listen in to the way children retell books to their partners during this first lesson and during reading workshop, I expect I will need to spend several lessons on teaching children the characteristics of good retelling. For example, retellings often sound murky and confused because students omit details, such as characters or settings. A typical retelling, early in the unit of study, might sound something like this: "He wanted a dog and they finally said okay. At first he was little but then he got really big. He got lost and they were sad." Instead, I want my students to distinguish characters in the retelling by using their names or some other characteristic, so that the retelling will sound more like this: "This boy named Henry wanted a dog, and his mom and dad finally said yes. They picked out a puppy and named him

Mudge. Mudge grew big, and Henry and Mudge had lots of fun together. One day, Mudge got lost, though, and everyone was sad, especially Henry."

Besides teaching children to identify characters as they retell, there are other things we can teach them in mini-lessons for this part of the unit of study.

❧ *Readers identify the setting when they retell.* When children read books that have several different settings and scenes, it's important for them to identify where the action is taking place when they retell. This helps the listener to better picture what is going on in the story.

❧ *Readers follow the events of the story when they retell.* When children sequence the retelling from the beginning, it helps the listener to better understand what happened in the story.

❧ *Readers know how to balance the details when they retell.* Teaching students about this balance can be tricky. We don't want them to belabor their retelling with exquisite details of character, setting, or action, yet we do need a certain amount of detail to help us picture the action. The way we can teach this is to introduce the idea of determining importance by asking, Is this an important part of the story?

❧ *Readers use time words when they retell.* We can help students retell by teaching them the language that is characteristic of retelling, words such as *at first, then, next, after that, suddenly, finally, in the end.*

❧ *Readers retell with expression.* We work hard to teach our children to read with fluency and expression, and we can use this work to teach them to retell smoothly and with expression. We can show them how to use characters' voices, how to use intonation to reflect the story, such as a tone of surprise, a quiet tone for sad parts, a suspenseful tone for building suspense.

❧ *Readers use text evidence to clarify, confirm, or revise the retelling.* When a child retells and gets stuck, we teach him to check the book to help him remember the part that he couldn't remember clearly. We also teach the listener to pay close attention to the retelling so that he asks, "Can you show me that part?" if he is confused by the retelling or thinks it was inaccurate.

The following are some possible mini-lessons or mid-workshop lessons to support partner retelling.

❧ *Partners read together and retell.* If partners are reading books that can be finished in one partner session, they can decide which book to read together and retell it together.

❧ *One partner retells, then both partners read together to confirm.* One partner retells the book she read during private reading time to the other partner. Then the partners read the book together and confirm the retelling.

- *Partners take turns retelling.* If partners are reading books that are too long to read together in one partner session (early chapter books, for example), we teach them how to take turns retelling and questioning each other. One partner retells her book, and the other partner asks, "Can you show me that part?" or "Why did that happen?" Then they switch roles.

- *Partners help each other retell.* In this lesson I teach partners how they can help each other retell by joining in, if they both know the story, or by asking to look at the book during the retelling. Also, partners can hold each other accountable for the qualities of good retelling by asking for characters' names, setting, important events, and so on.

After teaching the characteristics of good retelling in a few mini-lessons and in individual and partner reading conferences, I turn our retelling work toward the different kinds of retelling that readers can do after they finish a book. Until now, the retelling that my students have done has been mostly the start-to-finish kind. This kind of retelling is the oral equivalent of a storyboard for a television commercial: each scene is included in the retelling. This is the easiest kind of retelling to do because it follows the story closely, and if there is a hard part, the reteller can look back into the book for clarification.

Another kind of retelling we can teach children to do is what many teachers call a gist retelling or a summary retelling. When a child retells this way, she limits the detail and chronology to the most important parts. For example, a summary retelling may sound like this: "This is a book about two friends who have a play date that starts out good, turns bad when one of the friends, the red-haired boy, falls off a bike, and gets good again because the friends help each other".

Summary retelling—distilling a book to its essence or most important parts—can be quite challenging. To make this a little more concrete, I teach them to start this kind of retelling by saying, "This is a book about. . . ." When they start this way, they are less likely to launch right into a chronological retelling.

Another kind of retelling we can teach children is retelling from a point of view. This overlaps somewhat with a book review in that the reteller begins by making an opinion-based statement about the book. This kind of retelling might sound like this: "This book was kind of exciting because there was a lot of action, especially when one of the friends in the story, the red-headed kid, fell off a bicycle. These two friends were having a play date, and everything was fine until the redheaded kid fell off the bike. I liked how the other friend was helpful because I know if that happened to me, my friend would throw up because he hates blood."

You might want to postpone teaching children how to retell in different ways until the end of the unit of study because in order for children to do more sophisticated retelling, they need to have done more sophisticated thinking as they read. That is the subject of the next bend in the road. On the other hand, when I've taught the different kinds of retelling at the beginning of this unit, as I've described, it has served as an introduction to the topic of retelling, and I've been able to reinforce and demonstrate the different kinds of retelling as the unit progresses. Both ways—teaching this study at the beginning or at the end of this unit—have benefits as well as drawbacks.

Readers Have Thoughts as They Read

In this bend in the road we teach children about the thinking they can do while they are reading their books. All the things I plan to teach during this part of the unit of study have already been talked about and done during interactive read-aloud since the beginning of the year. For example, when I read aloud a picture book like *Crow Boy,* I stopped at a part when the other children are being unkind to Crow Boy and said, "Wow, right here the author made me get a really strong feeling. Did that happen to any of you? Why don't you talk to your talk partner about how this part makes you feel." When I read aloud a chapter book like *Charlotte's Web,* I stopped and said, "You know, I just need to stop here for a minute and picture what's happening in this part because it's getting confusing. I'm going to reread it and make a picture in my mind. As I reread it, why don't you do that, too, try to really picture in your mind what's going on so we can talk about it."

I want the talk work and the thinking work I'm asking my students to do to fit with the natural flow of the reading, and so my prompts need to be similar to what I could imagine my students thinking about in their own minds as they read independently. In other words, I don't want my thinking and talking prompts to sound too much like they could only have come from a teacher. It's hard to imagine a reader stopping during private reading time and thinking, "I'm making a personal connection to this part." Instead, I can imagine a child thinking, "Hey, this reminds me of when my sister and I had that big fight. I bet they're going to make up, just like we did." Of course, this child is making a personal connection that also enables her to make a prediction, but in the midst of her reading, I don't want her to pull out of her story in such a way that she labels her thinking. My hope now is simply that she does some thinking as she reads. I'll teach her to jot notes on sticky notes to keep track of her thinking in the same way that adults highlight, underline, or even attach sticky notes to text they are reading.

I might begin the work of this bend in the road by saying to my class, "I'm noticing something about all of you. You are getting to be such strong readers, and now you're becoming great at retelling the stories when you finish reading your books. But guess what? It feels like there is something missing. There is just so much more to reading than reading the words and retelling the story. Really careful readers don't just read the words and then retell the story; they also think, think, think about the story as they read. Does this make sense? Talk to your partner about what I just said, about what it means to think about the story while you're reading."

As the students turn and talk, I move around and listen in on their conversations. After a couple of minutes, if I find that they don't quite get what I'm saying, I bring them together again. One year, I used *Wolf Story*, the chapter book I was reading aloud at that time, to help make my point.

"Let me try to explain what I mean when I say that readers don't just read the words but also think about the story when they're reading. It's like when I'm reading aloud *Wolf Story*. As you listen to the story, you do lots of great thinking. I know this because you say such smart things about the book when you turn and talk to your partners and when we talk together about the story. What are some things you think about when you're listening to me read aloud a chapter book like *Wolf Story*?"

"I try to picture what's going on in the story in my head," Talia says.

"I picture how the wolf talks and how scary he is," adds Deanna.

"I try to figure out what's going to happen next," says Erik.

"That's a prediction," Vi reminds him in her best teacher voice.

"Well, all these things you're talking about, picturing the story, predicting what will happen next, feeling scared, all those things are the kinds of thinking that strong readers do when they read their own books. Readers have thoughts and feelings about the stories when they read. You do these things already when you listen to me read books aloud, but you also have to do these things yourselves when you're reading your own books. We're going to spend a couple of weeks learning how to be great thinkers when we read and learning how to be great talkers about our books. Today, when you're reading by yourselves, I want you to do more than just read the words. I want you to be sure that you think about the story in your books. I'm interested to see what kinds of thinking you do as you read."

After our talk, the children leave the meeting area, get their book bins, and settle down to read. Many of my conferences in the first day or two of this teaching topic are assessment conferences. I'm trying to see what the children are or are not doing so that I know what my teaching needs to focus on in the coming days.

I look around the room for a minute and watch the readers begin. I grab my note-taking clipboard and see that I need to meet with Natasha. I pull up a chair next to her and listen in as she reads several pages of *Baby Bear Goes Fishing*. She stops and looks at me.

"Natasha, how's it going?"

"Good," she says. I quickly compliment her on how smoothly she's reading and decide to move right in to find out what thinking work she's doing.

"So what are you thinking about as you read this book?"

"Well, I'm thinking about the baby bear goin' fishin'."

"What about that?"

"Well, if he goes fishin', is he gonna catch any fish?"

"You're wondering if he's going to catch any fish. Well, what do you think? Think he'll catch anything?"

"I bet he does catch one, just one though."

"So you're predicting that Baby Bear will catch a fish. Hmm. What makes you think so?"

"Well, then it would be a happy ending 'cause they'd have somethin' to eat."

"Wow, Natasha. Can I tell the class about what you just did?"

Natasha nods and smiles but looks tentative. It's clear to me that she's not really sure what she just did.

"Natasha, I want to tell the class about this because what you did was some really great thinking. As you read this book, you were thinking hard and wondering about the story so that you made a prediction. It wasn't any old prediction, like Baby Bear was going to run away and join a circus or something. No, you made a prediction that made sense with the way the story was going. I can't wait to tell the class about it during share time. I'm going to stop back to check what happens with Baby Bear, to see if he does catch a fish like you said or to see if he runs away and joins the circus. Okay?" Natasha rolls her eyes and says with certainty, "Ms. Collins, he's not gonna run away." I shrug and go to the next reader.

In this assessment conference, I wanted to find out what kinds of things Natasha thinks about as she reads. By asking, "So what are you thinking?" I made the assumption that she *was* thinking about the story as she read. I first complimented her on how smoothly she was reading and then named two things she did, wondering and predicting, without changing from the conversational tone of the conference. I decided to focus more on her prediction instead of the wondering because I felt the prediction was the stronger of the thoughts, and it was something that I could easily share with the class.

Next, I move on to Eliza, who has been reading the Poppleton series. Eliza is a strong reader who is reluctant to talk about books. She just doesn't want to interrupt her reading. I've heard her say, "I just want to keep reeeaaading!" under her breath on several occasions when I move the class from private reading time to partner reading time.

"How's it going, Eliza? I notice that you're reading another Poppleton book."

"I'm almost done with this one. It's my third one so far."

"How great you've found a series you like so much. That's what the big kids do, you know. You must really be into Poppleton if this is your third one."

"Yeah," Eliza says as she looks back at the text. I'm sure she's wishing that she could just "keep on reeeaaading."

"Tell me what you've been thinking about as you read this book," I say.

"Well, I'm reading it . . . and I don't know, I'm just reading," Eliza says.

"Eliza, I know you are such a strong reader of the words, but I want you to get really strong at thinking about the story, too. I want you to make sure you're having thoughts about the story as you read. Let me show you what I mean. Where are you in the book?"

Eliza points to the page. "Okay, let's read it together, and if we get a thought, we'll say it out loud, okay?" We each read the page silently, and I begin to whisper things like, "Poppleton seems to be getting tired of Cherry Sue," and "He just wants time to himself."

We get to the end of the page, and I ask Eliza what she had thought about. She shrugs. "Eliza, did you notice how when we read this part, it was like I was talking back to the story? I said, 'Poppleton seems to be getting tired of

Cherry Sue.' I was reacting to the story. As a reader, it's real important to react to the story, to kind of talk back to it. You might even say things out loud at first, like I did, until it becomes automatic in your head. Why don't you try it on this page; as you read, try to notice what you're thinking about as you read, and say it out loud, as I did. I'm going to sit here for a second to jot some notes, and I'm going to kind of listen in a little bit. Afterwards, I'll be here to ask about how you reacted to the story on this page. I'll want to know whether you tried the thinking work of talking back to the book. Go ahead now, and let me know when you're finished."

As Eliza reads, I move my chair away just a bit, and I jot down some notes. She looks up at me to indicate she is finished, and I ask, "So Eliza, how'd it go?"

"I talked back to this part."

"Oh, I didn't hear you. Tell me more."

"I said to myself that Cherry Sue must feel bad because Poppleton squirted her."

"Eliza, are you telling me you felt bad for Cherry Sue as you read this part?"

"Yep."

"So it was like you were talking back and saying, 'Poor Cherry Sue!' Eliza, that's exactly what it means to think about the story as you read. Great work. Keep it up. Listen for when your mind talks back, and remember you can even say your thoughts out loud a little bit, as I did. That helps you pay attention to them, especially when you're just beginning to do it."

It was hard for me to tell in this conference whether Eliza doesn't know how to do thinking work or if she just isn't able to notice and articulate when she does in fact think about the story. I decided to show her what it sounds like and looks like to think about the story. We did it together at first, and then I left her to try it on her own.

These assessment conferences with Natasha and Eliza were very helpful in guiding my planning. I knew I needed to do two things: show my students how it looks and sounds to think about a story, as I did with Eliza, and name a variety of things readers think about, as I did with Natasha. I also would have to continue to use my read-aloud time to model my thinking as I read.

After another couple of conferences with individual readers, I gathered the class in the meeting area for the teaching share time, even though we hadn't had partner reading time that day. I made the decision that today I wanted to spend more time working with and assessing individuals by conferring with a range of readers in the classroom. I knew that I could cheat a bit by integrating partner time into share time. To do this, I said, "Please bring the book you are reading to the meeting area, and sit beside your reading partner."

I began the share by saying, "I met with some readers today, and I learned what you are thinking about, and I learned that this thinking work can be tricky, so I'm going to help you. Right now, though, I want you to tell your partner about the thinking work you did today. You might show your partner a page where you did some thinking work and tell him or her what you were thinking about. Go ahead." I listened in on a few partnerships before I asked for their attention again.

"Can I tell you about Natasha? She was reading *Baby Bear Goes Fishing*, and she was thinking all along as she read. She wondered about what was going on, and she made a prediction about whether Baby Bear would catch a fish. Oh, Natasha, I forgot to check in. Did Baby Bear catch any fish?"

"Yup, he did, just like I told you," Natasha said.

"Your prediction was right! I guess he didn't run away to the circus as I predicted, huh?"

"Nope, Ms. Collins; that's a silly prediction," Natasha said.

"So, guys, I'm wondering if you're like Natasha because, as she reads, sometimes the voice in her head is a predicting voice. Sometimes the voice in her head says, 'I bet blah-blah-blah is going to happen next.' Making predictions like Natasha, well, that's just one of the things that careful readers can be thinking about as they read. We're going to spend the next couple of weeks getting really good at thinking as we read, and I bet that in two weeks, we'll have lots more to think about besides predictions."

For the next couple of weeks, we name for our students and demonstrate some of the different kinds of thinking that readers can do as they read to help them understand their books. Although there are infinite possibilities for what we could teach at this time, we need to prioritize and make choices about the kinds of thinking that we will spend whole-class time on during mini-lessons.

Besides deciding on which thinking strategies we'll focus on, we need to consider how we'll teach them. One of the things we can do to figure out how we might teach our students about the thinking work readers do as they read is to pay close attention to our own thinking as we read.

I was in a study group where we did just that. Our focus was developing strategies for teaching struggling readers, so Gaby Layden and Donna Santman, our group leaders, had us read a challenging text in order to experience as readers what it feels like to struggle, and to think about as teachers how we might teach our children the strategies we used to overcome our struggles.

While we read *Paradise*, by Toni Morrison, our job was to take notice of the thinking work we did that helped us understand the story and pay attention to places that presented difficulty. At our biweekly meetings we would share our observations about our own thinking and consider the teaching implications for our classrooms.

We found that as we read, we most frequently predicted, inferred, created mental images, questioned, wondered, synthesized, and talked about the book. The challenging thing about teaching these kinds of thinking, we realized, is that they don't happen in isolation. In order to predict, we often need to infer what the character is really saying or doing in a particular scene. In order to synthesize the events and undercurrents in a chapter, we need a mental image of what is going on. In other words, we must be versatile and able to do different kinds of thinking simultaneously.

The implication for our teaching is that we need to model how readers orchestrate a variety of thinking strategies and demonstrate what each one sounds like and looks like. We can use read-aloud with accountable talk as a time to show how thinking strategies work simultaneously. Then, in independent reading, before teaching how to integrate them, we can take some time to slow down and show our students what each strategy looks like and sounds like, and what it means to use it.

In many ways this parallels our work in the print strategies unit of study. We begin that unit by focusing on a variety of strategies, one by one, and then we move our readers toward using the strategies simultaneously and with flexibility as they integrate the sources of information so that they can read with accuracy, fluency, and comprehension.

When making decisions about what strategies to teach during mini-lessons in this bend in the road, I consider that I need to use the whole-class time (mini-lessons) wisely. For my strongest readers, the mini-lessons might provide an opportunity for maintenance learning, although for the rest of the class, the lessons will be for acquisition learning.

I often choose what thinking work to teach in whole-class lessons from things that my students have been exposed to already during interactive read-aloud or shared reading. When I revisit the strategies we've already learned in read-aloud or shared reading during mini-lessons to support my students' independent reading, I know that most children will be successful because they already have some level of familiarity with the work. For example, because we worked so much on visualization and creating mental images as I read aloud *Pigs Might Fly,* I can refer to those experiences in mini-lessons, by saying, "Remember when we read *Pigs Might Fly,* and there was the part about the flood that was so hard for us to imagine? Remember how I slowed down the reading so we could really try to make a picture in our minds? Well, that's what I'm going to teach you to do today with your own books." The challenge for my students will be to do this thinking independently as they read their own books rather than depending on me to facilitate it, as I do during interactive read-aloud.

I find solace in reminding myself that I can use individual conferences and small-group work to teach children the thinking strategies that fit particularly well with who they are as readers. So, if my more struggling children continue to be challenged by making pictures in their minds as they read, I can spend time in conferences and small-group work teaching them to do just that. My stronger readers might need to do more sophisticated inferring work because of the kinds of texts they are reading, so I can meet with them in reading conferences or strategy lessons, for example, to teach them how to do this, whether or not the rest of the class needs this work.

It can be difficult to sift through all the possibilities for our teaching in order to prioritize and decide upon what to teach our students. To make this easier, I take a deep breath and realize that I still have more of the year ahead of me to get to the things that I'm not able to cover at this time. So, although I know that determining importance is, well, important to teach young children, I am comforted when I realize that I can teach them to do that work in our upcoming nonfiction study. I also use read-aloud and shared reading to model the kinds of thinking that we don't deal with in these whole-class lessons. And then I find comfort in knowing that they will have second grade and beyond to continue to strengthen their thinking work as they read. My hope is to lay a solid foundation early in my students' reading lives that they can continue to build on in the grades and years that follow.

In this bend in the road, I typically teach my students how readers react, envision, predict, and make connections as they read because these things will help them to understand their stories. Other strategies, such as inferring, synthesizing text and determining importance, are discussed in Chapter 7. Of course, in your classroom, you might choose to prioritize differently and teach other thinking strategies, so I hope that the plan for my teaching offers support for you as you plan yours.

❖ *Readers react and talk back to the text.* I want my readers to have reactions to the characters and their stories—including wondering about or questioning the text—and to talk back to their books as they read.

I'll share two stories to clarify what I mean by "talk back to their books." When I lived in upper Manhattan, I used to regularly attend services at the Riverside Church. There were many reasons that I liked to go—stunning architecture, friendly congregation, moving music, inspiring services, and . . . the church lady. I would look for her and try to sit as close to her as possible. I liked how the church lady would talk back to the sermon as the Reverend Forbes preached. When I say "talk back," I don't mean disrespectful talk. No, the church lady would call out, "Amen," and "Tell it to us!" and "Yes, sir!" and "True that!" and other things. You see, as she listened on Sundays, she had thoughts and reactions to the sermon, and she chose to voice them.

Similar to the church lady are people at the movies who shout at the screen in the middle of a film. They call out, "Don't go down in the basement, fool!" when the mild-mannered protagonist investigates a strange noise, or "You didn't just say that!" when the character says something unexpected, or "hisss" when the bad guys enter the scene. I know some people find this kind of talking out during a movie (or a church service) annoying, but I enjoy it because it energizes my experience in some way.

In any case, whether or not one likes these forms of talking back, the church lady and the people who shout at the movies are doing the kind of work I want my students to do as they read. I want them to read actively and have reactions to the story and to the characters in their books. In class, of course, I would prefer that my students refrain from voicing their thoughts out loud when they talk back to their books. Instead, I want them to have an internal dialogue as they read. And I teach them to hold on to their thoughts by jotting them on sticky notes.

I was working in Liz Fuchs's first-grade classroom at P.S. 29 in College Point, Queens, and we had a reading conference with a student who needed to be a more active thinker as she read. We sat alongside Fiona, one of the two strongest readers in her class. Liz said that Fiona could decode most anything. Although she read through her books quickly, Fiona appeared to understand what she read, at least at a plot level, because she could accurately retell the action of the story.

Liz was concerned that Fiona wasn't really digging into her stories. She seemed to be skimming the surface of the text as she quickly moved from one book to another. Another worry was that as Fiona begins to read more complex texts with multiple story lines or subtleties, she would already be habituated to this way of reading, only demanding a surface level of understanding. Liz wanted to have a series of reading conferences with Fiona to teach her to slow down and pay attention to her thoughts as she reads so that she would have a stronger hold on (and investment in) her books.

In our conference Fiona was just beginning to read *Nate the Great and the Phony Clue*. We asked her to reread the first couple of pages aloud, which she did with accuracy, fluency, and phrasing, although we noted that she didn't read with much expression.

After the first couple of pages, I stopped her. "Fiona," I said, "sometimes right after I start a book, I like to stop after a few pages just to check in with myself to make sure that I'm really getting it. I ask myself, 'What am I thinking about so far?' I want you to do that, too. What have you been thinking so far as you read these first few pages?" Fiona shrugged and looked back at the text, ready to turn to the next page. Liz and I waited a bit until Fiona broke the silence.

"Well, Nate is a detective and he's going to solve a case," Fiona said. This was certainly true, but again, Fiona was reading as if she were holding on to the story by her fingertips. We wanted to teach her to dig in more as she reads.

"Fiona, as I listened to you read these first pages, I had a voice in my head that kind of talked back to the story. The author was telling us a lot about Nate in this first part, so I was really thinking about him. Let me show you what I mean. In this first part, where Nate talks about the things he ate for breakfast and keeps saying pancakes, the voice in my head said, 'That's kind of funny how Nate keeps saying pancakes. He must really love pancakes.' Don't you think so, too, Fiona? Then on this page, when you read how Nate wants to solve cases involving jewels and other stuff, I thought he must be a serious kid detective. Careful readers read the words like you do, but we also make sure that our minds are always thinking about what's going on in the story. When you think about the story as you read, it's like you have a voice in your head that kind of talks back to it, as mine did. I'm going to give you a chance to practice that."

I read the next couple of pages and told Fiona to stop me if the voice in her head was talking back to the book. I just wanted her to see what it felt like when that happened. As I read, she stopped me once to tell me about something she was thinking as she listened. I complimented her and said that even when she's reading herself, her mind needs to read the words and have thoughts about the story.

We want our students to be wide awake when they read so that they are actively thinking about much more than the words. When there's a funny part, we want our students to laugh out loud, or at least think, "Hey, that's funny how she did that." When there is an unexpected plot twist or character action, we hope our children will think, "Wow, I didn't expect that to happen." When the author describes a scene or character, we want readers to think, "Hey, that reminds me of my grandma's house, all warm and good-smelling," or "Junie B. Jones sounds like a brat right now!"

For young readers, there are times when it's important to bring a behavior, skill, or strategy up to the surface so that they can pay attention to what it feels like to do it or use it. During part of the unit of study, we help our students become aware of the voice in their heads that talks back to the story as they read. We ask them to put sticky notes on the pages when they hear the voice in their heads say something to the story.

During this part of the unit of study, I've done the following mini-lessons about the kinds of thoughts or reactions readers have as they read.

- *Readers notice when they get a feeling as they read.* We can teach readers to pay attention to when they're getting a feeling as they read, such as, "Hey that's funny! What a silly thing to do!" or "Henry must feel lonely now. I feel sad for him."

- *Readers make predictions as they read.* I teach readers to notice when they are predicting as they think, "Why'd she do that?" or "I didn't expect this to happen!" or "Now she's in trouble. The teacher's going to find out!"

- *Readers try to picture what's going on in the story.* When readers envision or picture the text as they read, they think things like, "That sounds kind of like our lunch room, all noisy and smelly. That must be why she never eats her lunch," or "I bet she looks mad right now."

- *Readers pay attention to when they are confused.* In this lesson I teach students that it's really important to notice when something is confusing as they read. The mind cues for this might be, "Wait a second . . . I'm not sure what just happened," or "What did she mean by that?"

- *Readers question things that happen or things that characters do.* When readers are thinking about their stories, sometimes they get questions in their minds to clarify meaning, to predict what's ahead, to figure out the author's point of view, or to figure out content (Keene and Zimmermann 1997): "How does she think she's going to win the spelling bee if she never does her homework?" or "Why would the kids be so mean to the new boy?" or "I wonder why the author wrote this story."

- *Answers to readers' questions come from the book or from readers themselves.* In this lesson (or series of lessons) we teach students that careful readers sometimes have questions about the story as they read. Some questions can be answered by reading on in the text, but others are not answered in the book. The latter require a reader to use what she knows already, to use what she's thinking about the story, or to use other texts in order to determine an answer. Teachers can model ways readers deal with both kinds of questions, the ones that can be answered from the text and the ones that cannot.

After these lessons I expect to see the children reading and putting sticky notes on pages where they've had a thought about the story. At first, I just have them mark the page with the sticky note, but soon I show them how to jot quickly on the sticky note to remember their thoughts so that they can easily share them with their reading partners.

Some teachers show children how to put symbols on their sticky notes to represent their thinking. For example, they put a happy face on funny parts, a question mark when they have a question or are confused, an exclamation point when they're surprised, and so on. Other teachers begin right away by teaching children how to jot down notes. The thing to avoid is inviting children to spend more time writing on sticky notes than they spend reading. As I've said before, any decision teachers make about what to teach in the classroom depends on the needs and strengths of the particular students.

Envisioning

Eavesdropping in a café one day, I overhead two women talking about a Club Med vacation that one of them, the tan one, had just taken. As she described the scenery and action, I couldn't help but picture palm trees, white-sand beaches, volleyball games, Brian from Michigan and his six-pack abs, and the other "hot" guys she'd met. Though I'd never been on a Club Med vacation in Mexico, I could envision it from her enthusiastic tale. Being able to envision, or create a mental image, is one of the fundamental ways we help ourselves understand something. So, whether we're engaged in a conversation (or eavesdropping on one) or reading a text, important mind work we do involves making a picture (or a movie) in our minds of what we're hearing or reading.

Envisioning: Readers Make a Picture in Their Minds
Words we can use
> "I'm imagining that . . ."
> "I can picture how . . . sounds, feels, looks, tastes."

Picturing . . .
> . . . helps us be in the story.
> . . . makes the characters and the events come alive.
> . . . clears up confusing parts.

When I read aloud *Pigs Might Fly* to my first graders, they loved the story and its dramatic plot and vivid characters. However, it was a lot of work to read aloud. There were long descriptive passages about the setting, a farm that got flooded, and I was certain that many of my students hadn't seen a farm and couldn't imagine a flood. I stopped often as I read to help them make pictures in their minds of what was happening in the story. When I had finished reading a particularly dense description, I would say, "You know, I didn't quite get that part. I'm going to read it again really slowly, and I'm going to try to get a picture in my mind. I want you to try it, too. Try to picture the scene, make it like a movie in your mind." To offer more support,

I used illustrations of farms and pig sties from other books, and I made enlarged copies of the little illustrations from the book itself. As I read the chapters, we would stop at times to take a close look at the enlarged illustrations together.

An essential thing to teach is that making a picture in your mind as you read is not like watching television with the volume turned down. When careful readers picture the story, they do more than visualize. They hear the characters' voices and tones in their dialogue, they smell, taste, and feel the setting when appropriate, and they experience the mood of the text (Keene and Zimmermann 1997).

One way we can begin to teach children to visualize is to reread a short text to them that they know really well. In my own class I've used *Mrs. Wishy-Washy* to help my students understand what it means to make a picture in their minds. We look back over the pages and think about how Mrs. Wishy-Washy sounds when she speaks, both her voice and her tone, and we apply our senses to think about how the setting sounds, smells, and feels.

Some mini-lessons I have done to support my children as they envision the scenes from their texts are the following.

❁ *Readers picture the story in their minds as they read.* In this lesson I suggest that reading a book is like watching a movie of the story. Readers need to have a pretend movie screen in their heads so they can watch the story.

❁ *Readers don't only see the story in their minds, but they also hear it, smell it, taste it, and feel it.* In this lesson I remind children to use their senses as they read. If the setting is a classroom, they can imagine what it might sound like, for example. When the characters go to the cafeteria, careful readers can practically smell it as they read.

❁ *Readers envision the characters, settings, and actions in the story.* This lesson works for children who are reading texts with relatively dense descriptive passages. I teach them how to slow down and picture what the author wants the reader to see.

❁ *Readers envision "between the pictures" scenes.* For this lesson, I use a familiar text, such as a Big Book we've read several times, to help children understand that they can imagine the behind-the-scenes things that are going on. For example, in *Birthdays,* each page shows a child opening up a present, but I help my students consider and picture what is going on around that page.

Many children may still be reading books that have comprehensive illustrations that support the text, so they do not need to create their own mental images of the story in the same way that a chapter book reader needs to do. Children who are reading these early books with high picture support can still use mental imagery and visualization to imagine how characters sound when they say things and to picture the action that might happen between pictures.

Also, the illustrations in these texts often just provide snapshots of the text, so children might need support in learning how to put the pictures together to make a whole story.

Predicting

We constantly make predictions, both in life and in reading. Predictions keep us safe. If we are at an intersection and we see a car speeding toward it, we might predict that it won't be able to slow down in time, so we'd better not cross the road. Predictions keep us sane. Every morning when we arrive at school, we can loosely predict which students will be in our class. We know we will see most or all of the twenty-five first graders who were there yesterday. We don't expect to see a roomful of college sophomores squeezed into our little tables and chairs waiting for a lecture on organic chemistry.

As we read, we make predictions, too. Predicting begins at the word level. If we read a line that says, "My favorite sandwich is peanut butter and . . . ," we fully expect the next word to be *jelly* rather than *jumping* or *money*. If the line actually read, "My favorite sandwich is peanut butter and beef," we'd be surprised because it wasn't as we predicted. When this happens, we have to reset our thinking to visualize a peanut butter and beef sandwich or reread to make sure we got the word right.

We also predict at the sentence level. For example, if a text says, "So many surprising things happened on that date," we would expect the next few sentences to detail the surprises rather than, say, provide information about how to operate an electronic toothbrush. If the passage did indeed continue with information on operating an electronic toothbrush, proficient readers would most likely reread to make sure they didn't miss or misunderstand something.

The kinds of predictions most people associate with reading are plot predictions. As we read, we might think, "Oh, I bet she's going to end up losing this job, too," as the main character, who has a sketchy employment history, calls in sick on the second day at her new job. If we listen to ourselves predict, we find that many of our predictions are subtle and short-term. We don't spend as much time trying to figure out the ending as we do predicting what might happen next, and next, and next.

At the plot level, careful readers make predictions that are based on their knowledge of how books and the particular genre tend to go, their sense of what's possible and probable within the world of a text, and their life experiences. For proficient readers, these predictions happen so quickly and so automatically that often the only time we realize we have predicted is when we're shaken up by something unexpected that happens in the text, which forces us to revise our thinking.

Recently, I had an unexpected chance to think about characteristics of good predicting that we could teach our young readers. I was working with a second-grade teacher to help her improve her students' accountable talk. Over a few weeks, she had been reading aloud books from the *Junie B. Jones* series to her class. She told me that while the children really loved Junie B. and laughed a lot, it had been very difficult to get any kind of conversation going that hadn't turned either into a retelling or a platform for personal connections. We decided that for the demonstration I would read from where she had left off in the current *Junie B. Jones* book so that I could see for myself how the talk was going and so that we could see some ways to get it to change. This read-aloud demonstration ended up teaching me a lot about prediction.

In the chapter I read aloud, Junie B. was upset because a boy in her class was not going to invite her to his birthday party even though he was inviting all the other kids, and she said she was going to run away. Junie B.'s parents were in the hallway outside of her bedroom, huddled and whispering about how to handle this latest crisis. "Hmm," I said. "Something is definitely going on here. I wonder what's going to happen." I asked the class to turn and talk to their partners about what they thought would happen.

I moved around and listened in as the students talked. The variety of predictions was fascinating. One set of partners said that they thought Junie B. would run away to Disneyland, and they talked about how cool it would be to go there themselves. Another set of partners said Junie B. would get punished (and maybe spanked) by her parents for saying she was going to run away. Finally, instead of predicting what would happen next, there were some children who were making longer-term predictions about whether Junie B. would finally get an invitation or whether she'd crash the party.

I learned in this moment that not all predictions are created equally. The children who predicted that Junie B. would run away to Disneyland were taking Junie B.'s empty threat literally. They were not considering whether their prediction was realistic, or based on what they knew about the character of Junie B. or how *Junie B. Jones* books tend to go.

Also, I learned how personal connections affect our predictions. Perhaps the children who made predictions about the parents' reactions to Junie B.'s tantrum were using their own experiences as a guide. Of course, we can't remove personal connections from our reading, nor would we want to, but we can teach children how to make predictions that are based more on the text than on their own lives.

Once when I read aloud *Little Polar Bear Finds a Friend,* I was at the part where the little polar bear was floating on an iceberg. The illustration showed one of the polar bear's legs hanging over the side of the iceberg. Reina blurted out, "Oh no, he's going to get eaten by a shark!"

"No, he's not," Zoe said matter-of-factly. "That wouldn't happen in this book."

"Why not, Zoe?" I asked.

"Well, this isn't that kind of book. It's a nice book," she said.

"Yeah, it feels like a happy ending book. I can tell," added Marissa.

Reina's prediction wasn't ridiculous because it was based on knowledge she had gathered in life. According to movies and some news reports, sharks are attracted to dangling limbs, and they have been known to bite them. In this book, the polar bear was, in fact, dangling his leg, so he could, in the realm of possibilities, get eaten by a shark. However, Zoe was right to say that it isn't "that kind of book." Zoe discarded Reina's prediction when she considered the world the author was creating within this particular book as well as her knowledge of how children's books, in general, tend to go.

When we teach children to predict well, we need to show them how to use clues from the text. In reading, we accumulate a sense of story as we go along, and this is the raw material that we use to guide our predictions. Personal experiences and a sense of genre are certainly helpful, but we need to make sure that we're also considering the information supplied by the text itself.

Predicting: Readers Predict as They Read

Words we can use
>   "I think . . . is going to happen."
>   "I predict that . . ."
>   "I bet the character is going to . . ."

Predictions . . .
>   . . . help us get into the story.
>   . . . make sense with the story.
>   . . . can be right ("It came true as I said").
>   . . . can be wrong ("That's not what I thought would happen").

When I teach my students about the thinking work of prediction, these are some of the possibilities I consider for mini-lessons.

❧ *Readers stay involved in the story by predicting.* When we read and we predict things that will happen, it's like our minds are really tuned into the story. We can't make predictions if we're not thinking about what's going on.

❧ *Readers predict by making pictures in their minds.* In order to predict, it helps us to really picture what's going on and how the characters are acting. We have to be able to really picture our prediction, too.

❧ *Readers use what they know about the text to make good predictions.* When we predict, we need to consider what we know about the character, the setting, and the story itself to help our predictions be strong.

❧ *Readers use what they know about the kind of story and about life to make good predictions.* Readers think about the kind of story they are reading (silly, sad, funny) because that helps guide predictions. For example, in an ABC book, we can predict that the N page follows the M page. In *Horrible Harry* books, we can predict that Harry will tend to do silly things and make mistakes.

❧ *Readers know that not all predictions are correct or helpful.* When we predict, our predictions can be kind of unhelpful sometimes. We might get lost in thought and forget to follow the story closely. As well, our predictions may turn out to be incorrect. In that case, when our predictions don't work out, we have to let them go. If we hold on to incorrect predictions, it makes it hard to pay close attention to what is happening in the story.

Making Connections: "Hey, That Reminds Me of Something"

From early in their reading lives, many children already know that readers make connections with a text. We might teach them that books can remind us of something in our own lives (text to self), in other books (text to text), or in the world (text to world) (Keene and Zimmermann 1997). When students make connections with their texts, they can say, "This reminds me of . . ." and then go on to explain the connection.

Of course, I want my students to make connections with their texts because it's another way of being an active and careful reader. Also, making text connections is a steady companion to the other kinds of thinking work that careful readers do. When we predict that the little brother in the book will finally stand up to his big brother, the prediction might be based on what we know about being a little brother who has reached the end of his rope. When we infer that the character is shy, not aloof, when she doesn't talk to children in the neighborhood, the inference might be based on a similar character we have seen in a movie who acted that way. The connections we make as we read help to clear the path for other kinds of thinking as well.

Besides teaching children about different ways that readers can connect to their texts, I also want to extend or deepen their connections in a way that helps them to better understand the text. Instead of simply saying, "This reminds me of . . . ," my students can go further by adding, "and this connection helps me to understand [the story, character, part, page] because. . . ."

So, when a reader says aloud or thinks, "This reminds me of . . . ," I consider it to be only the start of a connection with the text. What I want this reader to do next is think about how her connection helps her to understand the book better.

I sat down for reading conference with Frances as she was reading *Henry and Mudge and the Careful Cousin*. She had just put a sticky note on a page to mark a place where she had a thought, and I asked her what she had been thinking about at that point. "I was thinking that Annie reminds me of my cousin, Ne Ne." Frances had written, "Like Ne Ne" on her note.

"Can you say more?" I asked.

"Well, Ne Ne never wants to get messy either when we play, and that's like Annie," said Frances. Now, at this point, Frances could do a few things:

- Get lost in thought about some of the times she has played with Ne Ne, and end up moving beyond the bounds of the story.
- Ignore the significance of the connection altogether and keep on reading.
- Consider how her connection might help her to understand the text better.

The fact that Frances caught herself thinking as she connected Annie with her cousin, Ne Ne, is a good start, and it's even better that the connection she made between the two was not simply, "They're both girls," or "They both wear dresses like that," or "I have a cousin that comes over, too." Frances was able to connect Ne Ne and Annie by something more significant and important: the fact that they don't like to get messy. I could take Frances's good start and move her connection to the next step. After all, the real power of making a connection as Frances did is in extending it in a way that answers the question, How does this connection help me to better understand the story, the character, my life?

So, I said to Frances, "Wow, you've got a cousin like Annie? You actually know someone who doesn't like to get messy when she plays? I bet that helps you understand the story better. When I make connections as you did, I always think, 'Hmm, how does that help me understand the story better?' I want you to try to do that thinking right now. How does your connection help you understand the story better?"

"Well, when we play, Ne Ne's always sayin', 'Don't mess up my clothes 'cause my mom's gonna get mad.' It's not fun sometimes 'cause she's always saying that. It bugs me sometimes."

"So, Frances, let's use your thinking to think more about the story. If Annie is like Ne Ne, how do you think Henry must feel when he's playing with Annie? Maybe he feels like you do. I bet you can imagine how he might feel."

"Henry is probably tired of her bein' so worried about getting messed up. I bet he's not having a lot of fun with Annie."

"Frances, you're doing good thinking as you read. I love how you made a connection and then thought, 'How does this help me understand the story better?' That was powerful because now you can understand Henry's feelings. Keep on reading, and you might just keep on noticing ways that Henry and Annie are like you and Ne Ne, and that's going to help you understand the whole story better."

Making Connections: Readers Make Connections as They Read
Words we can use
   "This reminds me of . . . because . . ."
   "This is like [another book] because . . ."
   "This makes me think of . . . because . . ."
Making connections . . .
   . . . helps us stay in the story.
   . . . helps us understand the story.
   . . . helps us understand the characters.
   . . . helps us understand the world in the book.

Some mini-lessons I have taught to help children make connections that deepen their understanding of a story are the following.

❖ *Readers notice when books remind them of something.* In this lesson we can teach children to notice when they think, "That reminds me of . . . ," or "This makes me think of. . . ."

❖ *Readers explain their connections.* I teach students that when we are reminded of something as we read, it's important to think beyond the connection. After saying, "This reminds me of my dog," add "because my dog was such a frisky puppy, too. It was a lot of work to take care of him, so I think that the dog in this book must be a lot of work, too." I consider this to be the most important element of making connections as we read. I want readers to use connections to help them understand their books better. I teach children to do this by asking them to add, "My connection helps me understand the book or the character better because. . . ."

❖ *Readers make connections to understand the characters and the stories better.* When characters remind us of someone, we can think about the character and the person she reminds us of to try to learn more about the character. For example, I might make a connection to Noisy Nora and say, "Wow, she reminds me of my little niece. When her baby brother was born, boy, did she get crazy! She and Noisy Nora must feel the same way about losing their parents' total attention."

❖ *Readers stay focused on the story, not the connection.* In this lesson I teach students how connections can sometimes take our minds right out of a story. I usually give an example of a connection and then go on to talk more about it. I contrast this example by showing students what it's like when I make a connection but don't let it take me far away from the book.

Strategies for Checking Comprehension

All year long, we make checking for comprehension and monitoring for meaning constant companions to any reading skill or strategy that we're teaching. So, during the print strategies unit of study, when we're doing a shared reading lesson, the focus might be on reading across the word, but if the children make a nonsense guess, we're apt to say, "Does that make sense here?" During interactive read-aloud, we take time after each chapter to stop and think about what happened in order to help students accumulate the story across the pages. And during individual reading conferences, we check with our children to see that they're not only decoding the text but comprehending it as well. In all these examples, the teacher has supported and facilitated comprehension, but it's at this point in the unit of study that we teach children to take more ownership and hold themselves accountable for comprehension so that they are monitoring for meaning with or without us.

The tricky part about teaching children to check for comprehension as they read is that often when they read independently our youngest readers aren't even aware that they're experiencing confusion, that their comprehension has broken down, or that it is missing altogether.

The first thing we need to do is raise awareness about comprehension. We need to make sure our children realize the importance of understanding when they read independently. A great many of our youngest readers need to be reminded, time and again, that reading requires much more than just knowing the words. Although we may have emphasized this during read-aloud, shared reading, and many of our mini-lessons for reading workshop, in this part of the unit of study we spend a couple of days or so making a big deal out of the importance of understanding. Then we need to teach our students how to monitor their reading so that they are aware of when they are confused or not understanding parts in their books. Finally, we teach them strategies they can use to clear up confusion and to improve their comprehension when they are reading independently.

The Importance of Understanding

To begin, I take a little time to emphasize the importance of understanding and to teach children to be proactive about their own comprehension. Although it seems to be an obvious point to make—that it's important for readers to understand what they are reading—it's still worth taking time to make sure that each child realizes that a successful reading experience is more than just decoding the words; it's about understanding the story.

Once, when I was living in Japan, I had some friends over to watch the newest drama on television. These dramas were a cross between a mini-series and a nighttime soap opera, and this particular one was very popular. English subtitles were not available, but the action on the screen, the melodramatic dialogue, and my very basic skill in Japanese combined nicely to help me understand what was going on as I watched the show.

In this episode the two main characters, who were attractive co-workers in an otherwise drab office setting, had been exchanging looks during a staff meeting. Then, after the meeting ended, the two of them passed each other in the corridor. The man turned toward the woman and said, "Shall we have coffee in the morning?" The woman smiled and averted her gaze as she walked away. At that point, there was a commercial break.

I understood this scene completely—or so I thought. My Japanese friends were expressing shock and surprise; they said things in Japanese to the effect of "I can't believe it!" and "Uh-oh!"

"What's the problem?" I asked. "They clearly have an interest in each other. So what if they have a coffee date?" I thought it seemed like an innocent enough way to begin what I expected to become a torrid affair.

My friends laughed and explained to me the real meaning of "Shall we have coffee in the morning?" When taken literally, it is a straightforward question, but in this case the man was subtly asking the woman to spend the night with him. "Shall we have coffee in the morning?" is actually the Japanese equivalent of "Your place or mine?" Who knew? If it hadn't been for my friends' explanation, I would have thought I had understood the interaction perfectly.

I share this story because I think many children experience this same kind of surface-level understanding as they read, and they don't always realize when they don't comprehend. This happens often to young readers: they keep on reading although they aren't really catching the story.

First, our young readers don't have a vast and varied history of reading experience, so perhaps they haven't yet internalized a sense of what it feels like when they understand and when they don't. If we think about our own reading lives, it's most likely true that we developed this felt sense for comprehension over time. In other words, we're able to monitor our reading in such a way that we can tell when we're not quite understanding because we've had lots of experience with understanding. So, it's important that our students have lots of opportunities to read and reread their just-right books so that they acquire experience with what it feels like to understand. Then, when they don't understand, they will be more likely to notice it.

Another reason that I believe children may not realize that they don't understand as they read is that they're used to operating with a muted level of comprehension. When you think about it, children have lots of interactions in their daily lives in which they don't experience a high level of comprehension. Many of the most popular children's cartoons and movies have adult story lines and jokes that go right over youngsters' heads. Children may laugh at the jokes and one-liners right along with the grown-ups or the built-in laugh tracks even though they don't quite understand the real meaning of the words uttered by Shrek, Buzz Lightyear, Nemo, or any other beloved characters.

What we have to do, then, is help children desire and fight for comprehension as they read, to make them strive to really get the story. A mini-lesson I've done to start this part of the unit of study is the following.

Mini-lesson

Connection

Readers, you've all gotten so good at reading the words in your books and at having thoughts as you read. Those are two very important jobs for any reader. But you have another important job to do, and that job is to make sure you understand what you are reading. After all, if you don't understand the story, it is like you never read it in the first place. Today, I want to teach you the difference between getting only the words and getting both the words and the story so that you can do your job of making sure you really understand what you're reading.

Teaching point and demonstration

Watch me as I read this passage. Notice that I get the words. But watch and see if I'm able to understand what I read.

I use a difficult text to demonstrate this teaching point. I read along fine and decode the words, but when I'm finished I look confused.

Hmm, I was able to read all those words, but I'm not really sure what they were about. Thumbs up if you think I did my job as a reader. Oh, I'm glad I don't see any thumbs up. I did not do my job as a reader. Although I could read the words, I didn't quite understand the story. That means that this text was too hard for me, or it means that I have to do some extra work to figure it out.

Now listen to me as I read this. Watch and look for signs that I understand what I've read.

I choose a simple text and my reading voice is smooth and confident.

Oh, that felt like a real read. I understood what was going on the whole time. I could picture it in my mind. I got the words, and I got the story. Did you guys notice? I didn't just read the words, but I laughed at the funny part, and I knew what was going on the whole time.

Active engagement

Now I want you to try it out. I'm going to give you and your partner a poem by Valerie Worth, and I want you to read it together and see if it's a real read for you. I want you to make sure that you're not just getting the words but that you're also getting the meaning.

I choose a Valerie Worth poem because often the words in her poems are relatively simple, but the images are abstract or metaphorical, so it can be hard to understand the meaning.

You know, as I listened in, you were getting the words in the poem, but when I asked you what it was about, you looked confused. What you'd have to do if you were reading this poem during reading time would be to work hard to figure out the meaning. Just reading the words is not the only thing you have to do as a reader.

Link to ongoing work

So, today, I want you to really pay attention to your reading, to be the kind of reader who tries hard to understand the book. I want you to do all your jobs as a reader: to figure out the words, to have thoughts as you read, and to understand what you're reading. Are you ready?

Sometimes, as I start this part of the unit of study, my students shop for several familiar books that are easy reads, along with a few other books at their independent reading level. I want them to have familiar or easy books to make sure they experience what it feels like to truly understand what they're reading.

In the next couple of lessons, we'll study what it feels like when readers truly understand their books. I teach mini-lessons on some of the following ideas.

❖ **When readers really understand, their reading voices sound smooth.** In this lesson I teach children that when they really understand, their voices will reflect the story by sounding like the characters' voices, by showing the tone of the story, by sounding smooth, like comfortable talking.

❖ **When readers really understand, they can picture the story in their minds.** In this lesson my students learn that when readers understand their books, they can picture what's going on.

❖ **When readers really understand, they can retell their stories easily.** In this lesson I teach my students that when we really understand something, it's easy to talk about it, and we can usually retell it pretty well.

✿ *When readers really understand, they just know.* This lesson opens up an inquiry actually. I suggest to my class that everyone has their own particular ways to know whether they understand something, so it's their job to pay attention to their own reading and the ways they know when they understand. During share time, the students will talk about what they've discovered about themselves. Some of the things students have realized are

- They get immersed in their books when they really understand.
- They can predict things more easily when they really understand.
- They have a good feeling in their minds.

Over these few days of inquiry about ways of knowing that we understand a text, we create a class chart.

Ways to Know if You Really Understand
- Your reading voice goes along with the story, characters, feelings.
- Your reading voice sounds smooth.
- You can picture the story in your mind.
- You can retell the story easily.
- Your mind feels good.
 How else do *you* know if you really understand?

Monitoring Comprehension: "Do I Catch Myself When I'm Confused?"

One night when I was in second grade, my parents had company for dinner. As we ate, I waited for the grown-ups to stop talking for a minute so I could tell them the joke I had heard that day on the school bus. I knew the grown-ups liked jokes, and I was really looking forward to telling them this one. After all, the boys on the bus had been laughing really hard, so I knew it must be funny.

I will spare you the details, but as you might imagine, I proceeded to tell a table of grown-ups a dirty joke. Although I understood all the words of the joke, I didn't get the meaning one bit. I had no idea that it was a joke meant for the back of the school bus and not for the dinner table. It only occurred to me that I didn't really get the joke because there was something strange about the grown-ups' reactions. They laughed, but I had a sense that they weren't laughing at the joke. I knew right then that there was something more to this joke that I didn't quite understand. Later that evening, my brother explained the joke to me, and I'll end this anecdote by simply saying that I was horrified that I told such a joke to grown-ups at dinner.

In this example of lack of comprehension, the reaction of the grown-ups cued me to the fact that I hadn't really understood the words that had just come out of my mouth. When children are reading, we want them to be sensitive, too, to cues that tell them when they are not understanding something. We want our students to pay attention to when their comprehension breaks down or when confusion arises so that they can use strategies to help them reclaim meaning as they read.

In these several lessons we teach children about some of the ways they can tell whether they are understanding something as they read.

<table>
<tr><td>

Mini-lesson

Connection

Teaching point and demonstration

Active engagement

</td><td>

Readers, you know what? I was reading with Kadeem yesterday. He did something so smart when he was reading along in Little Bear. *Everything was going smoothly, but all of a sudden Kadeem said, "Huh?" I looked at the book, but the word* huh *wasn't on the page. I asked Kadeem what was going on, and he said, "I don't get this part." When Kadeem was reading, he was working hard to be sure he understood the story, so when it got confusing, he said, "Huh?" to the book. He ended up going back and rereading a part of it, which helped him a lot. That was so smart. Today, I want to teach you how careful readers can say, "Huh?" when they don't understand something in their books.*

Watch me as I read this page from My Father's Dragon. *I'm going to read merrily along, but then I'm going to get to a confusing part.*

I read a short passage from an earlier chapter. I choose not to read aloud from a new chapter because I don't want my students to be distracted by the ongoing story. I get to a part, stop, and model being confused.

Huh? Wait a second. What's going on here? Did you guys hear how I was reading along and that I stopped when I got to something that was confusing? I was being a careful reader, that's for sure. Now, the next part of my job is to go back and fix the confusing part, and I think I will reread like Kadeem did. Anyway, I want you to be the kind of careful readers who catch yourselves when you're reading and say, "Huh?" when something is confusing or unclear.

I prepare a text with a tricky vocabulary word and read it aloud to the group.

Readers, we're going to do a little pretending here. I'm going to read this aloud and I want you to pretend that it's you reading it. If it gets confusing, I want you to say, "Huh?" Okay? Let's try it. As I read, pretend you're reading. I want you to be careful readers and listeners who notice if you get confused. I want to hear you guys say, "Huh?" if it gets confusing. Okay? [I read about people jostling for seats on a subway.] Okay, I heard lots of you saying, "Huh?" Turn and tell your neighbor what part was confusing for you. I'm going to listen in.

 Readers, here's what I heard you say. Some people said the word jostling *was really tricky and it made you say, "Huh?" That happens when we read sometimes. There might be tricky words that we really need to think about. I heard some of you say that you couldn't really picture what was going on in the last part, and it made you say, "Huh?" When you can't picture something*

</td></tr>
</table>

as you read, that can be a big clue that maybe you're not understanding the words. We'll be talking about ways to help yourselves when you get to tricky parts of your books. Just as we have strategies we can use to figure out the words, I'll teach you strategies you can use to help you figure out what's going on in the story.

I want you guys to always be the kind of careful readers to notice the times you don't understand something you're reading so that you can fix it for your-selves. Anytime you're reading, you might say, "Huh?" when you don't understand. Today, when I meet with readers, I'll be looking for people who catch themselves when they are having a hard time understanding something.

Over the next day or two, I teach my students to look for the clues that will let them know they are not understanding something. Some other mini-lessons I might teach are as follows.

* *Readers catch themselves when they are daydreaming.* In this lesson I high-light daydreaming because when children daydream, they may miss part of the story. I share that I daydream sometimes as I read, and that when I do, it makes it hard for me to really understand what I'm reading. I teach them how to catch themselves daydreaming and to say, "Okay, back to the book now."

* *Readers stop and think after reading chunks of text.* In this lesson, which I usually do for two or three days, I teach children how to use a "stop and think" sticky note to remind them to check after reading a chunk of text. I show them how to move the note forward every few pages to cue themselves to ask, "What just happened?" or "What's going on in the story?" If they have a hard time answering these questions, they need to reread.

* *Readers check their retellings.* This lesson connects and extends the previous one. I teach children that when they have trouble retelling, they may have missed something or not understood part of the story. If this happens, they need to go back and reread.

* *Readers check their book talks.* In this lesson I teach children that when they have a hard time talking about the book with a partner, they may have not understood the story. When we read and understand our books, we will have thoughts we can talk about. When we don't have any thoughts to talk about, we may not have understood the book enough.

Strategies to Clear Up Confusion

So far, we've taught students about the importance of understanding what they read, and to be aware when they don't understand. Now, we take some mini-lesson time to highlight the strategies our students can use to help them understand parts that are confusing or tricky.

"Readers," I say, as we begin this series of lessons, "you have been working really hard to make sure you understand what you read. So, now I want to teach you some of the things that careful readers do to figure out the tricky parts when they don't quite understand what they're reading. Remember when we were figuring out words? Remember how we imagined readers have a toolbox full of tools or strategies to help them figure out hard words? Well, for the next week or so, we're going to take out the toolbox again and add tools that readers use to help them understand what they're reading. We'll study how careful readers have strategies or tools to figure out the story when it gets tricky. Our toolboxes are going to get so full."

For the next week or so, in each mini-lesson, I teach a specific strategy that helps readers regain their comprehension when their texts get tricky or confusing. For whole-group teaching, I do the following mini-lessons.

❀ *Readers go back and reread to understand.* In this lesson I tell students that sometimes we read and don't really catch the story. When this happens, we can reread to help us understand what's going on. I model what it means to reread for comprehension.

❀ *Readers read back and read on to understand the tricky parts.* This lesson is worth repeating over a couple of days because students need to know ways of figuring out what tricky words or tricky parts mean. One way to do this is to read back a little and then read on to use the context in the story to help us.

❀ *Readers stop and make a picture in their minds to understand.* The students have already learned about using "stop and think" sticky notes to remind them to check their comprehension. I revisit this idea, focusing this time on how stopping and thinking can help us figure out tricky parts.

❀ *Readers read tricky parts aloud.* Sometimes it helps us to say words out loud and to make a picture in our minds as we're reading them.

❀ *Readers talk to a partner about tricky parts.* Partners can help us figure out the tricky parts. First, we give our partner the setup (background information), and then we see if they can help us understand the tricky parts. In my demonstration I do exactly that with a tricky part so that the students can be my helpers to figure it out.

❀ *Readers talk to someone who has read the book before.* In this lesson I suggest that if students know someone who has read the book before, they can check with that person if they get stuck on a tricky part.

❀ *Readers make sketches to understand.* This is a lesson that I would tend to do for small groups of children who are reading complex texts with lots of characters, changing settings, or long stretches of dialogue without obvious dialogue markers. I show them the kinds of quick sketches they can make on sticky notes to help them keep track of characters, such as character webs, character equations (Timmy = Jason's big brother), sketches of settings, or dialogue maps (picturing the conversation to help figure out who is speaking).

❖ *Readers use clues from the book to understand.* This topic might need a few different lessons, each one featuring a text clue and how readers can use it to better understand the text. I often do these lessons in small-group strategy lessons for children who are reading the kinds of books that have these particular clues. *Series books* often start the same way, and authors describe series characters' relationships and behaviors early in each book. The *blurb on the back cover* can provide fill-in information. *Chapter titles, captions, and illustrations* provide insight into particular chapters. Sometimes *character or setting maps* are included at the beginning of books.

Assessment

Throughout this unit of study I try to make sure my assessments offer information about my students' levels of comprehension in addition to their proficiency with print. Often, when I meet with a child for a reading conference, I ask the child to read aloud the page that she read just before I got there. I jot a quick, informal running record and note the child's fluency. After asking the child to reread the most recent part of the book, I have a comprehension conference. To do this, I focus my assessment on the following things.

Retelling

When I sit alongside a child for a reading conference, I can ask the child to do a retelling. Depending on where she is in the book, the retelling might include just a part of the text. I assess whether the child uses the characteristics of good retelling and the depth of her comprehension based on the retelling.

There are limitations in using retelling as a gauge to check the comprehension level of a reader. Some children are great at retelling although their understanding of the text may be limited. They can retell the major events in an expressive way, yet they might not truly understand the story. Other children might not be as strong at retelling for one reason or another, so their retelling doesn't quite represent the level of their understanding. This can be especially true for children who are English language learners or children who have difficulty expressing their ideas. Although retelling gives us some information about children's comprehension, we can't count on it to give us all the information we need.

Thinking

During a reading conference I might choose to assess a child's comprehension or engagement with the text by asking, "What have you been thinking about as you read this?" The child's response can provide a lot of information. I also ask children to share some of the places where they have put sticky notes so that I can get an idea of the kinds of thoughts they have as they read. If I notice that a child always seems to predict or make personal connections, I may remind her of another kind of thought that readers may have as they read.

During this type of assessment, as in the retelling assessment, I also ask the child to read aloud the part he has just read. Again, I want to do a running record to note accuracy and fluency. As the child rereads, I also note the reactions he has to the text. For example, if a funny thing happens, I want to see if the child reacts to it in some way. I listen to see if his reading voice reflects an understanding of the meaning of the text. For example, if the child is reading a sad part of a book, I listen to see if his voice reflects that mood or tone.

Celebrations

At the end of this unit of study, it's time to celebrate the progress of the readers in our classrooms. Throughout this study the children have learned that careful readers have thoughts as they read, monitor for understanding, and have great book talks about their books. Here are some suggestions for ways that teachers have celebrated this progress.

Our Lines of Thinking

For this celebration, children collect the sticky notes of thinking that they put in one of the books they read. The teacher gives everyone a sentence strip, and the children attach their sticky notes to the sentence strip. Then, each child analyzes his line of thinking to answer the question, What kind of thinker am I? If a child often makes personal connections as he reads, he would notice that by looking closely at the sticky notes. After children analyze their lines of thinking, some teachers have them write a few sentences about what they've discovered about themselves. These lines of thinking are shared with reading partners, and then they are put up someplace for the school community to read.

Create a Big Book

Some teachers have closed units of study by having the students create a Big Book together. For this unit of study, the children might create a Big Book about thinking strategies. In pairs, they create pages for the Big Book about what it means to them to be thinking readers. Students have also made how-to Big Books that teach people how to do something as readers. For this unit of study, children can put together a Big Book about how to be a thinking reader.

Discussion Groups

For this celebration, teachers organize children into groups of four or so. Each member of the group brings a book to the celebration and shares the kind of thinking he did while reading a text. The child might say, "I'm the kind of reader who has a lot of wonderings when I read. When I was reading this book, I was wondering so much." The child might then share some of the things he was wondering about as he read.

Of course, it's important to set a date for celebrations in advance. This gives the unit of study a deadline of sorts and helps to build anticipation. When a celebration requires that the students make something (Big Book pages or lines of thinking notes), it's important not to use independent reading time in order to get ready for the celebration. In my class we use choice time to get ready for the celebration rather than using the time children need for reading their own just-right books.

Finding Reading Mentors and Setting Up Reading Centers

The next unit of study, Readers Pursue Their Interests in Books and Other Texts, actually comprises several units of study. At this time of year, we teach children how to do the kinds of things that readers do in the larger world outside of school. We teach strategies for reading different genres, such as nonfiction and poetry; show how readers can become experts about authors; and teach about the importance of understanding the characters in books.

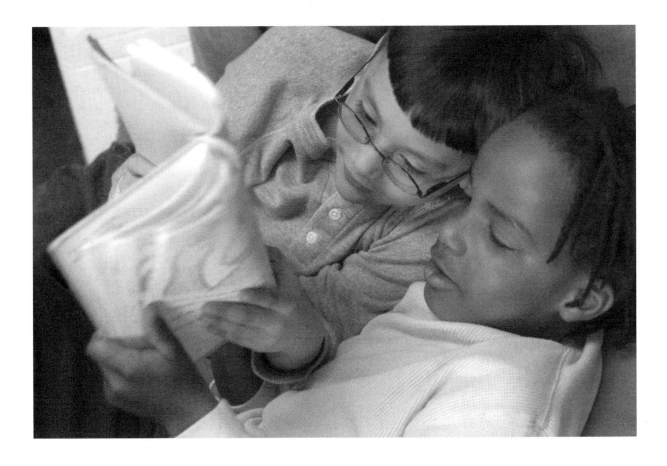

Within each of these units we teach children reading skills and strategies, such as determining importance, synthesizing text, and inferring.

Before launching this unit of study, we spend a week or so studying the reading lives of readers in the world around us and how to find reading mentors in our lives. Behind the scenes we gather the books we need for this study.

In the buffer days between the previous unit of study and this one, my class and I spend a little time finding reading mentors and researching the kinds of reading people do in their lives. During these buffer days the children read in the usual way during independent reading workshop. The mini-lessons for these few days might be discussions about reading lives. Then when I send them off to private reading time, the children read their just-right books as usual. This is followed by partner reading, time to read, think, and talk together about books. While my students read, I confer with and assess them in order to inform my instruction.

Looking for Reading Mentors and Examples of Reading

It's easy for children to be influenced by sports figures or pop culture celebrities because they are ubiquitous in the media and the marketplace, and their lives are thoroughly examined. Imagine how easy our job would be if reading became a pop culture phenomenon, if the release dates for new books (other than Harry Potter) garnered as much publicity and as many A-list celebrities as the premieres for Hollywood blockbusters, if authors had their own lines of high-priced sneakers or bookmarks. What if Sponge Bob lived a more readerly life? What if the paparazzi staked out bookstores to catch, say, J.Lo sitting on the floor against a bookcase lost in a romance novel? For better or worse, we teachers can't hold our breath waiting for stars and athletes to provide model examples of reading lives to entice children toward developing their own reading lives. Fortunately, we can look toward the people closest to us. There are interesting reading lives all around; we just have to find them.

Invite People in the School Community to Talk About Their Reading Lives

A teacher in one of my study groups asked his school principal to come in and speak to his first graders about her reading life. The principal brought in a bag containing all the reading material from her nightstand. She had a novel, a nonfiction book on leadership, two magazines, a cookbook, a catalog, and a pamphlet. She pulled each text out of the bag and told the kids why and how she was reading it. The principal explained that when she goes to bed, she loves to read the novel most of all, but if she's really tired, she'll often just skim through one of the magazines or catalogs before falling asleep. She held up the pamphlet and said it has information about a conference she wants to attend and that she has to read it really carefully and mail the application in soon. Finally, she held up the nonfiction book on leadership and said, almost in a whisper, that she only reads this book on the nights before she has a principals' meeting.

As the principal shared this glimpse into her reading life, the classroom teacher jotted notes for the class to refer to during their follow-up discussion. During the discussion, the children seemed to glean two big ideas about reading from their principal's talk. They learned that readers can juggle lots of different kinds of reading at the same time. Their teacher added to their thinking by suggesting that readers read things for lots of different reasons. He then shifted the conversation by asking, "Readers, how many of you read like our principal? How many of you have a few different things going at the same time? Tell us what that's like."

The power of these interviews is the power of suggestion. To hear the principal say that she reads lots of different kinds of texts may open up possibilities for the readers in the class to imagine themselves reading a variety of things. To learn that the principal has purposes for her reading may lead children to consider their own purposes for the texts in their lives.

Interview Family Members About Their Reading Lives

After a couple of guest speakers came to talk to my students, Anna, the little grassroots organizer of our class, asked if she could interview people in her family about their reading lives. I hadn't really thought about doing that, but it seemed like a great idea. I asked Anna and a few other children to think about how kids could interview people at home, and they came up with a plan. The interview would have five questions. Anna suggested that the class brainstorm questions besides the ones we asked our classroom guests, and then vote for the best questions. So we did. These were the top vote-getters:

1. What kinds of things do you usually read?
2. When and where do you usually read?
3. How does reading help your life?
4. What was your favorite book when you were a child?
5. What kind of advice about reading do you have for kids?
6. Interviewer's choice.

We decided to have an interviewer's choice option for the sixth question because the voting was so close, and we didn't want the interview to become too unwieldy.

Before the children took the interview form home, they practiced interviewing me as well as each other. It was very difficult for children to record their interviewee's responses during the interview, so we talked about ways of getting the information down on the page. I decided that it was okay to let the

---

Reading Interview

Interview someone at home about their reading life. You can tape-record your interview, have the person you're interviewing write his or her answers, or write the answers yourself.
If you tape-record, please bring in the tape. If the person you're interviewing writes the answers, have him or her read them to you.

Name of person you are interviewing ___dad___

1. **What kinds of things do you like to read?**

News papers & books about polar

2. **Where do you like to read? (Describe your most comfortable place.)**

His bed.

3. **When do you read in your life?**

In the morning & night.

4. **What is your favorite children's book?**

green eggs and ham.

5. **What was it like for you when you learned to read?**

It was a lot of fun.

6. **What advice do you have for young readers?**

Pick books you like.

If you have other questions to ask, please use the other side of this page.

---

family members write their own answers after they talked with their children. In the end, about one quarter of the students wrote the responses themselves, and the rest of the children had the adult interview subject do the writing. Alex tape-recorded his interview with his dad, and he brought in the tape for all of us to hear.

When the children brought their finished interviews to school, we had a whole-class talk about what they had learned from the grown-up readers. They talked to their reading partners about how they might use what they learned in their interviews to help them in their own reading lives.

Reading Detectives: Looking for Examples of Reading

Another way to show children that reading is an important activity for a lifetime is to look for examples of people reading in the world beyond school grounds. I decided to take my class on a 25-minute walk around the neighborhood to see that people read even when they don't have a teacher telling them to do so. I prepared the students by telling them they would be reading detectives. I said that we were going outside to search for evidence of people reading in the world. But before we went outside, I had the children predict some of the reading activities they might see. I wanted to get them warmed up before we launched our investigation.

As we walked down the street, I started things off by calling out reading behaviors I saw. For example, I noticed a man in the laundromat reading the *Village Voice*, so I gathered my class to take a peek in the window. "Why do you think he's reading in there?" I wondered aloud.

"He's probably bored doing laundry, so he's reading," John said matter-of-factly.

"Maybe he has nothing else to do in there," added Sarah.

"He didn't bring a book with him so he has to read that," Herbert said.

"Hmm, I wonder," I said. "Let's keep going and find other people reading."

We walked around and noticed lots of reading. We saw a couple of people stopped near an intersection reading a stoop sale notice on a telephone pole, a woman sitting near the window of a coffeeshop reading a book, a young man reading a magazine at a newsstand, and so on. Each time we saw someone reading, we'd take a minute to ask, "Why is she reading now?" or "What do you think he's reading that for?"

When we returned to the classroom, we made a class chart listing the examples of reading we had seen on our walking trip. Our chart was open-ended, so for the next few days or so, the children would add sticky notes to it when they spied other examples of life reading.

I know that many teachers might not teach at a school where there is an action-packed neighborhood community right outside the door. In that case, children could act as reading detectives over the weekend and report back Monday about the kinds of reading they had spotted at home.

Using Reading Centers to Support Our Studies

During this unit of study I rely on a structure called reading centers rather than the usual form of reading partnerships to support the reading work my students will be doing. The reading centers I describe here resemble the literature circles or book clubs one might see in upper-grade classrooms rather than the literacy centers that teachers put in place so they can do guided reading in primary classrooms.

The first thing to emphasize about such reading centers is that they are *not* a place in the classroom. I won't be talking, for instance, about a listening center where children go to hear books on tape, or about a shared reading center where children go to work with pointers and the shared reading texts. Reading centers as I describe them here are not a place where children go to do a prescribed task. Instead, a reading center is simply children gathered around a set of books that are connected in some way. It might be best to think of reading centers as reading that is focused on a topic, an author, a genre, or a character.

In other words, in a cycle of reading centers, reading partners meet to read and talk about books that are collected around a topic, an author, a character, or some other kind of unifying theme. Unlike regular partner reading time, when ability-based partners meet to read and talk about their just-right books from their independent reading bins, reading center time is for partners to meet to read books from their reading center baskets. These books are connected in some way, and they may not all be precisely at the children's independent reading levels.

For example, one year during our cycle of nonfiction reading centers, Wyatt and Anna wanted to learn more about the human body, so they gathered four books on the human body from the nonfiction basket in our library and put them into a smaller basket, which they labeled Human Body Reading Center. Jonah and John were interested in outer space, so they found books on Venus and Mars as well as a couple of books on the solar system for their reading center basket, which they labeled Space Center. Jonah also brought in an issue of an astronomy magazine from home to put in their reading center basket.

Sometimes, especially for nonfiction centers, reading center partners are not ability-based. When Cassidy was interested in dogs and wanted to create a dog center, Jennifer was his partner, although they were two readers at different ends of the ability continuum. Jennifer had pleaded that she, too, was interested in learning more about dogs. Jessica, my co-teacher, and I decided that for the two-week cycle Jennifer would benefit from reading alongside a reader like Cassidy. Even though the texts would be quite difficult for her to read alone, she and Cassidy could still do some good reading work together. As it turned out, Jennifer was highly invested, Cassidy was happy to work with someone as interested in dogs as he, and the two of them worked well together.

Would we let two very different kinds of readers like Jennifer and Cassidy work together in a character reading center if, say, Cassidy wanted to study the character of Junie B. Jones? The answer is no. In a cycle of nonfiction reading centers, there is so much that readers like Jennifer can get from the pictures, illustrations, and diagrams, whereas in text-dense books like those in the *Junie B. Jones* series, Jennifer would be unable to engage effectively. It's important to add here that even during a cycle of reading centers, there is still daily private reading time when children read their own just-right books.

Throughout the course of a school year, I usually had about four or five cycles of reading centers, which would last from two to four weeks. During the

Partner Reading Arrangements

	Partner Reading—Usual	Partner Reading—Reading Centers
Partnerships	Always ability-based	Mostly ability-based but exceptions made, especially during nonfiction reading centers
Text levels	At or near independent reading level (just-right books)	May be above or below reading level, especially in nonfiction reading centers
Types of text	Wide variety of subjects or stories	One theme, genre, author, or character connects texts
Number of texts	Guided Reading Levels A–H usually 8–10 books per week for each partner; readers above H usually 1–5 books per week	Between 3 and 6 books on a theme; if two partnerships are in the same reading center, more titles or double copies of book
Partner work	Read either simultaneously or independently the same text and talk about it	Read and talk about any or all books on a theme; have a project or line of thinking
Schedule	Every day after private reading time	One-to-three-week cycles, four times per week

time when my class was engaged in a cycle of reading centers, our independent reading workshop would change a bit. During a reading center cycle, my children read their just-right books during private reading time as usual, but during partner time they would meet with their reading center partners to read from the center baskets that they had put together. Usually, reading partners read and talk about the just-right books they've got in their book bins. This change is slight, but it's important. The table contrasts partner reading as it's usually done throughout the year and as it's done during reading center cycles.

Another difference between regular partner reading time and reading center time is in the configuration of the independent reading workshop. During a reading center cycle, I begin the workshop with a mini-lesson that teaches toward reading centers and then send the children off to read and talk with their center partners about the books in their reading center baskets. After a while, I pull my class together for the teaching share time, which will support my students' work in their reading centers. Then I send the class off again for private reading time, so that they will have the time they need to read their own just-right books. During private reading time I confer and meet with small groups as usual.

Supporting Students' Conversations About Books During Reading Centers
We encourage students to use text evidence to support their ideas.
   "Can you show me where?"
   "This is a big idea you guys are having. You should mark the places in the book where you notice this happening."
   "I don't get what you mean. Can you show me where you noticed that?"

We name what students are doing to help their work become more purposeful.

"So you two are gathering information on ants."

"Oh, I see, you and your partner are comparing the grown-ups in these two Donald Crews books."

We scaffold great partner talks by teaching some tricks of conversation, such as asking your partner's opinion, adding on to what your partner said, disagreeing with civility, and so on.

"Ask your partner what she thinks about your theory. Say to her, 'What do you think about Tom Little wishing she was his girlfriend?'"

"Are you agreeing or disagreeing with that idea? Tell your partner what you think about it. You could say, 'I agree with you because . . .'"

We teach partners ways to plan together.

"Why don't you two get a couple of sticky notes and mark the page where you're going to stop so you'll remember to meet and talk at that point."

"So, now that you've marked all the sad parts, what's your plan for tomorrow?"

We teach students to think more deeply about their books.

"So, you noticed that some dinosaurs have long necks. What do you think about that?"

"What does that make you think?"

Another important point about reading centers is that it's not absolutely necessary to have reading centers every day throughout a cycle. I usually schedule reading centers four times a week. On the day off, instead of reading centers, I have private reading time first and then the usual partner reading time when they read and talk about just-right books.

Readers Pursue Their Interests in Books and Other Texts

Chapter 7

I WAS WORKING WITH NEW TEACHERS at a reading institute last summer, and after a few days one of them approached me during a break. "This may be a weird question," she said, "but I keep hearing about lifelong reading. Everyone's talking about helping children become lifelong readers, but what exactly does that mean? What does a lifelong reader look like? Is it about having several books on your nightstand at all times? Is it about being well read? Maybe this is a dumb question, but for some reason, I'm not quite getting what lifelong reading means, and I sure don't know how to teach it."

I thought her question was brilliant. When we talk to other teachers, to our students, or to their families, we often sprinkle jargon like "lifelong reading" into our conversations and assume that our meaning is understood. But, really, what do we mean? I was sure that this teacher's question was not hers alone, so I posed it to the rest of the group after the break. I asked everyone to take 5 minutes and write about what they thought it means to be a lifelong reader, and then we shared our thoughts.

The group came up with a wide range of ideas, and I listed them on an overhead transparency. Even though we didn't come up with a concise definition or even something everyone agreed upon, our discussion helped to clarify the term for many of the teachers.

When I went home that night, I looked back over the list, and I realized that we had only just begun a very important conversation. We need to do more than have a list in our minds of what it means to be a lifelong reader. We also need to think about ways to teach children how they, too, can join the club of lifelong readers. Just because our students are only five or six or seven years old, they are not too young to understand that reading is not just school work but life work. It's important, then, for independent reading workshop and our reading curriculum to provide opportunities for our children to try on the habits of lifelong readers.

One way we can help our students to understand what lifelong reading means is to collect stories from reading mentors. Unfortunately, it can be hard to find them. People's reading lives tend to be quiet, private, and virtually invisible to the outside world. We don't often talk about how we read as much as about what we read. Even when we meet in book clubs, we naturally talk about the book more than we talk about the habits, idiosyncrasies, or ambitions we have as readers. However, when we ask the right questions and listen closely, we can find stories and reading mentors all around us among our family, friends, and colleagues.

This morning my mother called. She was typing a paper for her sociology class. Her assignment was to read *Warriors Don't Cry: A Searing Memoir of the Battle to Integrate Little Rock's Central High,* by Melba Pattillo Beals, and to write a reaction paper. The book details the author's experience as one of a small group of students chosen to integrate Central High School in Little Rock, Arkansas, and the struggles that she, her family, and the community endured through the tumultuous time after the Supreme Court's landmark *Brown vs. Board of Education* decision.

My mother read her paper over the phone to me, and all of a sudden she paused. I thought she was doing a quick edit right then and there, but then I heard her take a deep breath before she began reading again. Her voice was just a little shaky.

"Mom, are you okay?" I asked.

"I'm okay," she said, obviously on the verge of tears. "I can't believe I'm starting to cry. It's just that this book was so amazing to me. I feel so different after reading it. I'm humbled by this girl's life, by her grandmother, their faith, their strength, everything," she said before blowing her nose. "I feel foolish crying like this, but this book was so powerful. I'm buying it for you kids. You just have to read it. Everyone should."

Our phone conversation ended up being mostly about her paper and how to put in page numbers without deleting her hard drive. What I really should have talked about with her during that phone call was her reading experience. I should have told my mother that it isn't foolish at all to be powerfully moved by a book. It isn't unbelievable that a book, a single book, can change your thinking or even change your life. As a teacher, this is something that I want my students to experience. I want them to be profoundly affected by books. Reading mentors are all around us.

I have a very good friend who is HIV-positive. He reads everything available to collect information on the latest medical breakthroughs and treatment options. He has friends with whom he exchanges books, articles, and on-line resources about HIV and AIDS. My friend compares and contrasts all of the information and sources so that he can make the right decisions for his life. My friend's health, his survival even, depends on the work he does as a reader. Reading mentors are all around us, if we listen closely.

They might even be one of our students. Cassidy, a boy in my class, rushed into our room one morning all breathless and reported to everyone within earshot that his parents had told him that he could finally get a dog. I asked him what kind of dog, being a huge dog fan myself, and he said, "I don't know, just something cute." Well, that was my opening, so I just had to tell him about Casey, my very old and very cute cocker spaniel.

I lent Cassidy some dog books, including my favorite one, which is kind of like a dog catalog with lots of information and photographs about different breeds. Each day Cassidy would take that book home and come in the next morning with new information he'd gathered about different kinds of dogs. He was making lists: dogs that shed vs. dogs that don't, dogs that are good with children vs. dogs that aren't, huge dogs vs. small dogs. He was getting to know the breeds so well that I overheard him telling his reading partner what kind of dog Mudge might be. "Look at him," Cassidy said, tapping an illustration of Mudge. "I mean, he's either a St. Bernard, they drool a lot, you know, or a Leonburger, because they're really big like Mudge."

After a week or so of research, Cassidy announced that he wanted to get a cocker spaniel. "Ms. Collins, what kind of cocker spaniel is your dog?" he asked. "Is she a King James? An English spaniel? A Brittany spaniel?"

"Good question. I'm not sure what kind she is," I said.

"You mean you don't know what kind of spaniel she is?" he asked, barely hiding his annoyance. Cassidy told me to bring in a picture of Casey so he could figure it out, but I kept forgetting. A few days later, he brought in three dog books with sticky notes poking out of them. He opened each one to the spaniel section.

"Okay, Ms. Collins. We can figure out what kind of dog you've got. Which one of these spaniels is like Casey?" he asked. He narrated as I looked at the pictures he had marked with sticky notes. "If Casey's ears are shaped like triangles, she's this kind," he said. "Is her tail clipped? If it is, then she's one of these." I looked carefully at the pictures. I pointed to the one that looked most like Casey. "Well, if you'd bring in a picture of her, we can find out for sure," he said.

Later that week, Cassidy announced to the class that his family had settled on a silky terrier. He returned my dog breed books, which still included his load of sticky notes. He continued to read dog books, but he changed his reading focus from dog breeds to dog care, in order to prepare for when his family brought home their silky terrier puppy. Even at seven years old, Cassidy knew that reading could help him make important decisions in his life.

My mother, my friend, and my student—three reading mentors doing very different things as readers. When we think of our own reading lives or ask someone we know well about theirs, we can easily gather examples of the ways reading can affect, inform, or enrich life. It's these stories we collect from the reading mentors all around us that can help us teach children about what it means to be lifelong readers, which is the work we strive to do during this unit of study.

This unit of study is one of the times of the year when we ask children to orchestrate all they know about reading—how to read words, how to make sense of and have ideas about stories, how to hold conversations about books, how to fit books and life together—in order to do the work that lifelong readers do. We ask them to read for purposes that extend beyond simply practicing and improving their reading skills. In this unit we are moving beyond how to read to explore why we read. We provide opportunities for our students to do the things readers do outside of school, such as reading for information, reading to become experts about something, reading to pursue interests, and reading to support the projects in their lives.

Planning for This Unit of Study

The unit of study Readers Pursue Their Interests actually comprises several separate studies. Each study can last from two to six weeks. The curricular decisions we make about what to study and how much time to allot for it depends, of course, on the needs and interests of our students and the standards to which we are held accountable. Over the years, I've tried many different kinds of studies during this time. In this chapter, I describe three of them in detail:

- Nonfiction study
- Favorite author study
- Favorite character study

I also suggest ideas for some others.

When I plan for these studies, one of my goals is to make the study resemble, in a first-grade way, the kinds of reading work that people might do in the world outside of school. So, for example, when I plan the nonfiction study, I imagine the purpose readers have, like my friend who is reading about HIV/AIDS or Cassidy, who was trying to figure out what kind of dog to get. When I plan the author study, I think about what happens when people fall in love with authors' books. When a reader becomes very attached to the main character in a book and begins to feel the character's joy or pain, what is that reading like, and how can I integrate it into the character study? I need to consider the work that readers do in the course of their lives. In order to do this, I begin all of these studies by considering a few questions:

- What are the reasons or purposes that adults have for reading? Why do adults read nonfiction, for example? What causes readers to get attached to or repelled by the characters in books? What makes us fall in love with the books of particular authors? When I can get a kind of behind-the-scenes view of reading motivations, I feel like I'm better able to increase my children's level of engagement and enthusiasm around the study.
- What are the actions or habits of adult readers when they are reading nonfiction? When a reader loves an author's books, how is her reading life affected? When a reader reads poetry, how is his reading similar to or different from when he's reading a novel or a newspaper?
- What are readers' skills, strategies, behaviors, habits? My goal in these units is not only to teach children to love an author's books, pay attention to a character, or read poetry, for example. I am a teacher of reading, so I need to teach my first graders the strategies and skills they need to successfully interact with the texts they are reading. When children read nonfiction, for example, one of the most essential things they need to be able to do is to synthesize information and determine importance. During a character study, it's critical that children infer. In a poetry study, one of the things I need to teach toward is fluency.

To answer these questions, I turn to the readers I know best, the reading mentors from whom I've collected stories over the years. I am convinced that our teaching gets better and more focused when we lay the reading work we ask children to do in school against the reading work people do in their lives. When we make this home-school connection, the necessary reading skills we teach in each of these studies will have more staying power and make more sense to children. What we teach children about reading will no longer be limited to the "things your teacher makes you do in school." Instead, what we teach in school about reading becomes what our readers might do as lifelong readers.

Reading Center Studies

The focus of a teachers' study group I took part in was to consider the ways we launch and teach the whole-class units of study that take place at this time of year. We were looking at how we could use reading centers as a structure to provide the opportunities for children to think and talk about their books. Throughout our work together, the other teachers and I tried many different kinds of whole-class studies in reading centers, from nonfiction to fairy tale studies, from ABC books to series books studies, from poetry to character studies.

As our study group reflected on the work we and our students had done in these whole-class studies, we came to realize that no matter what the study, there were many ways in which they were similar. Before I go into detail about the work we can do within some of these studies, I'd first like to share the things they seem to have in common.

The Students Become Experts

In all these whole-class studies the students were enthusiastic because they believed they would become experts in some way about something. In an author study I assured my students that they'd become experts about the author they chose to study and that they could use what they learned in class to become an expert on any other author they became interested in for the rest of their lives. When we were studying characters, the students believed they were becoming experts about say, Poppleton, and that they could use what they learned about studying characters to get to know any other character in their books. Becoming an expert about something is very powerful and motivating for students and teachers alike. One thing that teachers can do to support children's growing expertise is to notice and help them extend their thinking.

Bends in the Road

All the units seemed to follow the same general bends in the road. Although the particular work differs, there is a consistent rhythm or pattern from one unit to another.

Immersion

During the immersion phase, which happens right before we launch a cycle of reading centers, we expose children to the kinds of texts they will soon be working with in the unit of study. So, for example, in an author study, we may pick an author to focus on for a week during interactive read-aloud. During the book talks the teacher focuses the discussions on the author. For shared reading, the teacher might go back to some Joy Cowley books, for example, so children can begin to think about Joy Cowley as an author for study. In

Thinking to Notice and Support in Reading Centers

Children are doing this	When we hear them say things like this
Noticing overlapping information and/or discrepancies between books	Nonfiction Biography Centers (MLK Jr.): "All these books about Martin Luther King Jr. talk about how he loved to read when he was little." Nonfiction Biography Centers (MLK Jr.): "These two books tell that he died, but this one doesn't."
Accumulating information about a topic from different texts	Nonfiction Centers (Ants): "So far we've learned that ants have different kinds of jobs in their ant farms, like doctors, builders, and other stuff."
Paying attention to surprising information, new information, information that contradicts prior knowledge or beliefs	Reading Projects Centers (Reading a Series: M&M): "I used to think I wouldn't like M&M because it's about girls, but they're pretty funny." Nonfiction Centers (Cats): "This book says that you have to wash your hands every time you touch your cat. That's just not true!"
Paying attention to new wonderings, developing new ideas	Nonfiction Centers (Insects): "This is weird. Ants have queen ants and bees have queen bees but they don't have kings. We're wondering why insects don't have kings."
Connecting the text to their own experiences in ways that deepen their understanding of the text	Favorite Character Centers (Henry and Mudge): "I can really understand how Henry must have felt when Mudge was lost because when my cat was lost, we had to look all over, too. I was so sad, just like Henry."
Attending to characteristics of the book, genre, author	Reading Projects Centers (Friendship Study): "We noticed that all these books on friendship always have troubles. Then they work them out and become friends again."
Looking for evidence to support their ideas	Favorite Author Centers (Miriam Cohen): "We're looking for all the places where Miriam Cohen makes Anna Maria seem mean."
Discussing/disagreeing	Reading Project Centers (Books that are sad): "We're talking about the places where the books get sad." Favorite Character Centers (Fox): "I think Fox is faking being sick, but Julia thinks he's really sick and not being a faker."
Planning their work	Favorite Character Centers (Frog and Toad): "We're going to put sticky notes on all the pages that show Frog and Toad are opposites. Then tomorrow we're going to find places where they act alike." Reading Projects Centers (Fairy Tales: Little Red Riding Hood): "We're going to try to read these pages and sound just like we think the characters will sound."

addition to reading several books by the same author during read-aloud or shared reading, the teacher encourages children to think about authors' books they know and love. The immersion phase of the study involves mostly teacher-initiated exposure during read-aloud and shared reading to the work the children will soon be doing. In the immersion phase we tend not to teach mini-lessons in support of the unit during independent reading workshop. Instead, our mini-lessons for independent reading might revisit and remind students of print or comprehension strategies as needed. For work time, the children read their just-right books and meet with their reading partners to think and talk together as usual. Again, immersion often takes place outside of reading workshop, during read-aloud and shared reading especially.

Launching

In the launching phase the teacher begins to do mini-lessons in independent reading workshop about the unit of study. The children explore the kinds of texts that they will read during the unit in their partnerships. So, for an author study, the teacher does mini-lessons to teach children about ways readers think about the author as they read their just-right books. Then, for partner time, readers will talk to each other about what they are thinking about their authors. Throughout the launching week, the class creates baskets of books for specific authors because by the end of the week each partnership will choose an author to study during the next part of the unit.

Reading Center Cycle 1

Each partnership has chosen a reading center basket, which they will read and work from for a week or so. For an author study, children may be reading authors ranging from Joy Cowley to Ezra Jack Keats, from Cynthia Rylant to Donald Crews, from Arnold Lobel to Lois Ehlert. The teacher does mini-lessons that support the students' work in the unit of study and that help them become experts.

Reading Center Cycle 2

In the second cycle the children often pick a new reading center from which they'll work. Some of the mini-lessons during this second cycle may be repeated from the first cycle, especially if the concept was particularly difficult. From cycle to cycle, I tend to repeat lessons on the reading skills and strategies children need while also finding ways to deepen their work in the unit of study.

Reading Center Cycle 3 (Optional)

Many teachers decide to have a third cycle of reading centers; however, the work the students do becomes more sophisticated. During an author study, this cycle might mean that the center baskets are reshuffled. Instead of containing books by one author, the baskets might contain books by a few different authors that share a theme, such as Authors Who Write About Kids, Authors Who Write About Friendship, Authors Who Write Funny Books, Authors Who Write Sad Books, Authors Who Use a Lot of Detail, Authors Who Are Illustrators, Too, and so on. The work the children do in these centers is to compare and contrast the books and to develop theories about the topic and the authors.

Projects or Celebrations

At the end of a study the children have become experts about something new. Teachers have found that it is nice to end the studies with some sort of project or celebration that provides opportunities for the children to share their expertise in some way.

Mini-lessons During Reading Center Cycles

We found it helped if we used one of the reading centers to make our teaching points and if we pretended the students were our reading center partners. In other words, during an author study, I demonstrated my teaching point throughout a cycle of centers by using texts in the Eric Carle basket. I chose this basket for two reasons: my class was very familiar with Eric Carle already, so I didn't have to spend lots of time reading the texts; and two readers who needed extra support were in the Eric Carle reading center. During my mini-lessons we pretended that we were reading center partners who were becoming experts on Eric Carle. My teaching demonstrations from the Eric Carle basket enabled me to show my students exactly what they could do in their own reading centers.

Keeping Track of Thinking

When working in reading centers, partners build upon, add to, and revise their thinking from day to day. For most young children, however, carrying on a line of work or thinking about an idea across days can be very challenging. Teachers have found that as students work in reading centers for days (or sometimes weeks) at a time, it helps if they have a place, a file of sorts, to keep track of their work and their thinking.

Some teachers began giving partners note-taking sheets that were simply different kinds of open-ended graphic organizers. These sheets gave children a place to hold on to their thinking across days. Teachers would show children how to record information or ideas on their note-taking sheets during mini-lesson demonstrations. So, during a favorite character study, for example, teachers gave reading center partners a blank T-chart on which to record theories they were developing about their characters in the left-side column and evidence from the text that supported the theory in the right-side column. During the nonfiction study, partners used a web organizer to keep track of the new information they were collecting about their topics. After a while, children were able to initiate their own note-taking systems. During a favorite character study, Ryan and Hal asked me if they could have a blank sheet of paper because they wanted to make a web to keep track of the character traits they were learning about Poppleton, whereas Victoria and Talia decided to create their own Venn diagram to compare and contrast their friendship with that of Mandy and Mimi, the best friends in the M&M series.

Teachers gave each partnership a manila folder to keep in their center basket so they would have a place to file their research during the cycle of reading centers. These files made it easier for teachers to monitor the work that all the partnerships were doing. If we didn't have an opportunity to confer with a partnership for a couple of days, we could check their folders for an indication for how their work was going. Some examples of note-taking sheets are included in the appendix.

In the rest of the chapter I offer ideas for how teachers might conduct various units of study in their classroom. I detail the nonfiction study the most and use it as a basis for the ways you could teach the other studies.

Nonfiction Study

Each morning, when my children arrive in the classroom, they unpack their bags and then check the message I've left in the top left-hand corner of the chalkboard to find out their morning jobs. When they finish their morning jobs, which is usually not much more than a 5-minute task, they go to the classroom library and read anything until it is time to gather for our morning meeting.

Year after year, I've noticed that the most sought-after books during that informal reading are nonfiction texts. Each day, one by one, Hans, Dito, Michael, Nicole, and Sam gather around our Big Book Atlas as Hans quizzes the others on United States geography. They all lie on the floor to study the two-page spread of the United States, and Hans says, "I'm thinking of a state that begins with *A*." His four "students" scan the map trying to find the *A* states. "Nope, not Alabama," Hans says as Michael taps the state with his finger. "No, not Arkansas either," he says as Sam points there. "It's kind of a tricky one, and there's lots and lots of snow there," Hans hints. "It begins with *A* and ends with *a*," he adds, as Michael again points to Alabama, saying, "I tried that one already but you said it was wrong."

"I'm not thinking of Alabama. Do you just want me to tell you?" Sam and Michael nod yes enthusiastically, but Nicole and Dito plead for just a little more time to figure it out themselves.

On another part of the carpet, Rohan and Abigail sit side by side to look through the Apartment Book, which is filled with illustrations of incredibly detailed cross-sections of apartments and apartment buildings. They play house, imagining themselves as Mandy and Mimi from the M&M series who live in the same apartment building. While they read this book, they pretend they're living just a floor or two away from each other. "I'm going to run up the stairs," Rohan says, as he uses his fingers to run up the stairwell in the illustration. "No, no, take the elevator," Abigail admonishes. "You've got to get here quickly!"

I once asked some children why they always read nonfiction during free reading time, and I received a variety of answers. "The pictures are cool," Eric told me while flipping through an Eyewitness book on insects. "I like to find out stuff," Molly said. "I don't have to get tired on the words," Patrick said. "I can just look at the pictures and think."

Nonfiction reading may be one of those rare things that is both loved by children and good for them, too. Becoming proficient readers of nonfiction has many payoffs, from enriching their lives with information and ideas to (dare I say it?) helping them score well on high-stakes tests. I would make the claim, too, that nonfiction is probably the genre that readers encounter more than any other. Even those of us who identify ourselves as the kind of readers who read novels or poetry also read more nonfiction than we realize. The headlines in the newspaper, downloaded maps, directions to operate our newest high-tech electronic purchases, liner notes to CDs, recipes, the fine print on coupons and contracts, all are part of the vast range of nonfiction that we are exposed to and interact with on a daily basis. Nonfiction reading is sort of like breathing: we aren't even aware that we're doing it most of the time.

When we teach nonfiction reading to our young students, it's critical that we don't take children's natural curiosity and playfulness about nonfiction texts and grind them into junior test prep. Nonfiction reading is about much more than helping children understand how to use the features of nonfiction texts and teaching them to synthesize, determine importance, and find the main ideas. Although it is important to teach children to do these things well, we also need to make sure we are teaching them how to read nonfiction for authentic purposes.

In the world outside of school, after all, readers of nonfiction don't choose to read the genre to get better at determining importance or finding the main idea. In another one of my unscientific and informal studies, I've asked some of my reading mentors why they read nonfiction, and they've told me that they read it for the following reasons: to learn about something unfamiliar, to learn more about something of interest, and to learn how to do something.

In planning a unit of study in nonfiction, we need to make sure we are accounting for the real reasons people read nonfiction as well as for the skills and strategies readers need to read it well, such as determining importance and synthesizing text.

My plan for this nonfiction study is as follows:

- Immersion: Getting ready to study nonfiction
- Launching: Noticing and naming the features, and sorting through and categorizing nonfiction texts
- Reading Center Cycle 1: Using nonfiction texts to learn about something
- Reading Center Cycle 2: Using nonfiction texts to develop ideas

Immersion in Nonfiction

In the week or so that leads up to the official starting date of the nonfiction study, I want to whet my students' appetites for nonfiction reading. Although at this time I do not do very explicit teaching about the genre of nonfiction, I do invite the children to think about the differences between nonfiction texts and other kinds of texts they know. So, for example, I might read a picture book like *Cinderella Penguin* and then later read a nonfiction text about penguins. I then ask my students to consider and discuss the differences between these texts. It's worth mentioning that I've never had to spend too much time teaching my students the differences between fiction and nonfiction because their kindergarten teachers and the school librarians had done wonderful jobs teaching children to make the distinction.

In any case, aside from making sure children understand the difference between fiction and nonfiction, there are some other things to do to get children ready to study nonfiction. For homework during this immersion phase of our study, I ask children to bring in different kinds of nonfiction texts they have found in the world so that they can understand how much nonfiction they encounter in their daily lives. We set up a nonfiction museum in a small corner of our room, and some of the artifacts we display are things like cereal boxes, a phone book page, an instructional booklet on how to play the harmonica, a microwave popcorn packet, a dictionary, and so on.

Here are a couple of other suggestions for ways we can get children ready for the upcoming nonfiction study during the immersion phase.

Select Nonfiction Texts for Shared Reading

There are many nonfiction poems and Big Books available to use during shared reading. As I read these with my class, I might say, "This is a nonfiction Big Book about clouds, and one of the things I know about nonfiction is that it gives us information to think about. As I read, let's notice when it gives us some information about clouds." We can also begin to show children how to use the features of nonfiction texts by saying, "Hmm, this book on insects has a table of contents, which tells us what kind of topics we can read about in the book and which pages to go to so that we find the information we're looking for. Let's see, I'm kind of interested in butterflies. I'm going to check the table of contents to see if there's a part on butterflies." During shared reading we can also model how to negotiate a nonfiction text. I once used a *Magic School Bus* Big Book to introduce my students to the idea that some books are loaded with information and we need to figure out just where to start reading on the page.

Select Nonfiction Texts for Interactive Read-Aloud

As we read aloud nonfiction picture books or chapter books, we consider comparing and contrasting them to fictional texts that cover the same topic. For example, I might say, "We just read *Officer Buckle and Gloria* and loved it and then something weird happened. I was looking through this dog book and it had this little part about working dogs. I noticed there were police dogs in it. I thought we could read it together to see what it says." After reading that part, my class and I discussed how the books were different. I also pointed out how we can read fiction and nonfiction differently by showing them how we only read a small part of the nonfiction book on dogs, but we read *Officer Buckle and Gloria* from start to finish.

During the interactive read-aloud, I also try to read different types of nonfiction. For example, I show the children nonfiction books that are read like stories (from start to finish) as well as nonfiction texts that don't require a cover-to-cover reading.

Children Shop for Nonfiction Books

During the immersion phase it helps to let children pick one or two nonfiction books for their independent reading bins. During private reading time, children will read their just-right books as always, but then during partner reading time, can explore their nonfiction books together. Alternatively, we can make a few baskets that contain a variety of nonfiction texts and put them on table-tops during partner reading time so that children have a chance to explore the range of nonfiction in the classroom.

At the end of the immersion phase, I say, "Readers, I know that so many of you want the chance to read nonfiction yourselves, and we're going to have the chance to do just that. It's time for you guys to become experts at reading nonfiction."

Launching the Nonfiction Study

I want to begin by emphasizing that throughout any of these studies, my students still shop for just-right books to read during private reading time. This is non-negotiable. Even during a nonfiction study, I make sure that my students have daily time to read the just-right books that are at their independent reading levels.

The difference during these studies is that instead of following the usual schedule of mini-lesson, private reading time, partner reading time, teaching share time, our independent reading workshop begins with a mini-lesson that supports partner time by teaching partners how to work together on their topic. After partner reading time, I gather my class again in the meeting area to do a brief teaching share about their nonfiction work. Then, without a grand mini-lesson, I send my students back to work for private reading time so that they have daily opportunities to read their just-right books. During this time I confer with readers and meet with small groups for guided reading and strategy lessons.

In other words, as I launch the nonfiction study, my mini-lessons and my teaching share time support my students' work with their nonfiction texts. And after the teaching share, the children read their just-right books during private reading time. To support private reading time, I may do very brief mini-lessons, which might simply be reminders of print and comprehension strategies.

During the launching week I put baskets containing nonfiction books on the tables for reading partners to explore. Each basket has about a dozen nonfiction texts that vary in terms of reading level, topic, and structure. For example, in one basket the students might find a few leveled books I've pulled from the leveled library, several books with a variety of topics from insects to mummies, and books representing different nonfiction structures, such as nonfiction stories, non-narrative Eyewitness books, or hybrids like The Magic School Bus series.

During the immersion week, when we read nonfiction texts during shared reading and read-aloud time, the children inevitably noticed some of the features of nonfiction texts. My objective during the immersion phase was simply to help them recognize and identify the main features of nonfiction texts, but now as we officially begin our nonfiction study I will teach them how careful readers use these features to help them read their books.

As I begin launching the nonfiction study, I send my students off to their partner spots to explore the nonfiction book baskets that I've placed on the tables around the room. My mini-lesson might go as follows.

Mini-lesson

Connection

Boys and girls, last week I read aloud tons of nonfiction books and poems, and it was like we were really getting into nonfiction. I thought it would be only fair if I gave you your own turn to read nonfiction. I can't hog all the fun. Anyway, for the next few weeks, you and your partner will spend partner time becoming experts at a few things. You'll become experts at reading nonfiction books, and you'll become experts at doing research in nonfiction. What that means is, you will learn how to read nonfiction in a way that helps you learn a lot about a topic that you're interested in. I'll say more about that in a few days, but for now, I want to spend some time exploring nonfiction books with you. We'll begin by naming the features of nonfiction that we see in our books because these features can help you read nonfiction. Today, I'm going to teach you how to find the different features in nonfiction books so when you read them you'll know how to use them to help yourself.

Teaching point and demonstration

Watch me. I'm going to pretend that I'm a first grader and these are the two nonfiction books I borrowed for the week. I'm going to flip through the pages and take a book walk to see what features of nonfiction I can find. I'm going to put a sticky note on the features I notice that will help me read the book. [I demonstrate.] Hmm, here's that thing . . . what's it called? Oh, the table of contents. That's right. I remember it from the book about dolphins we read last week. I'm going to put a sticky note on that page because I know that can help me find information that I'm looking for. Okay, let's see, on this page, there are photographs, and they help me to really understand what the words are saying. I'm going to put a sticky note on the photographs.

Boys and girls, did you see how I flipped through and put a sticky note on the features that I noticed? You guys are going to get a chance to do that, too, with the nonfiction books you shopped for, but first I want you to try it with me.

Active engagement

I'm going to continue flipping through this book, and I want you to give me a thumbs-up when you notice a feature that you think will help you read the book. [I continue the book walk, and as children put their thumbs up, I stop flipping through.] Turn and tell your neighbor what feature you noticed on this page. [I listen in and report back.] You guys noticed the captions under this picture, and some of you said that the caption tells you what the picture is about, so I'm going to put a sticky note on this page right here next to the caption. Captions can help you read nonfiction. Good job. When you're reading, and you find a photograph or illustration in your book, and if you're not quite sure what's going on in it, you can always check the caption.

Okay, I can tell that you'll be able to find the features that will help you read nonfiction texts. You already know how to find the table of contents, captions, and photographs. You'll notice these things in most of your nonfiction books, and I know you'll find lots of other features.

Link to ongoing work

Readers, when you read nonfiction, you'll notice some features in the books that are there to help you read the books. For the next couple of days we'll take some time to notice and name the features and learn how we might use them to help us read. Today, though, your job with your reading partner is to find a nonfiction book from the basket on your table. I want you and your partner to flip through the book as I did and to put a sticky note on the pages when you notice a feature that you think would help you read the book. We're going to share them at the end.

After the mini-lesson, when I send the students off to partner work with nonfiction books, I confer to support the children as they discover the features. Often, one of the things I need to do in these conferences is to name the features for them. For example, many children will put a sticky note on the glossary because they recognize that it's a feature often found in nonfiction texts, but they don't always know its purpose or what it's called. In the conferences I provide the name for the feature and make a quick teaching point about how to use it.

When we reconvene at the meeting area for share time, I ask partners to bring the books that they were exploring during partner time so that we can share the features that we noticed. I also start a chart entitled Features of Nonfiction and How They Help Us Read. To make the chart more helpful, I include copies of the different features from actual texts in the first column, so that children can easily remember what the feature looks like.

Although my students and I create a list that includes a wide variety of features of nonfiction during our launching week, I tend to focus my lessons for the next several days on just a few of the features: the table of contents, the index, photographs, illustrations, captions, and section headings. I teach the children how to use these features and then send them off to try it with their partners. Their job during partner time will be to flip through their nonfiction books together to find one with an index, for example, and then to use the index to find particular information.

One thing to consider as we focus on the features of nonfiction during this portion of the study is the idea that teaching the features is simply a warm-up to our work in nonfiction. Studying the features of nonfiction together is a lens that provides opportunities for children to explore the wide variety of nonfiction texts available. We don't need to spend lots of time teaching our students about each of the features during this launching phase of the study.

Features of Nonfiction and How They Help Us Read

Nonfiction Feature	Where to Find It	How It Helps Us Read the Book
Table of contents	Front	Helps us find the part of the book we're looking for
Index	End	Helps us find the information we're looking for, by giving page numbers
Photograph	Anywhere	Helps us picture the information
Illustration	Anywhere	Helps us understand the information
Diagram/map	Anywhere	Helps us understand the information
Caption	Near photos, illustrations, diagrams	Helps us understand what's going on in photo, illustration, diagram
Glossary	End, usually	Helps us understand tricky words
Section heading	Beginning of new sections	Helps us to get our minds ready for the information that follows
Different kinds of print (**bold,** *italics,* <u>underlined,</u> large)	Anywhere	Helps us notice that certain words or text parts are important

In the reading center cycles that follow, we ask children to choose a topic of interest, and we teach them to do research. During these reading center cycles, the students will have authentic opportunities to use features of nonfiction to help them get information or to better understand their topics.

For the next two lessons in the launching phase, I teach my students that reading nonfiction books can be a lot different than reading other kinds of books, such as chapter books or picture books. I show them how readers don't have to start on the first page in many nonfiction books but instead can go right to the part of the book that interests them. A typical mini-lesson might go like this.

Mini-lesson

Connection

Readers, you have been noticing the features in your nonfiction books, and we've talked about how they help us read the books. Want to know something else that's really interesting about nonfiction? Well, the way we read nonfiction books can be different from the way we read other kinds of books. For example, when I read aloud Charlotte's Web, *I started from the very beginning of the book and read from one page to the next, right? And when you read your just-right books during independent reading, you did the same thing: you started from the beginning and read to the end. But when we read nonfiction, it can be different because we don't always have to start at the beginning of nonfiction books. When we read nonfiction, sometimes we have a target. We know just what part we want to read. In lots of nonfiction books we can go right to the part we want. Today, I'm going to teach you that when you read some kinds of nonfiction, you can start reading in different places in the book depending on your target.*

Teaching point and demonstration

Watch this. You know, all week I've been reading this book about the ocean. When we looked at the table of contents, we saw how this book has information about lots of different kinds of animals, like sharks, dolphins, and whales. Today, though, I am in the mood to learn more about dolphins because I saw something about them on the Discovery Channel last night. I'm thinking that I can go straight to the dolphins part instead of reading the book from beginning to end. After all, if I want to know about dolphins, I don't have to read about everything else like the parts about sharks and whales. Watch how I do this. [I open to the table of contents and think aloud as I find the part on dolphins.] Hmm, let's see . . . whales . . . sharks . . . dolphins, there's the part on dolphins . . . it's on page 33. I'm going to go straight to page 33 because I want to focus on dolphins when I read.

Did you notice how I decided I didn't want to read everything about ocean animals, but I just wanted to read about dolphins? Dolphins were my reading target. Did you see how I used the table of contents to help me? I looked for dolphins, checked to see what page that section started on, and went straight to it, page 33. I didn't go from page 1 to page 33. Instead, I went straight to page 33 because that's where the dolphin section starts and that was my reading target.

Active engagement

I want you to try it right now. You and your partner are going to pretend right now that you're reading this ocean book together. I've made copies of the table of contents for you to use because you and your partner are going to do what I did: you're going to decide what you want to focus on, your reading target, and you'll figure out what page you will have to start reading on. Right now, as I pass out the table of contents to you and your partner, I want you to decide what you're interested in learning more about . . . whales, sharks, dolphins, ocean birds, jellyfish, or other things. [I pass out copies.] Okay, if you've decided together what you want to learn more about, figure out what page you'd have to turn to if you had the ocean book in front of you. [As they look at the table of contents, I move around and listen in.] Wow, many of you want to learn more about sharks, so the pages about sharks are your reading target. What page did you have to go to? [The children call it out.] Okay, let me check in the book to make sure that's the shark section. [I go to the page and show it to them.] Good job, guys, you'd be ready to learn more about sharks.

Link to ongoing work

So, readers, today when you and your partner go back to read your nonfiction book, I want you to decide about your reading target, which is what you want to focus on, like I decided to focus my reading on dolphins. Then you have to figure out whether you need to start from page 1 or whether you can check the table of contents and start in another place. That's a cool thing about some nonfiction books. In some nonfiction books, when you have a reading target, you can start reading in places other than the beginning. I'm going to listen in and see how that goes for you guys.

Here are some suggestions for follow-up mini-lessons.

❖ **Readers use the index to find the page with information they're looking for.** In this lesson I say that I still want to get information about dolphins, but what I really want to know is what dolphins eat. The index can help me find the exact information I'm looking for. I ask the children to watch how I use the index to help me, and then I give them a chance to try it during active engagement. I can do this kind of mini-lesson a few more times if I want to highlight other features and how to use them.

❖ **Readers decide where to start reading on a nonfiction page.** Many nonfiction books have pages that allow readers to begin reading in places other than the top left-hand part of the page. There are text boxes, illustrations, and captions as well as text paragraphs, so in this lesson I teach children that they can make a plan for where they are going to start reading.

Categorizing and Sorting Nonfiction Books

The last thing we do in this launching week is sort through and categorize our nonfiction texts into more specific topical baskets. Until now, my classroom library featured a couple of baskets that contained a variety of nonfiction topics. Alongside those miscellaneous nonfiction baskets I also have a couple of more specific baskets, such as insects (which supported our science study on insects), sea life, and plants and trees. Because the children will soon be choosing a topic of interest to study with a partner, I want them to have a role in creating some other nonfiction baskets on specific topics. To do this, I send them back to their tables to look through a basket of miscellaneous nonfiction books and find books that go together by topic.

When the children do this, they may often categorize and create very broad topical baskets, such as books about animals. Then, we need to sort through the books again to find subtopics within these larger groupings. So, for example, from the animal book basket my students will realize we can take dog books to create a dog books basket because we have four different books on dogs. They can create a bird books basket because we have several books about birds. It's these topics that the students will choose to research in the upcoming bend in the road.

When we sort our nonfiction books into topical baskets, I ask my library monitors to make new labels for the baskets during their morning jobs. I teach them to write the words (Dog Books or Books About Birds or Planets) in big, clear letters on a large index card. They also draw pictures to go with the words on the labels. I affix these labels to our new baskets.

In subtopic baskets, such as dogs or birds, it makes sense to have from four to six different books with the possibility of getting one or two more. It's not necessary to fill the basket with dozens of books about the topic because that can be overwhelming for our young researchers. It's extremely helpful to have a range of reading levels represented in each basket, so that children have at least one or two accessible texts.

Some teachers may be concerned that most of their nonfiction books are well beyond the reading levels of their students. "What kind of work can they do in books that are too hard for them to read?" teachers may wonder. This is a good question.

In even complex nonfiction texts, children can use the pictures, illustrations, and captions to anchor their work. One year, Jonah and John wanted to study space together. I was concerned because my books on outer space were all above their reading levels, and I wondered if they'd get frustrated or if their reading work would be a waste of time. The opposite occurred. Jonah and John were highly engaged as they went through these books on outer space because it was a topic that interested them. They spent time comparing photographs of the planets across texts, and making theories about why Mars looks so red sometimes. They became particularly interested in the planets that were closest to Earth, and so they went through the books in their basket and put sticky notes on the sections about Mars and Venus. Jonah brought in a highly technical astronomy magazine for their reading center, and they spent one whole partner reading time studying the magazine even though the articles were fit for an astronomer. They studied the table of contents to see if there was an article on either Mars or Venus. When they discovered there were no articles about their planets, Jonah and John studied the ads for telescopes in the back of the magazine to figure out which one they wanted to buy so that they could see Mars and Venus on their own.

Although Jonah and John were not spending their partner time decoding text, I felt comfortable knowing they were doing important reading work together. They were pursuing an interest through reading, comparing information across books, developing questions, and theorizing about the answers. Also comforting was my knowledge that Jonah and John (and all the other readers in my class) would have daily opportunities to read their just-right books.

Reading Center Cycle 1

"Boys and girls, this is a big day for us," I say during our morning meeting as we get ready to run through our schedule for the day. "Today is the day you guys are going to begin research, just like the big kids do, about something you're interested in learning more about. Remember how we made some nonfiction baskets, like Bird Books, Books About Dogs, Outer Space, Butterflies, Ants, the Human Body? Well, today, you're going to decide which of those things you want to learn more about, and I'm going to teach you how you can do some research. I've made a list of the baskets we put together, and I want you to take a few moments to think about the topic you're interested in learning more about. Whatever basket you choose will be your reading center for the week." I quickly read aloud the choices on the chart while pointing out the corresponding baskets in the classroom library.

Later that morning, at the start of reading workshop, the children pick the topic that they want to study. It's important to say that we teachers have a choice here: we can either keep our ongoing ability-based reading partners together, or we can let children choose topics of interest individually and then assign the partnerships within each topic. The benefit of keeping the ongoing partnerships together is that they have a habit of working together and that they are ability-based. On the other hand, it can be a good idea to use these cycles of nonfiction reading centers to switch partnerships a little bit. If one of our readers who struggles really wants to learn more about space, it might be a nice change of pace for her to be partnered with a stronger reader who is also interested in the planets. During our nonfiction work in my class, I tended to partner my students according to their interests rather than require that they stay with their ability-based partner. But, like anything else, this is a decision that a teacher needs to make based on the needs and strengths of his class.

I gather the children at the meeting area and ask my library monitors to put out the nonfiction baskets on the tables around the room. Before starting my mini-lesson, I provide about 5 minutes for my readers to choose the topics that they would like to study.

"Readers, this morning I said that today is going to be a big day, and now it's time to begin doing our big work together. I asked you to think about which topic you want to research or learn more about, and now is the time you get to pick. The library monitors have put the baskets around the tables, so I want you guys to take a quick tour of the baskets to see what interests you most of all. You might already know, but even so, I want you to take a quick look at the baskets because you might change your mind. Let me show you exactly what I want it to look like when you are looking around." I get up and model how to flip through the books in the basket, and I think aloud by saying things like, "Oh, the human body. Maybe I'll be a doctor when I grow up, so I bet these books have some good information about what to do if you get sick," or "Birds . . . I love birds . . . birds would be fun to research," or "Wow, it's so hard to decide because there's just so much interesting stuff to learn."

"Did you see how I checked out the baskets, and thought about some things I could research in them? I didn't go through each basket because I want to make sure you guys get your own time to check them out. So, here's your job for right now. Walk around and check out the baskets, and when you decide what you want to study, come over here to this chart and put a sticky note with your name on it under the topic you want to study." I don't make a big deal at this point about the fact that they'll have a research partner. I want to avoid the popularity contests and hurt feelings that can often occur when children choose their own partners. Besides, I am the ultimate partner broker, and I decide on the partnerships. As the children sign up for their topics by putting sticky notes on the chart, I do the work of arranging them into partnerships.

I've rarely had any problems with the nonfiction partnerships I've assigned. Often, it's simply obvious how to arrange the partnerships, but sometimes I have private conversations with children about their partnerships. I remember meeting with Meaghan because I could see that she was disappointed that she and Cassidy weren't partners, even though they had both signed up to study dogs. "Meaghan," I said, "I know how much you love to work with Cassidy, and I know that you're such good friends, but I decided to put Cassidy with Jennifer and you with Silver. I did that because Cassidy and Jennifer never really get a chance to read together, and I just know that you and Silver would work really well together. I am confident that it's all going to be fine." She smiled weakly, but in the end, her partnership with Silver did work out well, and Cassidy and Jennifer had a grand old time themselves.

So now that the social engineering is out of the way, I gather the children again at the meeting area to do a mini-lesson that will set them up to begin their research. After the mini-lesson the partners will go to their reading center baskets to begin their work together.

Mini-lesson

Connection

For the next week, you and your partner will be doing research together about the topic you chose to study. I'm going to teach you some really grown-up ways that readers do research, and I know that you're ready to learn how to do them. As we do this research, I'm going to pretend that you guys are my reading partner and together we are studying the topic of ants. Today, I'm going to teach you how you and your partner might get started by warming up your minds before you read.

It's really helpful to choose one center basket for mini-lessons to model the work we want children to do in their own reading centers. It can be extremely helpful to choose the same basket that our readers who struggle might be reading from because our work in the mini-lessons can offer them extra support and reinforcement for their own independent work.

Teaching point and demonstration

Remember how when we read any book, we get our minds ready to read by looking at the cover, thinking about the title and the illustration, and flipping through the book? Well, when we read nonfiction, there are other ways to get your mind ready to read about your topic. Something I do is think about what I already know about the topic, so that when I read the books, I have an idea of what I might expect to see, and I also think about some things I'd like to learn so I can focus my mind. Watch how I do this. Before I even open up the books in my ants basket to do research, I want to get my mind ready to study ants, and I'm going to think about what I already know about ants and about some things I'd like to learn more about. Hmm, let's see. Well, I know that ants are hard workers and that they have different jobs in the ant colonies. I remember reading about that once. I am kind of interested in finding out more about their jobs. I think it's so cool that they have jobs, but I don't know too much about the kinds of jobs they have.

Readers, did you hear how I said something I already know about ants and then I said something that I'm interested in learning more about? That's important work that you can do when you go off to read and do research together.

Active engagement

But first I want you to practice it right here. Remember we're pretending that we're studying ants together, so right now, I want you and your partner to name some things that you already know about ants and think about stuff you'd like to learn. I'm asking you to do this because it can help get your minds warmed up for your research. Okay, turn and talk to your partners right now. What do you know about ants, and what do you want to learn more about? [I listen in.]

Readers, eyes this way. I heard you guys saying some really interesting things. Some of the things you already know about ants are that there are lots of different kinds, that ants like sweet food, that ants can bite, that ants die if you spray them. You know some big things about ants. Then some of you were talking about stuff you'd like to learn. I heard you say things like you want to learn about whether there are poisonous ants and where they live, you want to learn about how they make their ant colonies, you want to learn about how they have babies. Now, if you were going to read the ant books, you'd have something to focus on as you read. Wow, I'm so excited, you guys! I can tell that you'll be powerful researchers and that we're going to have lots to think about and learn together.

Link to ongoing work

Okay, readers. This is your job today, and anytime you might be starting to research something, like when you're in college. It's really helpful to get your minds warmed up for the research by thinking with your partner first about these two questions: What do I already know about the topic, and what am I interested in learning more about? Today, I want you and your partner to meet and talk about those things together to get your minds warmed up for your research. I think it will really help.

Some teachers may be thinking, "Well, that's nothing more than asking the students to talk their way through the K-W part of a K-W-L chart." Well, that's right, in a way, but I think there's more to it than that. When I ask children to consider the things they already know about a topic, it helps them anticipate the words and concepts they might encounter as they read the books on their topics. This prior knowledge can serve as an anchor or a safe haven in nonfiction texts, which may or may not be at the children's independent reading level.

When I ask children to think together about what they want to learn about their subject, they are deciding on an initial focus for their work. To help them have a focus for their work, I have learned over the years to make

Reading Center Reflection

Name _____

What reading center were you in?

☑ Bodies and Bones   ☒ Butterflies

☒ Space   ☒ Ants

☒ Snails   ☒ Animals

☒ Water   ☒ Plants

Who was your center partner?

Anna

What was something you learned in your center?

Thare Are no Bohes in your hose or ears

How did your partnership work out?

it was fihe We Cahatid the books

---

sure I say, "Think about what you're interested in finding out more about," rather than, "Think about questions you have about the topic." When we ask our students to list questions they have about a topic, they often come up with questions that they may never be able to answer. For example, one year, Julie and Michelle were studying butterflies together. I had asked my students to think about the questions they had about their topics, and Julie and Michelle wondered, "How many colors do butterflies have on their wings?" This was a perfectly fine kind of first-grade question, but if they had really focused their work on answering this question, they would have been frustrated because it's quite possible that they would never have been able to find the answer.

Instead, I've learned to turn these very particular kinds of questions into broader wonderings. Rather than their trying to find the number of colors on butterflies' wings, I could guide Julie and Michelle into broadening their inquiry by saying, "Hmm, your question makes me think that you're really interested in learning more about their wings. I bet you can find lots of information about butterflies' wings in these books."

When we ask children to consider the questions about their topic before they begin their research, they may also come up with questions that are quite easy to answer. Consequently, they may lose interest in their topic. Anna and Wyatt were in the Human Body reading center, and their question was simply, "How many bones do we have?" I knew that question would be easy to answer, so I tried to help them broaden their wondering. "That question makes me think that you're really interested in bones and, well, the human skeleton. I'm sure some of your books will tell you how many bones we have, but I bet you can find tons of other interesting information about bones and the skeleton, too."

So, after realizing that asking children to come up with specific questions to guide their research can have limitations, I have learned to rephrase that request by asking them to consider what they're wondering about or interested in learning about their topic. It tends to give them a broader point of entry into their research.

Other whole-class mini-lessons that I might teach my students during the first reading center cycle on nonfiction are as follows.

❖ *Readers research their topics by starting with the easiest books in the basket.* In this lesson I teach my children that when they start with the easiest books in their basket, it helps them warm up for the harder books. It's like the easy books are training wheels that help readers read the harder books. I can demonstrate this by showing students how to find the easier books within the ants basket, the center basket that I'm planning to use for mini-lesson demonstrations.

❖ *Readers use the features of nonfiction to help them find information.* In this lesson I remind my students that they can use the features of nonfiction to help them find the information they want to know about their topics. For example, I demonstrate this teaching point by using the index in one of the ants books to find a section on the jobs ants have in ant colonies.

❖ *Readers read nonfiction in special ways to learn about their topics.* In this lesson I teach children that often in nonfiction, a reader can go straight to a particular part of the book and read specific sections. This is actually an extension of a lesson I taught during the launching phase of our nonfiction work. In my demonstration I can tell the class that I've been wondering about the queen ant. I tell them that I want to learn more about what she does all day. I model using the index or the table of contents to go directly to the information, and then, almost as a secondary teaching point, I introduce the idea of synthesizing the text into one's own words.

✿ *Readers notice when they are learning something new.* In this lesson I teach children that when they do research, they have to read in a wide-awake way. It's like being a detective who has to look for clues. One way to do this is to listen when their minds say, "Hey, I didn't know that!" as they read about their topic. I give them sticky notes so that they can mark places in their books where they learn new information.

✿ *Readers jot notes on sticky notes.* This lesson usually takes two or three days, depending on the class. In one of the lessons on this topic I teach my students what it means to jot down a note. I show them how jottings hold only the most important information. In the next lesson I teach them that when we jot, we put the information in our own words. I show them how to read a portion of text, say to themselves, "So, what's the author really saying here?" and to jot that down. I repeat this lesson two or three times throughout the nonfiction study because it's a rather complex idea for first graders.

✿ *Readers look at different books to accumulate information about their topics.* In this lesson I demonstrate how to read through and make sense of two different books on the topic of ants. I show my students how books often have overlapping information and how they can also have different information about the same thing.

At the end of this first cycle of research, I provide an opportunity for children to "teach" what they've learned about their topic. Usually, after this first cycle, it's a simple and informal celebration. I often just combine partnerships and have them tell each other four important things they learned about their topics. This also serves the purpose of attracting children to other topics for the next cycle of reading centers.

Reading Center Cycle 2

When I get children ready for the second cycle of reading centers, I let them decide if they'd like to change topics or if they'd prefer to stay with the same one for another week or so. For the mini-lessons in this reading center cycle, I repeat the teaching points from many of the lessons I taught during our first cycle of centers. In this cycle I provide my students with more opportunities to practice using the very important reading and thinking strategies, such as synthesizing text, putting text into your own words, determining importance, jotting notes, and comparing and contrasting information. In this cycle I also introduce reading center note-taking sheets so that children can accumulate their thinking. A blank form for collecting new information, which works well in a nonfiction study, is provided in the appendix.

Reading Center Cycle 3

Depending on the needs and strengths of the students and the time available, teachers may decide to have a third cycle of reading centers during a nonfic-

Collecting New Information

Names _____ and _____

Fact

EVer thg ho
4.T.B male stag
beeles have
bigger jaws
the femal heas more
stag beetles bite

Fact

even
thow the Feamle
stag Bcetle
has a stoner
Bit the male
stell Bits

Stag beelles

Research Topic

Fact

twomale
stag beet les
fight over
one feamale
stag beetle.

Fact

stag Beetels
Live in lots
and lots
of plases

Questions we have:
WLy does the feamales bite hurt More
then the males?

tion study. During a third cycle of reading centers, we help our students to develop their own theories about their topics. Admittedly, developing theories is very easy for some students to do, whereas other students may struggle with this.

One year, Julian and Zoe gathered four books on Martin Luther King Jr. because they wanted to learn more about him. "Ms. Collins," Julian said, "every book talks about when Martin was little, and they all say that he loved to read. Look!" They showed me that they had put sticky notes on all the pages that mentioned Martin's childhood reading.

I said, "So, guys, what does that make you think about?"

"Well, he must have been a smart kid if he read all the time," Zoe said.

"Yeah, he must have really loved reading if all the books say so," Julian added.

"Well, you know something, when people write biographies, they choose what information to include and what information to leave out. I think you guys were so smart to notice that all the books tell you that Martin loved to read when he was a kid."

"Maybe the authors want to teach kids a lesson that if we want to be like Martin Luther King, we should read a lot when we're kids," Julian said.

"Hmm, that's an interesting theory, you guys. Are you saying that in these kids' books about Martin Luther King Jr. the authors make sure they say that Martin loved to read when he was little so that maybe it will make kids want to read, too?"

"Yeah, that's what we're thinking about," Zoe said.

As the week progressed, Julian and Zoe went on to notice that only two of the books mentioned that Martin Luther King Jr. was assassinated. They went on to theorize that perhaps the authors didn't always mention this because it was so sad and some kids might get really upset. "Yeah, it's violence, too, and maybe grown-ups don't want their kids to read violence stuff," Zoe continued. It helped Zoe and Julian to go beyond simply collecting facts about Martin Luther King Jr. when they were developing theories by thinking and talking about the question, What does this fact or information make me think more about?

In this third cycle of centers children may also reconfigure the books in their baskets so they are not strictly topical but organized instead in a more thematic way. For example, over the years, my students have created baskets of books in order to pursue their ideas and their theories. One partnership became interested in baby animals because in a previous center they had studied dolphins and learned a lot about baby dolphins. They gathered various animal books and marked off the sections about baby animals. They were trying to figure out the reason that some animals stay with their mothers for a long time, while other animals go off on their own much sooner.

The main work I do during this third cycle of reading centers is to reinforce reading strategies and teach children that when they learn something about their topics, they should go further and ask themselves, What does this information make me think about? To start this cycle of reading centers, a mini-lesson can go like the following.

Mini-lesson

Connection

Readers, you've spent the last few weeks learning how to research and become experts about different topics. You've learned how to do some very important reading work that will help you for the rest of your lives. It's like you know how to collect information and add it to all the stuff you know. Well, now, I think you're ready for the next step: this is something that all careful researchers know. Did you know that researchers don't just collect information, but that they also go further to think about it and develop an idea about it? It reminds me of the rock collection I had when I was a little kid. I used to collect rocks from different places. The thing was that I didn't just collect them and stick them in a box. No, I would collect rocks and then really look at them and think about them. I began to get ideas about the different rocks, like I noticed that the rocks I found near water were all really smooth but the rocks I found on trails and in the woods were all jaggedy. I got an idea that the water made the rocks smooth. See how I didn't just collect the rocks but that I thought about them? Well, you can do that, too, with the information you collect. You can think about it. Today, I want to begin to teach you how careful researchers don't just collect information but they also think about it by asking themselves, "What does this make me think?"

Teaching point and demonstration

When careful researchers get information as they read, they say to themselves, "Hmm, what does this make me think about?" Let me show you what I mean. Yesterday after school, I was reading this book about snails. I put a sticky note on this part that says that chalk can help snails' shells grow. Hmm, I thought, what does this make me think about? Well, I got to wondering what would happen if we fed our snails colored chalk . . . would it make their shells different colors, like the snail in The Biggest House in the World? *Then I thought that colored chalk might be bad for the snails because maybe the stuff that makes the chalk colored might make the snails sick. Anyway, did you see how I didn't just collect the fact that chalk helps snails' shells grow? Did you notice how I asked myself, "Hmm, what does this make me think about?" Did you hear how my thinking stretched?*

Active engagement

Okay, I want you guys to try it right now. Pretend you're my partners and we're studying snails together. I'm going to read a little part that gives us information, and then we'll think together, "Hmm, what does this make us think about?" Okay, let's try it. [I read aloud a brief part about snails' burying their eggs underground and then ask students to turn and talk to their partners. I listen in.]

You guys, I noticed that you were saying, "Hmm, what does this make me think about?" The cool thing that happened when I listened in was that you guys had lots of different kinds of thoughts. Some of you were thinking about the reason that snails bury their eggs underground, and you said that it's because they don't want other animals to eat them. Some of you were wondering how snails remember where they buried their eggs. Others were thinking about how the little babies get out from under the dirt when they are born. What great work. You didn't just collect that fact and stick it in some box in your brain, No, you did the work that careful researchers do—you thought, "Hmm, what does this make me think about?" and talked about your thinking with each other. You stretched your thinking. Great job!

Link to ongoing work

So, readers, whenever you get information as you read, I want you to remember to ask yourselves, "Hmm, what does this make me think about?"

and then talk about your thinking with your partners. This is big tough work, but I just know that you guys will be great at it.

Some other possibilities for whole-class mini-lessons to teach students in this cycle are as follows.

❧ *Readers think about the information they collect and find new questions.* In this lesson I remind my class that when we thought about the fact that snails bury their eggs underground, some kids wondered about the information. I remind them that they wondered how the snails would find the eggs again and how the baby snails would get themselves up above ground when they are born. I teach them that they can read on to find out the answers, or they can talk to their partners and come up with theories about this. In this lesson we ponder one of the questions together, and then we'll read on to see if the text supplies an answer.

❧ *Readers connect the information they collect with other things they know.* It can be powerful to use the same information across these mini-lessons. So, we could stay with the idea that snails bury their eggs and say, "You know, I realized something. I've been thinking about how snails bury their eggs, and I remembered that ostriches do the same thing. I decided to look up some information about why ostriches do that to see if snails and ostriches have the same reasons."

❧ *Readers make theories about their information.* When we develop theories, we try to answer the question, Why? Sometimes the text goes on to tell us, but other times, we need to do this work ourselves. We can again use the "snails bury their eggs" information and try to develop theories about "why?"

Project: Making a Big Book

At the end of our nonfiction study together, my class decided to make our own nonfiction Big Book. The problem was that there wasn't really any unifying theme across our reading centers. The topics during our nonfiction study ranged from outer space to various animals to the human body to Martin Luther King Jr. We looked at a variety of nonfiction books to find one we could use as a model for the book we'd like to put together. We realized that books about specific topics, like butterflies or Martin Luther King Jr., weren't what we had in mind. We then studied books with broader topics, like the insect books, which had information about lots of different kinds of insects. Those books were still not perfect for us to use as a model for the kind of book we'd put together.

One day, Alex brought in a book from home that contained a hodge-podge of random information for kids. He said that maybe we could use that book as our model, and the class decided that it would work.

During choice time that week, each partnership decided what topic they'd like to design a page about for our book. We reminded ourselves about the features of nonfiction by looking at several different kinds of nonfiction texts, so partners designed their pages in a variety of ways. Some included text boxes, illustrations, captions, labels, and so on.

When all the pages were done, we took some time to choose a title for our book. For a couple of days children jotted options on sticky notes, and then we had a class vote. The winning title was "First Grade Facts About Lots of Stuff." Our next job was to figure out how to put the book together. We grouped the pages that were related in some way and decided that our book would have sections called Human Beings, Animals, Outer Space, Insects, and Other Stuff. During choice time one of the options was Bookmaking, which several students chose. Their job was to design the cover page, the table of contents, and the pages to divide the sections of the book. They also created an index and wrote a blurb for the back cover. The book became a favorite part of our nonfiction collection, and we even lent it to the school library for a couple of weeks.

Now, I offer an overview of a couple of other units of study that we might teach at this time of year. All these study units tend to parallel the way I taught the nonfiction unit of study, although of course the details of the teaching will change.

Favorite Authors Study

In order to plan for the favorite authors study, it helps to think about the reading work people do outside of school when they love and pursue the work of a particular author. In addition to considering my own approach to the books of authors I love, I've spoken with my reading mentors and others, too, about the ways they conduct their own private author studies.

There are a variety of reasons readers pursue the books of particular authors. We might deeply appreciate an author's writing style or craft. David Sedaris is an author who immediately comes to mind for me. I'm likely to buy or borrow every book that he writes. His writing makes me laugh, and I enjoy retelling the funniest parts to other people who like to read his books. In fact, one of my best reading memories is lying in bed, unable to control my laughter as I read a particular passage in *Me Talk Pretty One Day*. I was laughing so hard that I was crying. I passed the book over to Ian and pointed to the funny part. He read it aloud and laughed just as hard as I did. We had a reading moment! I've learned that I can rely on David Sedaris to consistently make me laugh, so I eagerly anticipate his new books.

We also pursue the work of an author because he or she might serve particular purposes for us. A few summers ago, when I was planning a trip to Ireland with my mother and brother, I wanted to read a contemporary Irish author to get myself in the mood for the trip. Around the same time, coincidentally, there was a review of the latest Edna O'Brien book in the *New York Times*, so I decided to start with her. I've read at least three of her books since then. I look forward to her new releases, but in between I've read some of her older titles. She's an author who transports me to other places and times, and sometimes as a reader, that's just what I want to happen.

We may also have favorite authors across genres. I'm sure many of us can name our favorite poet, nonfiction writer, editorial columnist, journalist, feature article writer, dead author, and so on. When we find favorite authors, we tend to look forward to their next project. We may even try to find out personal information about them. Although there aren't too many *National Enquirer* articles or *Entertainment Tonight* segments about the escapades or fashion faux pas of authors, it is still possible (and intriguing) to get a hint of their personal lives in other ways. We can find out information about authors on their Web sites, during their talk show appearances, in book reviews, at book signings, and during book talks.

Once we gravitate toward a particular author's works, we tend to do some predictable things as readers. These are the things that can inform our teaching and become the work our first graders can do in their own author studies.

❖ *Readers gather and read texts by authors they love.* When we are attracted to an author's works, we often search out other texts the author has written, and we have a heightened awareness of when the author publishes again in the future. We might look at the new-releases shelves in bookstores or access Web sites to find out when our author's new book will come out. We notice times when our author crosses genres. For example, Barbara Kingsolver might write an editorial for the op-ed page of the *New York Times,* and Anna Quindlen has crossed over from writing syndicated columns to writing novels. We notice when our favorite poet writes an article about travels in South America for *Outside* magazine, or when our favorite political columnist writes a historical fiction novel about generations of a family entwined in the politics of the Middle East.

In our classrooms, children notice with admiration how Cynthia Rylant writes picture books, books of poetry, and chapter books. A child may come to school on a Monday eager to share that over the weekend he went to the library and found an Ezra Jack Keats book that hadn't been read to the class yet. We want to encourage our students to be vigilant in their pursuit of authors' works they love and appreciate.

❖ *Readers notice similarities and differences among the texts by authors they love.* As we read and accumulate texts by an author, we start to notice the ways authors leave their imprints on texts. For example, we might notice the author's folksy tone in all his books that we've read. Perhaps the author's subject matter across texts often features a stormy father-son relationship. Because we've grown aware of things the author usually does in his texts, it stands out when he does something unexpected. If our favorite author usually writes happy-ending stories, we take notice when her latest book ends with an ambiguous or unresolved situation.

In our classrooms as children read a few texts by their favorite authors, they begin to see trends and habits of the author, as well as times when the author writes differently. Partners who are studying Judith Viorst might discuss how her books are often silly stories about kids' lives, and they might look deeper for similarities among her characters. Others who are Lois Ehlert fans will discover that her books often have the same look but that she writes stories and nonfiction books, and that some of her books even have both a story and nonfiction information in them.

❧ *Readers try to find out more about their favorite authors' lives.* In years past, we might have been able to find out about an author's life and experiences only through the small blurb at the end of the book or on the cover. If the author was prominent, there might have been scholarly texts written on her life and work. Today, it's easier for authors to become media darlings who claim (at least) their 15 minutes of fame. And it's easier for readers to learn about authors they're interested in because they may very well be guests on *Oprah,* be featured in *People* magazine, or be given thanks in an Oscar speech for an adapted screenplay. For readers, it can be interesting to learn about favorite authors' lives because this knowledge can offer insights into their stories, their writing process, and even why we like their books in the first place.

In our classrooms we can provide our children with information we've accumulated about authors they love. When we tell our students that we heard Patricia Polacco speak at a teachers' conference and that she told the audience that she had had a hard time learning to read, we talk about how that information helps us to understand her books better. If we tell children Miriam Cohen has two sons and she based her First-Grade Friends books on stories from when her sons were young, the children can reread those books with that information in mind.

We may need to do behind-the-scenes research about the authors our students will be studying, such as looking on the Internet for information. We can print out our findings, insert them in plastic sheet protectors, and put them in the author baskets.

❧ *Readers wonder where authors get their ideas.* When my book group read *We Were the Mulvaneys,* one of the things we talked about was where Joyce Carol Oates got the idea for the story. The story contained so many disturbing events and interactions, and we wondered if the author herself had experienced some of the events in the text or knew someone who had.

When children read *Koala Lou,* and other texts by Mem Fox, they, too, wonder where she got her ideas. They note the fact that Fox is from Australia and infer that's why she knows about koalas, platypuses, and gum trees. They wonder and talk to their partners about whether *Koala Lou* might be based on Fox's own life when she was a child.

❧ *Readers look for themes that run through favorite authors' books.* Part of the reason we like an author's books may be that we're attracted to the themes in them. Some authors write beautifully about themes such as redemption, religious or sexual awakening, overcoming hardships, self-destruction, and many other things. As we read more texts by the authors we love, we may notice how they revisit themes or particular threads across the works.

Children may notice, for example, that many of Lois Ehlert's books are about nature, and that Arnold Lobel usually uses animals for characters. When they become aware of these themes or threads, we can teach them to take their work further by thinking, "Hmm, why might the author write this way?"

❀ *Readers notice their favorite authors' writing style and craft.* When I read Barbara Kingsolver, I always notice the incredible detail and knowledge with which she writes about the settings in her books. Whether it is the African Congo in the *Poisonwood Bible* or mountains in *Prodigal Summer,* Kingsolver writes wonderfully vivid and informed descriptions of the scenery and the natural world. This is something I've come to expect and enjoy in her work.

We can help our children notice an author's style by looking across books for similarities. They may notice surface-level things, such as authors who use lots of dialogue or authors who use lots of descriptive words. They may also notice structural things, such as how an author tends to begin her books or how an author teaches us lessons through her stories.

❀ *Readers recommend favorite authors to other people.* As we grow to appreciate an author, we often become marketing experts for her books. We promote the author to others, and to do so, we need to have selling points. We use the knowledge we've collected by reading several of the author's texts as the selling points. We try to play matchmaker, and set the author up with family, friends, and acquaintances whom we think will enjoy the author's work.

In our classes the children know each other's reading lives and habits rather well, especially by this time of year, and we can create venues for them to recommend authors to each other. We can also teach them that it's okay if some authors do not appeal to them. We can help them notice and name the things that make an author more or less likely to be one of their favorites.

It is these things, the real-life ways readers engage with authors, that we can teach our students during an author study. When we are getting ready to launch author studies in our classrooms, we might begin during the immersion phase by revealing to the children the simple notion that readers often have favorite authors.

"First graders, I heard some very big news," I say. "You'll never guess what it is. Are you ready for this? I heard that Mem Fox is working on another book! I'm not sure if it's public news or not, but I heard it from a reliable source. I'm so excited. You all know I'll be the first one at the store to buy it when it comes out. This news has got me thinking about how much fun it is to have an author that you really truly love. Do you guys have any authors that you like as much as I like Mem Fox?"

"I love J. K. Rowling," said Charlie. "I can't wait till the next Harry Potter book comes out."

"I love David Shannon," said Herbert, as he looked over at Max and they giggled because of their continuing fascination with the butt shot in *No, David!*

"I love to read about Frog and Toad," Deanna said.

"Frog and Toad aren't authors," Alex corrected.

"I forgot the author's name," Deanna said back to Alex.

"That happens to me, too, Deanna, but it's okay because we can check and see who wrote *Frog and Toad*," I said as I pulled a book from the library. "Oh, right! The author is Arnold Lobel. I can understand how you'd forget his name. Frog and Toad are such strong characters that they almost overpower the author. Arnold Lobel does such a great job with those books, doesn't he?"

"Right now, why don't you turn to your partners and say who the authors are that you love." While they turned and talked, I moved around as always and listened in to their conversations. For most children, I realized, it was hard to think of a particular author. They mostly named the titles of books that I'd read aloud, books that they had read, or a genre that they liked to read.

"Guys, you know what?" I said. "When I was listening to you and your partner talk, I realized that a lot of you haven't really found favorite authors yet. I'm thinking that it's time for all of us to find authors we love because that's what strong readers do. They have favorite authors, authors whose books they know really well. For the next couple of weeks, we'll all find authors we really love, and we'll get to know their books really well, too."

"Yeah, we'll become experts on our authors, right?" Molly said.

"We *will* become experts, Molly," I said. "And by the way, did you know that there are people in this world whose job is to be the best expert in the world on an author? I know someone who is an expert on Shakespeare. My friend went to college and then even more college to learn everything she could about Shakespeare's life and about the plays he wrote. Now she's such an expert on Shakespeare that she teaches college kids about him. What a job she's got—talk about getting to know an author!"

"Yeah, that's a lot of reading 'cause Shakespeare's hard," Silver said under his breath.

For the next couple of days, we created and kept adding to a two-column chart entitled Authors We Know. In the left-hand column we wrote the authors' names, and in the right-hand column we listed the kinds of text they'd written. We tried to put only authors on our chart who had written more than a couple of books; otherwise we'd have had the literary equivalent of one-hit wonders. It would be hard to do an author study of a writer who has written only one book.

During the immersion phase, I pick an author for read-aloud that I will stick with for the week, and we have whole-class conversations about what we notice about his or her books.

To launch this study, I do a quick mini-lesson to support the children's independent reading work, which they do as usual, but during partner time we work at putting together author baskets for the upcoming reading center cycle. The children look through their independent reading bins to find books by authors who have a body of work worthy of our author study. It's important to put together baskets that reflect the range of readers in the classroom.

One year, for example, the author baskets ranged in difficulty and tone from Harriet Ziefert to Cynthia Rylant, Joy Cowley, and Seymour Simon.

Each basket had from three to eight books by a particular author. For authors like Cynthia Rylant, I made sure the contents of the basket represented the range of her books, including picture books and some chapter books. If the basket were filled only with Henry and Mudge books, the author study might turn into more of a character study.

When children choose an author to study, they need to put together only some of the books the author has written because, in the case of certain authors, like Cynthia Rylant or Eric Carle, it would be overwhelming for students if they included every single book. When we set up baskets with about a half dozen books or so, the children have time not only to read but to talk about the books.

After a few days of putting together author baskets so that each basket had no less than three and no more than eight books, the children and their partners chose an author they wanted to study. In some cases, I had to be heavy-handed in guiding students toward an author whose books they could actually read. When Jennifer and Reina headed toward the Arnold Lobel basket, I had to redirect them toward an author with easier books. I did a little public relations pitch to help build their enthusiasm for the author whom I directed them toward. In some cases, however, I might let partners read an author's books that are beyond their independent reading level. If Jennifer and Reina, for example, really wanted to choose Mem Fox's books, I'd let them because I know they are already very familiar with her books. I have read them aloud many times, so I know the experience of listening to her books and talking about them with the class would scaffold their work in the author study. Besides, during private reading time in independent reading, Reina and Jennifer would be reading just-right books at their reading level.

When we do an author study, as with any whole-class study, it's important to choose an author basket that we can also use for our mini-lessons. In effect, we are choosing an author to study with the class during our mini-lessons so that we can model the work that we expect our children to do in their partnerships with their own authors.

Pat Garvey, a teacher I worked with at P.S. 29 in Brooklyn, used Ezra Jack Keats as her class author. She had read aloud many of his books throughout the year, so the children were quite familiar with him. Pat made a wise decision to use a familiar author because her children were able to focus more on the work of the author study rather than getting bogged down by the novelty of unfamiliar texts. Also, by choosing Ezra Jack Keats, a very familiar author, Pat didn't have to read the books in their entirety during mini-lessons. She was able to get to her teaching point more quickly and efficiently.

Favorite Characters Study

When I think back to the books I remember most from when I was a child, I think less about titles and story lines and more about the characters that made

Plan for Favorite Authors Study

Reading skills, strategies, habits	Making connections across books. Gathering and synthesizing information from various sources. Developing opinions and tastes about authors' books. Comparing books by one author with books by other authors.

Immersion Phase
Usually a week or so
	Read-aloud or shared reading suggestions
	    Read 2 or 3 books by the same author.
	    Think about similarities/differences across the books.
	    Share information about the author; think about the books.
	Homework suggestions
	    Name authors you know and love.
	    Interview grown-ups about authors they knew and loved as children.
	Class charts
	    List favorite authors and kinds of books they write.

Launching Phase Usually 2 or 3 days	Partners check just-right books to see if some are by same author. Sort through library to create author baskets. Partners choose an author to study together.

Reading Center Cycle 1
"When we read different books
by an author, we can notice
things the author often does."
	Mini-lesson topics
	    When we know an author's books, we discover similarities in them.
	    When we know an author's books, we discover differences in them, too.
	    We can learn information about an author.
	    We can use information about an author to help us think about her books.

Reading Center Cycle 2
"When we become experts about
authors, we think about reasons
the author writes certain things."
	Children may change author, or stay with same from previous cycle.
	Some mini-lessons may have to be repeated.
	Mini-lesson topics
	    We can figure out the order in which books were written.
	    We can develop theories about where the author got his ideas.
	    We can wonder why the author chose certain settings.

Reading Center Cycle 3
(optional)
"We can put together books by
different authors that have some-
thing in common."
	Teacher or children select new categories for center baskets.
	Categories for center baskets
	    Authors who write about friendships, families, kids' lives.
	    Authors who write books that are funny, sad, fantastic.
	    Authors who teach us lessons.
	    Authors who use many details.
	Mini-lesson topics
	    Different authors' books may have things in common.
	    Compare authors' writing styles for similarities or differences.
	    Compare authors' lives with what happens in their books.

Project/Celebration (optional)	Author promotions: "If you like books on friendships, read . . ." Book reviews: partners write review of favorite author's books. Children share why a book or author is their favorite. Partners contribute a page to a whole-class "Guide to Authors" book.
Other Considerations	Author baskets represent range of readers in the class, so all can have accessible texts. Readers may sometimes choose a favorite author's books that are too hard for them to read independently because the books are well known from read-aloud. Demonstrate partner work with books from author baskets. Provide daily private reading time for just-right books.

Plan for Favorite Characters Study

Reading skills, strategies, habits	Identifying main characters, secondary characters. Inferring to identify character traits. Inferring to determine character motivations. Comparing a character across books to find similarities and differences.

Immersion Phase
Usually a week or so
	Read-aloud or shared reading suggestions
	    Read 2 or 3 books with the same main character.
	    Think about similarities/differences across the books.
	Homework suggestions
	    Name characters you know and love.
	    Interview grown-ups about characters they knew and loved as children.
	Class charts
	    List favorite characters on a chart.

Launching Phase Usually 2 or 3 days	Partners follow characters in just-right books and talk about them. Sort through library to create character baskets. Partners choose a character to study together.

Reading Center Cycle 1
"Readers can get to know characters they care about."
	Mini-lesson topics
	    Identify characters' appearance and personality traits.
	    Read "between the lines" to understand characters.
	    Use text evidence to prove your thinking.
	    Study characters across books to find similarities.
	    Notice characters' relationships with other characters.

Reading Center Cycle 2
"To become experts about characters, we try to understand them and why they do and say the things they do."
	Children may change study character, or keep one from previous cycle.
	Some mini-lessons may have to be repeated.
	Mini-lesson topics
	    We can make connections with a character: Am I like him? Do I know anyone like her?
	    We can develop theories about why a character does or says things.
	    We can think about how characters change within and across books.
	    We can think about characters' relationships with others.

Reading Center Cycle 3
(optional)
"We can put together baskets of characters that go together for some reason and think of ways they connect."
	Teacher or children select new categories for center baskets.
	Categories for center baskets
	    Characters who are bullies, detectives, shy, quirky.
	    Characters who have problems and solve them.
	    Characters who are animals.
	    Characters who change in the course of a book.
	    Teachers as characters.
	    Pets as characters.
	Mini-lesson topics
	    Different characters may have things in common.
	    Compare characters for similarities or differences.
	    Study characters' relationships with others.

Project/Celebration (optional)	Come as your favorite character: dress and talk like a character. Children post riddles about characters on bulletin board.
Other Considerations	Character baskets represent range of readers in the class, so all can have accessible texts. Readers may sometimes choose a favorite character in books that are too hard for them to read independently because the books are well known from read-aloud. Demonstrate partner work with books from character baskets. Provide daily private reading time for just-right books.

big imprints on my reading psyche. I wanted to be Harriet the Spy. I loved her life of minor intrigue. I admired her independent spirit. Mrs. Piggle-Wiggle made me feel safe. I had such a vivid image of her in my mind, the lilting voice I imagined, the soft crinkly skin, the tender way she loved all kids. Then there was Pippi, nutty, living-on-the-edge Pippi. Pippi was like an antidote to my natural tendencies toward caution and obedience, the Thelma to my Louise (or vice versa), and I loved the feeling of joy-riding that I had when I read her stories. And I can't forget to mention my man, Encyclopedia Brown, my first literary crush. I wanted to work alongside him. I wanted to be the one who stood at his side with my hands on my hips, saying, "Yeah, take that, Bugs Meany!" after we had solved the case.

I remember fantasizing that Harriet and Pippi lived in my boy-infested neighborhood. I wondered what it would be like to hang out with them, but then I started to worry because I wasn't so sure that Pippi and Harriet would get along well enough to be friends. I sure hoped they'd get along because I didn't want to have to choose between them. When I think back to what made these characters come alive for me, I realize it's the fact that I put my life alongside theirs. I imagined us crossing paths, playing together, and going to each other's houses.

As a reader, I've always gotten attached to characters. Scout and Atticus Finch, characters from *To Kill a Mockingbird,* one of my Top Five books, are two of my all-time favorite characters. If I had more nerve (or if I were a Hollywood actress), I would have named our child either Scout or Atticus in honor of those wonderful characters. These days, as I read *Middlesex* for my book club, I find myself thinking about Calliope/Cal, the main character, even when I'm not reading the book. Characters can keep us tethered to the world of a book even when we put the book down.

When we do a favorite character study in our first-grade reading centers, we want not only to make children aware of character as a story element but also to help them learn how to make characters come alive as they read, how to understand their characters in a way that helps them to understand the stories better. This study also provides a strong contextual background for teaching readers how to infer as they read. This study follows the same kind of rhythm as the study on nonfiction reading and favorite authors.

Other Studies

In the preceding sections I've laid out details of studies on nonfiction, favorite authors, and favorite characters. During this time of year, there are many other kinds of studies teachers might want to launch, depending on the interests, strengths, and needs of her class. It is my hope that the plans for the studies that I've suggested will offer guidance for teachers who want to develop poetry studies and reading projects.

❖ *Readers fall in love with poetry.* The chart offers a suggested plan for a poetry study. It's important for teachers to assemble classroom baskets of poetry

Plan for Poetry Study

Reading skills, strategies, habits	Becoming familiar with poems and poets. Reading poetry with fluency and feeling. Inferring to determine poet's message, meaning. Comparing poems on the same topic. Making connections with poems. Noticing the poet's craft.

Immersion Phase
Usually a week or so
	Read-aloud or shared reading suggestions
	    Read and reread poems: vary poet, topic, shape, tone.
	    Practice reading poetry fluently and with feeling.
	    Talk about poetry: interpret, synthesize, notice poet's craft.
	Homework suggestions
	    Interview adults about what they know about poetry.
	    Take home a poetry book and put sticky notes on poems that interest you.
	Class charts
	    What we have discovered about poetry.
	    Who are the poets we love?

Launching Phase Usually 2 or 3 days	Partners find poems they love. Partners notice how poetry books are arranged: by author, by topic, anthologies. Sort through library to create poetry baskets: by poet, by topic, nature poems, family poems.

Reading Center Cycle 1
"Poetry is meant to be read aloud with feeling."
	Mini-lesson topics
	    Poems give us clues about how to read them: line breaks, tone, rhymes, punctuation, shape.
	    Readers think about poem's meaning and read aloud to reflect meaning.
	    Different poems need to be read in different ways.

Reading Center Cycle 2
"Readers appreciate the work the poet has done to write a poem."
	Children may change poetry basket, or keep one from previous cycle.
	Mini-lesson topics
	    Readers notice, appreciate word choice in poetry.
	    Readers notice, appreciate parts of poems that evoke pictures in the mind.
	    Readers notice, appreciate poems that change our thinking.
	    We can compare poems by same poet to find similarities or differences.
	    We can compare poems on same topic to find similarities or differences.

Reading Center Cycle 3 (optional)
"Readers collect poems they love and share the reasons they fell in love with these poems."
	Mini-lesson topics
	    Talk about why we love a poem and what we love about it.
	    Notice similarities across poems we love.
	    Name the feelings poems evoke in us.

Project/Celebration (optional)	Class anthology: each child illustrates a favorite poem. Poems as gifts: each child gives a poem to someone special. Poetry "slam": all children read aloud favorite poems with feeling.

books representing a range of poets, topics, and styles that appeal to the children. If we cannot find enough books to meet these needs, we can create mini-anthologies of poetry for partners to share, consisting of a dozen poems or so representing different poets, topics, language, tones, shapes, and so on. Partnerships may be interest- or compatibility-based rather than ability-based. If there are a great many struggling readers in the class, poetry can be a particularly tough genre to read because of the specialized word use and language structures. For readers who struggle, teachers can provide copies of familiar poems from shared reading in plastic sheet protectors. During these reading center cycles, it's important to continue to provide daily private reading time for children to read their just-right books.

❧ *Reading projects.* Because of the variety of projects in this study, it's difficult to do whole-class mini-lessons to support all readers. I might do more small-group strategy lessons for children who have chosen similar projects. However, there are some things I teach everyone. I teach children to set goals for their projects, make a plan, and then reflect on how the project they've created has helped them grow as readers.

Of course, any or all of these lessons can be taught throughout the year during small-group instruction and individual reading conferences for students who need this kind of support.

❧ *Readers explore books by authors they haven't read before.* Children who choose a project like this tend to replicate the work we've done during the whole-class author study.

❧ *Readers explore new genres.* I tell children that really great readers read a range of things and that it's important to have variety in our reading diets. Some children have chosen to explore nonfiction if they rarely read it on their own. Others have chosen to read picture books, especially if they've been locked into chapter books for a while. I've had several children who decided they wanted to stretch themselves to read mysteries or biographies.

❧ *Readers work at strengthening a skill, a behavior, or a strategy.* I've had children who decided they wanted to work on a reading skill, behavior, or strategy. Some of their projects focused on fluency ("reading aloud with a storyteller's voice"), stamina ("pushing myself to read more"), or talking about books ("reading in a book club").

❧ *Readers engage in an advanced print work study.* Based on their assessments of the readers in their classes, many teachers wisely decide to create a unit of study on print strategies late in the year to support children in dealing with the more challenging words in their books. Some of the things we teach in these advanced print work studies are

- Strategies for reading polysyllabic words
- Strategies for dealing with unfamiliar words and vocabulary
  "I can read it, but I don't know what it means."
  "I can't read it, but I have a feeling that I know what it means."
  "I can't read it and I have no idea what it means."
- Strategies for word collecting
  "Readers learn new words in books that they can use for talking and writing."
  "Readers build vocabulary by paying attention to new words when they read."

- ❖ *Readers engage in an advanced comprehension study.* Based on assessments, a teacher may decide that her class would benefit from another exposure to the comprehension and thinking strategies that proficient readers use to understand their texts. In this study a teacher might revisit some of the strategies already taught, such as retelling, predicting, wondering, making connections, making mental images, determining importance, synthesizing text, inferring, dealing with confusion, and so on. Although the children have been exposed to these strategies all year long during read-aloud and shared reading, and have had a whole-class unit of study on these strategies in December, it is often the case that children can use a reminder, or booster shot, in the form of another focused study.

- ❖ *Readers create their own reading projects.* A study on reading projects can be challenging to teach because its nature requires that children pursue diverse things of interest to them. When this happens, it can be difficult to plan mini-lessons that support everyone's work.

  When I've done this kind of study, I've only planned for two weeks, usually in late May or early June, right before the final unit of study, Readers Make Plans for Their Reading Lives. Each time I've done this study, it has worked out very differently because of the work the children have chosen to do. So, instead of including a planning chart, I offer some possibilities for what this study might look by describing some of the projects that my students have done.

Readers Make Plans for Their Reading Lives

Chapter 8

IT WAS THE LAST DAY OF MY FIRST YEAR of teaching. It had been a good, hard year, and I'd fallen deeply in love with my class. I was exhausted and exhilarated, and yet I also felt sad to be saying good-bye to this class, the one that broke me in. All year long, I had held on to the remarks of Peter Heaney, my principal at the time, who told me that teachers never forget their first class. He told the new teachers this very early in the year, and I remembered it through the good days as well as the hard ones.

Of course, this being the last day of school, it felt hectic and hurried. Unlike the more experienced teachers who had much of their rooms packed away and were enjoying a rather calm day with their students, I was still passing out work and finishing up loose ends with my class. And then there was the Distribution of the Snails.

We had raised snails all year, and the children were finally taking them home. Unfortunately, I hadn't thought to get the snails ready to go home before this, so during that last hot, sweaty day of first grade, my students were building snail terrariums.

Like the Jeffersons, our snails were moving on up. They were leaving the overcrowded, communal housing of the glass tank and moving into their own single-family homes, large clear plastic containers and covers, donated by a neighborhood merchant. Dirt and stones, twigs and leaves were all over the table-tops and on the floor as the children landscaped and designed their snails' new homes. While they did this, I went scurrying around trying to get all the report cards, last-minute handouts, and leftover schoolwork into their book bags.

Finally, the snails were relocated and the children's book bags were packed. We were just about ready to go out for our final dismissal together. There were 15 minutes left of the last day of first grade. "Leave your snails at your tables and your book bags on your chairs, and let's meet at the carpet for one last time," I said above the din. My class gathered, and as I looked at their sweaty, slightly grimy faces, I felt myself getting choked up.

"I just want you to know how special you are to me, and how much I enjoyed being your teacher this year," I began. I went on to tell them what Mr. Heaney had said about how teachers never forget their first class, and I assured them that they would always be in my thoughts and my heart. I mentioned a couple of the most joyful memories I had from the year. By now, I wasn't quite sure that I'd be able to fight off a little bit of a cry. I knew the children could tell something was up as they looked at me, wide-eyed and quiet.

Just then, Marissa, compassionate, gentle Marissa, raised her hand. "This is it," I thought. "She's going to say something sweet, and I may lose it."

"What is it, Marissa?" I asked, nonchalantly reaching for a box of tissues.

She cleared her throat. "Well," she said, "there's a snail coming out of the garbage can. Can I have it?" All twenty-six pairs of eyes darted toward the garbage can, and about a dozen kids lunged to salvage the wayward snail.

"Is it time to go yet?" Julian asked.

No memories, no feedback, no sharing, no epiphanies, no group hug. That was it. Like a snail retreating into the safety of its shell, my tears receded, and my sensitive emotional state was jolted back into the reality of the last day of school with a bunch of first graders who are only thinking about summertime. "Yes, Julian, it's time to go. Everyone, grab your book bag and your snail, and let's line up. Quietly." We left the building together to meet moms or dads, grandparents or babysitters, and I spent quite a bit of time in the warm sun saying good-bye to children and their families. When I got back to my classroom after the farewells, my tears finally came, as I expected they would. Looking back, I'm not quite sure if it was saying good-bye to everyone or facing the snail mud and the cleaning up I had left to do in my classroom that brought the tears to my eyes.

I share this story of unrequited emotion to highlight why I spend some time in the last month of school looking back over the school year with my class. I realized then that the ritual of reminiscing and reflecting is important to me, but for young children the last day of the school year will never be the time for a montage of memories.

In the way that we began the year by building our community, I like to end the year by wrapping up our community. I believe the act of remembering and reflecting is important as we put together stories of our lives, and I want my class to leave first grade with a shared story out of the year we have just spent together.

With regard to the teaching of reading in particular, I value this time in June to look back over the way my students have grown. We think about the work we've done in reading and about how each one of us has changed as a reader over the course of the year. I credit Hannah Schneewind, a colleague at P.S. 321, with showing me the power of looking back with our students. It is with thanks to Hannah and others, that I share some of these ideas here.

In order to reflect on the year of reading, it helps to have saved some artifacts from the reading work we've done since September. It's easier to talk with first graders about things that happened in the past when there is something concrete and visual to go along with the conversation. I always hold on to the chapter books we read aloud (if they aren't mine, I make color copies of the covers), along with any charts or sticky notes that arose from our work in the read-alouds. I keep a hanging file folder for each child, and every month or so I make copies of a page or two of my students' reading logs. I save any reading reflections they write or draw and also hold on to some work that represents our whole-class studies, so that when we think back on the year, we've got material to look at together.

Reading Artifacts to Save Throughout the Year
- Sample pages from each student's reading log (monthly, especially September, January, May samples)
- Students' written or sketched reflections on books, thinking, reading work
- Charts that go along with reading work
- Texts read aloud to the class (chapter books, picture books, poems, nonfiction)
- Parent responses about reading

- Photos of students reading alone, with partners, with adults
- Photos of the changing library
- Color copies of book covers, favorite pages

Looking Back at Books We've Read Together

In the beginning of June my mini-lessons change. Instead of making precise teaching points and following an architecture, my mini-lessons become time for class discussions. I still teach reading during reading conferences and small-group work with students, but I often use mini-lesson time during these last few weeks for some reflection and accountable talk. There are a few kinds of discussions we tend to have during this time.

One of the easiest ways to begin reading discussions is to recall the chapter books the class has read together. To prepare for this, I gather a basket of chapter books I've read aloud to the class. "Boys and girls, does this ever happen to you? You know how when you go someplace, or do something cool, and take pictures, it's so much fun to look at them and get the memories back in your head?"

"Yeah, like when my family went to Baltimore to see my uncle, and we went to see this big huge ship. We got a picture of that," Chelsea said.

"So when your mom got the pictures, did you look at them together and remember the time when you visited the big ship?" I asked.

"Yeah, we remembered that it was so big and my baby cousin was cryin' 'cause she was scared."

"Could you see her crying in the picture?" I asked.

"Yup. Her face was like this," Chelsea said, as she scrunched up her chin and mouth to provide a visual.

"One time we got pictures back from Christmas when we were opening presents, but my grandma threw the picture out 'cause she didn't have her teeth in and she was mad that my dad took the picture," Wyatt said.

"I know, Wyatt, I can imagine how your grandma must feel. Sometimes pictures might not make us happy, or we think we look funny, or they might remind us of bad things, too," I said. "I thought that just as we look back at pictures and talk about them, we could look back over the chapter books we've read and talk about them. We can see if they bring back memories."

I pulled our first chapter book out of the basket, *The Drugstore Cat*.

"Hey, I remember that one," Jacob shouted.

"You guys, this was the first chapter book we read together. Remember it?" I asked, as I showed the cover and flipped through the pages with them. I showed some of the illustrations, which jogged many children's memories about the story. We remembered characters' names, and I reread some of the chapter titles.

"I liked that book 'cause the cat could talk," Kadeem said. "I wish my cat could talk, too."

"I remember the part when the mommy cat made Buzzy leave and I felt sad," added Julia.

"Oh yeah, remember how surprised we were that a mommy cat would want to send her baby away? That seemed weird, but I remember that we had a great talk about it," I responded.

"Yeah, animals, like cats and dogs, they go away from their moms when they're little, and they get used to their new homes. I know 'cause we just got a new kitten, and she likes it now, but at first she cried for her mom," said Jonathan.

"Yeah, cats aren't like kids 'cause a kid would be really sad if he had to go," Laura said.

"Buzzy must be like Jonathan's kitten because Buzzy liked it when he went to the drugstore to live even though at first he wasn't sure and he was sad," said Daniel.

"At first he was sad 'cause he missed his mom and his other brothers and sisters, and the people weren't nice," said Sabrina. "That book reminds me of *Charlotte's Web,* kind of."

"Why?" I asked.

"Well, it's like Buzzy had to go away from his mom, and Wilbur went away from his, too, and it was sad at first, but then Wilbur made friends and got used to it."

"Wow, what a comparison! I never thought of that!" I said, genuinely surprised by her connection.

We spend a few days talking in this way about some of the other books we've read together. My expectations for these talks are that my students use the reading and accountable talk skills and strategies we've learned all year long. I expect them to make their points with text evidence, use specific information, listen to and build on what their classmates say. I am a minor voice in these talks, although I still may have to nudge a bit and redirect the conversations sometimes.

Besides discussing the texts, the children often request that I reread a favorite part. We also might think about what we learned from reading the book, about reading itself, and about life. For example, at the end of our *Drugstore Cat* talk, I posed this question to my class: "Well, what did this book teach us about life?"

Silence.

"I guess what I'm thinking is that sometimes we learn things about life when we read a book, and I was wondering if that happened in this book," I explained.

"Well, I learned that cats can go away from their moms when they're really little cats," Kadeem said.

"Little cats are called kittens," Sela said.

"Little dogs are called puppies," Julie added.

"Hmm. That's interesting, Kadeem. Kittens often live in a different place than their moms. When Buzzy went away from his mom, how'd it go for him?" I asked, trying to redirect the conversation before it turned into a comprehensive listing of baby animal vocabulary.

"Well, he was sad and scared at first, but then he made friends and had fun," Alex said.

"It started out bad, but it got good for him," Jacob added.

"Yeah, it reminds me of when I first went to school. I was like Buzzy because I was so scared. I missed my mom, and I didn't know what would happen, but I made friends and had fun, just like Buzzy," Laura said.

"Me, too," said Sammy. "I was new to this school, and at first I was shy and scared."

"But you were my buddy boy," Kadeem said, smiling at Sammy.

"Yeah, you were my first friend, and then I made more friends. Now it's good," Sammy added, looking down at his sneaker. Still shy but friend-rich.

"So, I wonder if one of the things this book taught us is that sometimes we have to do things that feel hard, like going to a new school, or being away from our moms for a whole day, but it gets easier if we make friends. It can be fun, even."

"Yeah, I learned that, too. My mom says to give things a chance," Chelsea said.

"Today, I'd love for you guys to think about whether the book you're reading teaches you something, whether you learn something. It can be a tricky thing to figure out, but sometimes that's like the hidden treasure inside of a book," I said, and sent the children off to read. As they read, I conferred or finished up my year-end reading assessments.

I realize that if a first grader is left to her own devices, she may never naturally say, "The life lesson I learned from *Jamberry* is. . . ." Nonetheless, learning about our lives and the lives of others from books is the great joy and power of reading. I also know that with my support and scaffolding, the children can begin talking in authentic childlike ways about whether they learned about life from their books.

After reminiscing this way over several days, I asked the class a big question: "You guys, I need your help. I'm starting to plan for my class next year, and I'm wondering which of these books you think I should read to next year's class. I mean which books were your favorites, books that you think the new first graders just have to hear?" Once again, I line up many of the titles on the chalkboard tray and look across them with the class.

"I think *Wolf Story* was so good," Alex said.

"Say more," I said.

"It was scary and funny, and I just liked it," he explained.

"So, you're recommending *Wolf Story*. Does anyone else?" I asked.

"*Wolf Story* was good because it wasn't too scary, but just a little," Gaby added.

"So, you and Alex both think I should read *Wolf Story* next year. Thanks. Anything else?"

"Yeah, but make sure you tell the kids first that the book is a little scary so they can be ready," Julia advised.

"I think The Littles were good, too, because there was a lot of adventure," Sela said.

"Yeah, the Littles were fake but they felt real 'cause they were like a regular family only they had lots of crazy stuff going on," Laura added.

"I liked *Mrs. Piggle-Wiggle* because it was so funny," Langston said.

"Yeah, you made your voice really weird, Ms. Collins," Gaby said, remembering how I changed my voice for the different characters.

"Right now, why don't you turn to your partner and take a minute to talk about the books you absolutely loved from this year. Make sure you tell your partner why you loved it or about the parts you remember that you loved. Also, you know, if you didn't like a book, you can talk about that, too," I said.

The partner discussion went on for a few minutes as I listened in. "I love how you guys have strong opinions about books and can tell me what you like and don't like," I said. "That's what grown-up readers do. They can tell you why a book is a favorite or why they didn't like it. You guys are getting good at doing that. Now, today, when you're reading your own books, I want you to think about how you feel about the book. Did you like it? Was it so-so? And remember, you need to think about what makes you feel that way."

So, the mini-lessons in June might be like book talks going down Memory Lane, but I try to take our conversation and apply it to the work the children can do on their own. I do this by linking the conversation to the kind of talks my students could have during partner reading time.

End-of-Year Conversations About Books We've Read Together
"What did we learn about life from this book?"
"What books would you recommend I read to next year's class?"
Talk about why books, or parts of books, are favorites.
> "Sometimes it's fun to reread favorite books. I'll reread some of our favorites."
> "Sometimes it's fun to reread favorite parts of books. I'll reread some of our favorite parts."

Looking Back Through Book Logs

After we spend a few days looking back over our read-aloud books and talking about them, I give students copies of some of their book log pages that I've saved throughout the year. As I mentioned earlier, once a month I usually make a copy of a reading log page for each student and put it in her hanging file folder. I staple these copies together and hand them out for this reflection. I distribute just two or three pages from each file because I don't want to overwhelm students with a huge pile of log pages. Instead, I give them representative pages.

Because we've already done the whole-class work of looking through the books we've read together, it's easier to guide students toward reflecting on their own work. "Boys and girls, these packets are like snapshots or photographs from your reading lives this year. Just as we looked back and thought about the books we've read aloud, we're going to take a look back at ourselves as readers by thinking about the books we've read on our own this year."

I pass out the logs while the children are still with me at the carpet because the only thing they notice at first is how funny their handwriting looked at the beginning of the year. I want them to quickly get over laughing at this so we can begin to concentrate on the content.

"All year, I've made copies of some pages from your reading logs. I saved them because I thought they would bring back memories for us. Take a look at the first page. These are the kinds of books you read back in the old days, back in September. Talk to your partner about what you notice." The children sit side by side and look over their pages together. I give them a few minutes, and then we start to share out.

"My handwriting is crazy," Natasha said, and I knew I needed to be careful to get us back on the right track.

"I know, everybody's handwriting has changed so much this year. But, Natasha, what do you notice about your reading from the old days?"

"I used to read those easy books," she said.

"Like what?" I asked, hoping she'd be more specific.

"You know, books like *Mom* and *Baby Animals*. They're so easy," she said, laughing and looking at her partner.

"Natasha, you've changed 'cause now you're reading *Little Bear*. I saw you!" Anna said.

"Yeah, I'm like Natasha, too, because I used to read those easy books, but now I can read stuff that's a lot harder," said Zoe.

"I bet lots of kids have books like Natasha's on their September page, but now you've all grown as readers and you can read different kinds of books," I said.

"Yeah, I used to read books with, like, one or two words on a page, but now my books are, like, chapter books, and now I read them instead of the easy books," Hal explained.

"So, do you think we can say that we all used to read books with only a couple of words on the pages, but now we read harder books?"

I heard a chorus of "Yes!" as I started a then-and-now chart. "Take a few more minutes and think with your partner about your reading in the old days and how you've changed since then." As they talked about what they notice, I moved around to listen in. We ended up adding a few more things to the chart, such as, "We used to read really short books." I reminded them of how they used to read for only 5 minutes by themselves and now they could sustain their reading for longer.

How We've Changed as Readers This Year

We used to read books with only one or two words on the page.
Now we read books with many more words on the page.
We used to use pictures a lot to help us read.
Now our books don't always have pictures, and we use many other strategies to help us read.
We used to read really short books.
Now we read longer books with more pages.
We used to read by ourselves for only 5 minutes.
Now we read by ourselves as long as 30 minutes.

For the next few days, I ask the children to look over their reading log pages, and we do some of the following things together:

- Highlight your three favorite books, and tell your partner why you liked these books.
- Find a book from your log that you love, and reread it. See if it brings back reading memories.
- Look for trends in your reading. Is there an author that you seem to love? a kind of book? a genre? What is missing?

As I mentioned earlier, during these last weeks of school, mini-lessons are venues for discussion rather than platforms for making a teaching point. After we talk about a book or a reading issue, I might say, "You know how we just talked about the reasons that we like or don't like certain books? Well, I want you to really think about the book you're reading in the same way. Decide why you like it, what makes it good. Or maybe you'll realize that it's not the best book you've read. That's fine, too." As they read, I do individual conferences and meet with small groups to support them with their reading needs.

Looking Ahead: Making Plans for Our Reading Lives

One of our ultimate goals as first-grade teachers is for our students to realize that reading is not just a school activity, something to do because the teacher tells you to do it. We want children to know that reading is a life activity, something you can choose to do because it brings you pleasure and knowledge. I know it doesn't work to say, "Boys and girls, make sure you read over the summer," even if we say it over and over. So at the end of the year I spend a couple of days helping my students figure out how they can fit reading into their lives.

Now, let me just take a moment to address the concerns of teachers (and parents) who might say, "They're only seven, they should be outside catching frogs/running through the spray of an open fire hydrant/playing with their friends/traveling with their families over summer vacation. They've got a whole life ahead of them to work, so let them just be kids." I agree with this statement with every fiber my being. Let kids be kids, of course! However, research indicates that young children do need to have consistent reading practice over the summer so that when they go back to school in September, they haven't lost any ground. When children don't read in the summer, they often begin the next school year a couple of levels behind where they were in June. This puts unnecessary stress on students and their families, not to mention next year's teacher.

So, if we believe children need to read over the summer, we have to do more than just tell them to do it. We have to help them (and their families) imagine ways they can fit reading into their lives. To do this, I usually begin by saying to my students, "Every day when you walk into class, there is a daily schedule on the chalkboard." I pull off the magnetic card that says "Independent Reading Workshop" and continue. "I put this card on our schedule every day so that we remember to make time for reading. But, when you're home over the summer, will you have one of these cards that says 'Independent Reading Workshop' to help you remember to read?"

"No!" say the children, laughing.

"So, there's not going to be a card on your refrigerator every day reminding you to read?"

"No!" they shout again.

"Well, what are you going to do? How are you going to make sure you find time for reading every day?" I ask them with an exaggerated tone of curiosity. This is how I begin the discussion about planning. Children begin listing suggestions about finding time to read. For homework, I send home directions such as, "Talk to a grown-up at home about times when you will fit in reading on summer days." This, I hope, sends the message to families that their children are expected to read over the summer and that they'll need family support.

Over the next couple of days we generate a set of suggestions for finding time to read. We talk about the benefits of nighttime reading vs. morning reading, keeping books and magazines in cars for long drives, reading after day camp, and making sure that you take books whenever you visit people or places so you're never caught without one.

Then we turn the discussion toward making specific reading plans. I share with them how I spend lots of time in the bookstore in June figuring out what I'm going to read over the summer, and then I either order the books from the library or buy them so I am never left empty-handed. We talk about how people have reading goals, too, that help them make reading plans. I tell them how after I read *Wild December* by Edna O'Brien, I wanted to read everything by her. Reading Edna O'Brien's books became a reading goal for me and helped me make my plans to find her books and read a few of them in a row.

For homework, I ask students to think about their goals by talking them over with someone at home: "Talk to a grown-up at home about a plan or goal you have for your summer reading." Some of the plans children have made involve authors or series ("I want to read all the Junie B. Jones books"); topics ("I want to learn more about horses because we're going south to visit my uncle's farm, so I'll read books about horses"); reading goals ("I want to read chapter books this summer," "I want my dad to finish the Harry Potter series with me this summer"); or social goals ("Me and Brittany and Tara want to have a book club and meet every week").

After a couple of days of talking about these goals and plans in order to create a range of possibilities, I send a "contract" home for homework. I ask the children to write out a few reading plans for the summer. When they bring these back to class, we try to find out if anyone has similar plans, and I help them imagine ways to stay in touch to help each other. We talk about how it's like having a book club when you've got other people doing the same things in reading.

Now, I fully realize that it's fantasy heaven to believe that every reading plan will be followed through and every reading goal will be met. These are young readers, and I'm trying mostly to get them to imagine the possibilities for reading and to educate families about the importance of helping their children continue to read over the summer.

Over the years, I've compiled the following list of summer reading suggestions from teachers with whom I've worked:

- *Get library cards.* Teachers can take students to the local library to get library cards and familiarize students with what's available. Then they send home information about summer hours and programs so that families are aware of their options.
- *Open a school lending library.* Westminster Community School, a public school in Buffalo, runs a summer school program, so the building is open daily during the summer. In the mornings, for half an hour before the start of summer school, time is allotted for parents and caregivers to bring children to the school library to borrow books.
- *Make reading journals.* Some teachers provide time for students to decorate reading journals that they'll keep over the summer. They might tape in a class phone list so that children can keep in touch, as well as a list of their classmates' reading plans. In some schools next year's teachers write a note to their soon-to-be-students suggesting titles for summer reading and previewing some of the studies the class will do. The children then use their reading logs as inquiry journals, too, where they gather questions, thoughts, and information about the studies they will do in their next grade.

Assessment

Although all schools and districts have their own expectations and mandates for year-end assessments, there seem to be four broad categories of assessments that we all have to do:

- Assessments that go home (report card)
- Assessments for next year's teacher
- Assessments for school record cards
- District/state assessments

Although the district and state assessments are particular to each school, teachers everywhere need to inform families about their children's progress. In my year-end report card to parents, I make recommendations for summer reading that are personalized for each child and based on the independent reading level as well as what I know about the child's interests and taste in books. I also include a copy of the child's "contract" for summer reading plans.

For the assessment that moves on to next year's teacher, I want to include more than just the child's reading level. I know that teachers may be most interested at first in what level their new students are reading at, but I also want to inform them of a child's reading strengths and weaknesses, habits and interests. After all, we know that two children who read at the same level can have completely different strengths and weaknesses around reading.

Also, it's important to include information about children's habits and interests as readers because teachers are thinking not only about the individuals they are going to see in the fall but also about the community of learners they will have. I want to let them know why Jasmine was difficult to partner with all year long, and that although Gregory is a struggling reader, he is also one of the most engaged and eager learners during shared reading and interactive read-aloud. I try to inform next year's teacher about my students in a way that will provide a picture of the child as a person, not just as a reader.

For year-end assessments that move along to next year's teacher, here are suggestions for giving a more complete picture of the students.

Instead of saying, "Brianna is reading at level J," we can say, "Brianna reads independently at level J. She is great at using a variety of strategies to figure out unknown words, but she has a difficult time inferring. She loves to try to challenge herself, and she wants to read chapter books like Cayla, her best friend."

Instead of saying, "Milo had difficulty with partners," we can say, "Milo struggled in partnerships this year because he tries to always be the leader, especially with passive children. It helps to partner him with another child with a strong voice."

Instead of saying, "Jarrod loves to read nonfiction," we can say, "Jarrod is very interested in books about animals. His brother has an internship at the zoo, so he'll often go there over the summer. He is particularly interested in bears and monkeys."

Year-End Reading Celebrations

We celebrated our growth as readers throughout the year, and it may seem like there's nothing left to celebrate. By June I would draw a blank about reading celebrations and end up doing nothing. Then, when I taught at the summer institute at Teachers College, I decided to ask teachers to share ideas they have for year-end reading celebrations. I've collected the following ideas over the last few years.

Readers' Theater: Performing Scenes from Literature

To prepare for this celebration, teachers and students look back over the books that have had a powerful presence in the classroom, which may include chapter books that have held the class over time and picture books that the students wanted to hear over and over again. Together, the students determine their favorite parts or scenes from these books to perform for an audience. The celebration is actually a series of vignettes acted out by the children. They work in small groups to develop their scenes and put together scenery, props, and costumes. It helps to have another adult or two to help the groups get ready.

Bookmark-Making Party

Because there is an expectation that students will read over the summer, some teachers have them make their own fancy bookmarks, or two bookmarks—one for themselves and one for someone else. The extra bookmarks may go to kindergarten children reading buddies, pen pals from another school, a pediatric ward of a hospital, the public library, and so on. One year, my class made bookmarks to sell at the Spring Fair, a PTA fund-raiser. I precut 2" × 8" bookmarks out of off-white posterboard, and then the children painted them with watercolors. I laminated the bookmarks after they had dried and children punched a hole in the top and made a yarn tassel. The bookmarks looked beautiful, and we sold out of them.

Book Donations

Students collect books that they are no longer reading, or books that no longer fit them as readers, and donate them to another school, to the public library, to an after-school program, or to anyplace in the community that needs children's books. The students can write a little note about why they love a book and tape it to the inside cover. To add a sweet touch, if the books are being donated to individuals rather than to an institution, the students can wrap them in white butcher paper and decorate them.

Year-End Book Clubs

Because talking and thinking about books was emphasized during the school year, some teachers have a year-end book club meeting that involves families. One teacher sets this up in May by gathering multiple copies of four to six titles. The students pick which book they want to read and share with their families, and then on one day in June the parents come to school to meet in book clubs with other children and their parents who read the same book. Some teachers ask the students to act as facilitators in each group to help the conversations move along. After the book club meetings, students and their families have snacks, of course!

Reading to Kindergarten Buddies

Many kindergarten teachers take their children to first-grade classrooms toward the end of the year so that the children have a sense of what to expect in first grade. Instead of having the kindergartners just look around the room, some first-grade teachers arrange for their students to read to a kindergarten buddy. The first graders prepare by selecting a favorite book, and they practice reading it in a great voice. Then, when the kindergartners come in, they meet their first-grade buddies and listen to a story. It's helpful if the kindergarten teacher and the first-grade teacher strategically match the students beforehand.

When I plan for a year-end celebration (or any celebration), I consider the following questions:

Does the celebration allow my students to use what they've learned as readers?

Does the celebration provide an opportunity for sharing, either within the class community or beyond?

Is the celebration comfortable for the whole range of readers in the class?

Is there a way to fit snacks into the celebration?

It was another June of my teaching, and I remember a particular recess. It was one of the only days the students had been outside in over a week because the weather had been unusually wet. On this day my students and I kept looking out the window all morning hoping that the sliver of sunshine would last until recess.

The sun persevered, and I took my class out to the playground in front of our school. It felt so great to watch my students unfurl as they ran toward the monkey bars, slides, and freeze tag games as if it were their first time. I walked around as usual and stopped to watch some children in their games. A group of them were playing *Titanic. Titanic* was the big movie that year, and many children had gone to see it.

How do kids play *Titanic?* you might be wondering. Well, it's simple really. It involves a lot of hanging off the playground equipment and squealing, "Iceberg ahead!" It was clear to me that this was a game they had played before because their roles seemed clearly established: "No, I'm Rose, and I should be right here; you're that other lady; go over there and fall in the water," I overheard Victoria yell to Lauren. I was happy to see Raymond included and playing with the others because he had begun the year alone during recess. He had a hard time interacting with other children and would often play by himself.

I stayed on the periphery and tried to act as if I weren't paying much attention to their *Titanic* remake. I didn't want them to ham it up for my benefit or become inhibited because they were being watched. It was privately hilarious to observe them negotiating roles and acting out their understanding of the movie. But after watching for a little while, I couldn't help myself. I approached the group.

"Can I play?" I asked.

The action stopped. The *Titanic* kids looked at me for a couple of seconds and then looked at each other. After what seemed like too long, Victoria (who wasn't about to relinquish her role as Rose to anybody) said, "Yeah, Ms. Collins, you can be a dead body."

"Over here, you can have this spot," Raul said, pointing to the ground under the slide. The other kids looked around and nodded, and then they all went back to their roles.

A dead body? That's all?

Earlier in the year, my children nagged me to play tag with them, challenged me to race across the monkey bars, begged me to lift them up the side of the jungle gym, and otherwise hung on my sleeves at recess time. And now, all I can get is a nonspeaking role in their pretend game? What happened?

But at that moment, on this June day, it became abundantly clear to me what happened. It was the end of the year. My students didn't need me as much or in the same way anymore, and that was okay. With our guidance and teaching, they develop skills and strategies, cultivate relationships, initiate projects and games, and create their own sets of expectations for interactions. Our students' ability to work and play, to read and think independently has grown.

And isn't this what we've been teaching toward all year long?

Appendix

Recommended Professional Literature

The following are professional books that have been more like colleagues than reference texts for me. I constantly return to them when I need to replenish, refuel, and refine my teaching. I list them by categories for which they are particularly helpful.

Reading Development

Clay, Marie B. 1991. *Becoming Literate: The Construction of Inner Control.* Portsmouth, NH: Heinemann.

Goodman, Kenneth. 1996. *On Reading.* Portsmouth, NH: Heinemann.

Primary Independent Reading Workshop

Calkins, Lucy. 2001. *The Art of Teaching Reading.* Boston: Allyn and Bacon.

Duthie, Christine. 1996. *True Stories: Nonfiction Literacy in the Primary Classroom.* Portland, ME: Stenhouse.

Keene, Ellin, and Susan Zimmermann. 1997. *Mosaic of Thought: Teaching Comprehension in a Reader's Workshop.* Portsmouth, NH: Heinemann.

Miller, Debbie. 2002. *Reading with Meaning: Teaching Comprehension in the Primary Grades.* Portland, ME: Stenhouse.

Owocki, Gretchen. 2003. *Comprehension: Strategic Instruction for K–3 Students.* Portsmouth, NH: Heinemann.

Taberski, Sharon. 2000. *On Solid Ground.* Portsmouth, NH: Heinemann.

Primary Writing Workshop

Calkins, Lucy. 1983. *The Art of Teaching Writing.* Portsmouth, NH: Heinemann.

Calkins, Lucy, et al. 2003. *Units of Study for Primary Writing: A Yearlong Curriculum.* Teachers College Reading and Writing Project. Portsmouth, NH: Heinemann.

Fletcher, Ralph, and JoAnn Portalupi. 1998. *Craft Lessons: Teaching Writing K–8.* Portland, ME: Stenhouse.

Heard, Georgia. 1989. *For the Good of the Earth and the Sun: Teaching Poetry.* Portsmouth, NH: Heinemann.

Ray, Katie W. 2001. *The Writing Workshop: Working Through the Hard Parts (And They're All Hard Parts).* Urbana, IL: National Council of Teachers of English.

Reading and Writing Conferences

Anderson, Carl. 1999. *How's It Going?* Portsmouth, NH: Heinemann

Calkins, Lucy. 2001. *The Art of Teaching Reading.* Boston: Allyn and Bacon.

Calkins, Lucy, et al. 2003. *Units of Study for Primary Writing: A Yearlong Curriculum.* Teachers College Reading and Writing Project. Portsmouth, NH: Heinemann.

Interactive Read-Aloud with Accountable Talk

Fox, Mem. 2001. *Reading Magic: Why Reading Aloud to Our Children Will Change Their Lives Forever.* Orlando, FL: Harcourt.

Short, Kathy G., and Kathryn M. Pierce, eds. 1991. *Talking about Books: Creating Literate Communities.* Reissued 1998 as *Talking about Books: Literature Discussion Groups in K–8 Classrooms.* Portsmouth, NH: Heinemann.

Trelease, James. 2001. *The Read-Aloud Handbook.* 5th ed. New York: Penguin.

Interactive Writing

McCarrier, Andrea, Irene C. Fountas, and Gay Su Pinnell. 1999. *Interactive Writing: How Language and Literacy Come Together, K–2.* Portsmouth, NH: Heinemann.

Word Study, Phonics

Cunningham, Patricia M. 1999. *Phonics They Use: Words for Reading and Writing.* 3d ed. Boston: Addison-Wesley.

Snowball, Diane, and Faye Bolton. 1999. *Spelling K–8: Planning and Teaching.* Portland, ME: Stenhouse.

Wilde, Sandra. 1991. *You Can Read This! Spelling and Punctuation for Whole Language Classrooms, K–6.* Portsmouth, NH: Heinemann.

Shared Reading

Holdaway, Donald. 1979. *The Foundations of Literacy.* Portsmouth, NH: Heinemann.

Parkes, Brenda. 2000. *Read It Again! Revisiting Shared Reading.* Portland, ME: Stenhouse.

Small-Group Instruction: Strategy Lessons, Guided Reading Groups

Calkins, Lucy. 2001. *The Art of Teaching Reading.* Boston: Allyn and Bacon.

Fountas, Irene, and Gay Su Pinnell. 1996. *Guided Reading: Good First Teaching for All Children.* Portsmouth, NH: Heinemann.

Other Titles of Interest

Bomer, Randy, and Katherine Bomer. 2001. *For a Better World: Reading and Writing for Social Action.* Portsmouth, NH: Heinemann.

Hindley, Joanne. 1996. *In the Company of Children.* Portland, ME: Stenhouse.

Vygotsky, L. S. 1962. *Thought and Language.* Cambridge, MA: MIT Press.

Print Strategy Guide Sheet

Tracking print
- Using finger to point under the words (pointing is useful until child's independent reading level is Group 2/GR D; after that, children should point only to help themselves with difficult parts of text)
- Using eyes to track print

Using pictures/illustrations
- Using the pictures to help figure out words
- Using the pictures to help deepen understanding of the story

Noticing and holding the patterns in text
- Using patterns, such as repeating lines/phrases/rhyming words to help read the words
- Using spelling patterns to help figure out unknown words

Searching for and using visual/graphophonic information
- Using the beginning of words, saying the sound of the beginning
- Using the beginning and ending of words
- Looking through words (beginning sounds, medial, ending)

Searching for and using syntactic information
- Noticing when something doesn't sound right
- Making it sound right

Searching for and using semantic sources of information
- Noticing when something doesn't make sense
- Making it make sense

Self-correcting
- With prompting
- Without prompting
- Rereading so the text sounds smooth

Growing flexible with strategies
- Trying another strategy when first one doesn't work
- Knowing when and how to help yourself

Rereading the text
- Rereading a word/group of words to self-correct
- Rereading to improve phrasing and fluency
- Rereading for meaning

Improving fluency/phrasing
- Reading smoothly
- Reading in a way that shows understanding of the story

Encountering unfamiliar words
- Using picture and text for support
- Using features of the word
- Using context

Recalling details of the text
- Flipping back to remind oneself of the pattern
- Flipping back to remember a word
- Noticing details in text and illustration, and holding them for talk

Assessment Template

Name _____   Date _____

Title and Author _____   Level _____

Accuracy Rate _____   Self-correction ratio ____ : ____

Typed text (double-spaced to take running record) or a space for a running record (without typed text)	M	S	V

Notes on retelling/Evidence of comprehension   **Notes on fluency**

Other observations   **Implications for instruction**

Planning Chart

Unit of Study:

Goals	
Bends in the Road	
Classroom Library	
Materials and Resources	
Workshop Structures	
Other Literacy Components	
Work Students Are Doing	
Support for Struggling Readers	
Support for Strong Readers	
Home/School	
Assessment	
Celebrations	
Standards That Are Addressed	

Reading Interview

Interview someone at home about their reading life. You can tape-record your interview, have the person you're interviewing write his or her answers, or write the answers yourself.

If you tape-record, please bring in the tape. If the person you're interviewing writes the answers, have him or her read them to you.

Name of person you are interviewing _____

1. What kinds of things do you like to read?

2. Where do you like to read? (Describe your most comfortable place.)

3. When do you read in your life?

4. What is your favorite children's book?

5. What was it like for you when you learned to read?

6. What advice do you have for young readers?

If you have other questions to ask, please use the other side of this page.

Growing Readers: Units of Study in the Primary Grades by Kathy Collins. Copyright © 2004. Stenhouse Publishers.

Collecting New Information

Names _____ **and** _____

Fact	**Fact**

Research Topic

Fact	**Fact**

Questions we have:

Reading Partner Checklist

Names _____ **and** _____

☐   **We read one book together.**

☐   **We made a plan together.**

☐   **We worked out a problem together.**

☐   **We talked about our books.**

Reading Partner Reflection

Name_____ **Date**_____

Who is your reading partner?

What did your partnership do really well?

What is your partnership going to work on next week?

Reading Center Reflection

Name _____

What reading center were you in?

☐	**Bodies and Bones**	☐	**Butterflies**
☐	**Space**	☐	**Ants**
☐	**Snails**	☐	**Animals**
☐	**Water**	☐	**Plants**

Who was your center partner?

_____

- -

_____

What was something you learned in your center?

How did your partnership work out?

Growing Readers: Units of Study in the Primary Grades by Kathy Collins. Copyright © 2004. Stenhouse Publishers.

Bibliography

Professional Literature

Anderson, Carl. 1999. *How's It Going?* Portsmouth, NH: Heinemann.

Calkins, Lucy. 1983. *The Art of Teaching Writing.* Portsmouth, NH: Heinemann.

———. 2001. *The Art of Teaching Reading.* Boston: Allyn and Bacon.

Calkins, Lucy, et al. 2002. *A Field Guide to the Classroom Library A–G.* Teachers College Reading and Writing Project. Portsmouth, NH: Heinemann.

———. 2003. *Units of Study for Primary Writing: A Yearlong Curriculum.* Teachers College Reading and Writing Project. Portsmouth, NH: Heinemann.

Cambourne, Brian. 1988. *The Whole Story: Natural Learning and the Acquisition of Literacy in the Classroom.* Auckland, NZ: Ashton Scholastic.

Clay, Marie M. 1991. *Becoming Literate: The Construction of Inner Control.* Portsmouth, NH. Heinemann.

———. 1998. *By Different Paths to Common Outcomes.* Portland, ME: Stenhouse.

———. 2000. *Running Records for Classroom Teachers.* Portsmouth, NH: Heinemann.

Fountas, Irene, and Gay Su Pinnell. 1996. *Guided Reading: Good First Teaching for All Children.* Portsmouth, NH: Heinemann.

———. 1999. *Matching Books to Readers: Using Leveled Books in Guided Reading, K–3.* Portsmouth, NH: Heinemann.

Goodman, Kenneth. 1996. *On Reading.* Portsmouth, NH: Heinemann.

Goodman, Y., D. Watson, and C. Burke. 1987. *Reading Miscue Inventory: Alternative Procedures.* New York: Richard C. Owen.

Hindley, Joanne. 1996. *In the Company of Children*. Portland, ME: Stenhouse.

Holdaway, Donald. 1979. *The Foundations of Literacy*. Sydney, Australia: Ashton Scholastic.

Keene, Ellin, and Susan Zimmermann. 1997. *Mosaic of Thought: Teaching Comprehension in a Reader's Workshop*. Portsmouth, NH: Heinemann.

Miller, Debbie. 2002. *Reading with Meaning: Teaching Comprehension in the Primary Grades*. Portland, ME: Stenhouse.

Parkes, Brenda. 2000. *Read It Again! Revisiting Shared Reading*. Portland, ME: Stenhouse.

Pearson, P. David, and Margaret C. Gallagher. 1983. "The Instruction of Reading Comprehension." *Contemporary Educational Psychology* 8: 317–344.

Short, Kathy G., Jerome C. Harste, with Carolyn Burke. 1995. *Creating Classrooms for Authors and Inquirers*. Portsmouth, NH: Heinemann.

Smith, Frank. 1987. *Joining the Literacy Club*. Portsmouth, NH: Heinemann.

Vygotsky, L. S. 1962. *Thought and Language*. Cambridge, MA: MIT Press.

Children's Books Mentioned in the Text

All the Small Poems. Valerie Worth.

Baby Bear Goes Fishing. Beverley Randell.

Bedknobs and Broomsticks. Mary Norton.

The Biggest House in the World. Leo Lionni.

Birthdays. Joy Cowley.

Biscuit series. Alyssa S. Capucilli.

Charlotte's Web. E. B. White.

Cinderella Penguin. Janet Perlman.

Crow Boy. Taro Yashima.

The Drugstore Cat. Ann Petry.

First-Grade Friends series. Miriam Cohen.

Frog and Toad series. Arnold Lobel.

Goodnight Moon. Margaret Wise Brown.

Guess How Much I Love You. Sam McBratney.

Henry and Mudge series. Cynthia Rylant.

Hooray for Snail! John Stadler.

Horrible Harry series. Suzy Kline.

How to Make a Sandwich. Patricia Tefft Cousin, Claudette C. Mitchelle, Gracie R. Porter.

Jamberry. Bruce Degen.

Jim's Dog Muffins. Miriam Cohen.

Junie B. Jones series. Barbara Park.

Koala Lou. Mem Fox.

Little Bear. Elsa Holmelund Minarik.

Little Polar Bear Finds a Friend. Hans de Beer.

M&M series. Pat Ross.

The Magic School Bus series. Joanna Cole.

Max's Box. Celebrations Press.

Mrs. Piggle-Wiggle. Betty MacDonald.

Mrs. Wishy-Washy. Joy Cowley.

My Father's Dragon. Ruth Stiles Gannett.

Nate the Great and the Phony Clue. Marjorie Weinman Sharmat.

No, David! David Shannon.

Officer Buckle and Gloria. Peggy Rathmann.

Pigs Might Fly. Dick King-Smith.

Poppleton series. Cynthia Rylant.

Rattlebone Rock. Sylvia Andrews.

Shortcut. Donald Crews.

Wolf Story. William McCleery.

Index